THE TURCOTTES

THE
TURCOTTES

THE REMARKABLE STORY OF
A HORSE RACING DYNASTY

CURTIS STOCK

FIREFLY BOOKS

A Firefly Book

Published by Firefly Books Ltd. 2023
Copyright © 2023 Firefly Books Ltd.
Text copyright © 2023 Curtis Stock
Photographs published with the permission of Gaetan and
    Yves Turcotte, except as listed below

First printing

Library of Congress Control Number: 2022917768

Library and Archives Canada Cataloguing in Publication
Title: The Turcottes : the remarkable story of
    a horse racing dynasty / Curtis Stock.
Names: Stock, Curtis, author.
Description: Includes index.
Identifiers: Canadiana 20220439273 |
    ISBN 9780228104247 (hardcover)
Subjects: LCSH: Jockeys—Canada—Biography. |
    LCSH: Horse racing—Canada. | LCGFT: Biographies.
Classification: LCC SF336.A2 S76 2023 |
    DDC 798.40092/2—dc23

Published in the United States by
Firefly Books (U.S.) Inc.
P.O. Box 1338, Ellicott Station
Buffalo, New York 14205

Published in Canada by
Firefly Books Ltd.
50 Staples Avenue, Unit 1
Richmond Hill, Ontario L4B 0A7

Cover and interior design: Stacey Cho

Printed in China

Photo Credits

AP Images:
133t: Uncredited, 135: Uncredited,
136t: Uncredited, 138: Uncredited,
139: Uncredited, 140: Dave Pickoff,
141: Uncredited, 143: Uncredited,
144: Horst Schafer, 225: Uncredited,
230: Ray Stubblebine

Getty:
136b: Doug Griffin

Provincial Archives of New Brunswick:
129t: Uncredited, 129B: Uncredited

Postmedia:
238–39: Bruce Stotesbury and
Kim Stalknecht

 We acknowledge the financial support
of the Government of Canada.

For Barb, Dallas and Maia.
You always believed in me.

Contents

The Turcotte Family

	BORN	DECEASED
Alfred Turcotte	July 29, 1911	August 15, 1990
Marie-rose Turcotte	October 4, 1914	March 8, 1996
Camilla Turcotte	March 1, 1940	
Camille Turcotte	March 1, 1940	Februrary 24, 2002
Ron Turcotte	July 22, 1941	
Noel Turcotte	December 23, 1943	August 8, 2001
Odette Turcotte	June 16, 1945	
Aurele Turcotte	November 17, 1946	
Raymond Turcotte	March 27, 1948	February 1949
Rudy Turcotte	January 28, 1950	February 13, 2019
Albert Turcotte	August 3, 1951	
Raymonde Turcotte	March 7, 1953	September 16, 2018
Joseph Turcotte	1947	1947
Roger Turcotte	September 10, 1955	May 11, 1996
Gaetan Turcotte	February 11, 1957	
Yves Turcotte	March 13, 1960	

Prologue

I t couldn't happen.

Five brothers from New Brunswick. Five sons from an impoverished lumberjack town. Five children from a devoutly Catholic mother who bore 14. One by one, they would leave their little forested corner of the world to compete as jockeys all across North America.

They were the Turcottes: Ron, Noel, Rudy, Roger and Yves.

Ron was the most famous and celebrated of the quintet. He won 3,032 races — 106 of them in higher prized stakes. Just two years removed from picking worms on a Toronto golf course, where he was paid $3 for a thousand, he was Canada's leading jockey. He was the rider of Secretariat, the greatest thoroughbred of all time — a horse so brilliantly fast and powerful that many of his records still stand today, including his bewitching 31-length victory in the 1973 Belmont Stakes. The week before the Belmont, Secretariat was on the covers of *Time*, *Newsweek* and *Sports Illustrated*.

The other Turcottes soon followed their older brother.

Noel was one of Ontario's top jockeys. He rode Canadian Hall of Fame horse Belle Geste and had 945 career wins.

Rudy won 1,740 races. He led the standings just about everywhere he rode up and down the Atlantic seaboard. Once, he won six races on a single card. Many believe he was an even better jockey than Ron. He guided his mounts to career earnings of $11,600,379.

Roger, at the age of 18, was 1975's leading apprentice rider in North America, winning 290 races that year.

Yves, the youngest of the family, was a Canadian Derby–winning jockey — aboard Elmtex in 1988. He was one of Alberta's top jockeys, winning 1,347 races.

Each Turcotte found success, collectively winning a staggering 8,251 races for purse earnings just shy of $60 million. If only their story ended there.

But the jockey's life takes a toll. Each brother was in a never-ending battle with weight. All used every means to reduce: downing diuretic pills, soaking for hours in saunas in rubber suits, running miles wearing several layers of clothing and purging themselves after meals. Noel, Rudy and Roger all fought the bottle.

And then came the losses, the injuries and the heartbreaks. The unlikely triumph of one of horse racing's greatest families was not without tragedy.

It couldn't happen. But it did.

Chapter 1

"It's just the wind," says Alfred Turcotte, stealing back the quilt from his wife, Rose, and draping it over his ample shoulders.

"Just the wind," he murmurs again, rolling back to sleep, the bedside clock reading 11 p.m.

Rose knew otherwise. A mother always knows.

Rose slides away from the complaining of the narrow bed, grabs her housecoat and slips across the cranky wood floor and through the darkness. In socked feet, she heads to the tiny bedroom where Gaetan, the 22-month-old baby of the family of 11 children, has wrestled himself awake one more time.

Cheeks flushed red as gooseberries, tears scampering down his face, Gaetan is hungry.

Outside, the wind breathes heavily, still not exhausted from its long, icy slide down the Salmon River. The gale has been relentless — howling and shrieking for days on end, tearing and scrapping at everything in its wide swath — while the snow, which has been falling for days, is now knee high, burying just about everything.

It is Friday, December 8, 1958.

"Mama is here," Rose says in French, the only language spoken in the Turcotte home in the tiny village of Drummond,

New Brunswick, just down the road and across the long, high CN bridge from Grand Falls. Drummond, just a brisk walk from the U.S. border into Maine, is barely large enough to swallow the school, the Credit Union, Wilfrid Guay's general store and the Saint-Michel church — a brown cobblestone and wooden chapel that had been built by Alfred's great grandfather Napoleon Turcotte and two of his sons, Adelard and Pierre "Pete" Leone, in 1906.

Before the turn of the century, Napoleon, Adelard and Pete — all architects and carpenters whose ancestors were from France — left their Ile D'Orleans home in the Saint Lawrence River, which was about 5 kilometers east of Quebec City and one of the first parts of Quebec to be colonized by the French. Heading south, first by boat across the Richelieu River and then in wooden carts pulled along by a team of sturdy horses, they traveled around Lake Champlain on what would become the Trans-Canada Highway until where Quebec meets the rise of Vermont's Green Mountains. The men built churches as they journeyed.

Not all of them kept going, Alfred had told Rose many times. Some of the men stayed behind to finish the churches and to start small communities with schools, farms and houses. Adelard and Pete, however, went all the way southeast to New Brunswick — first through Edmundston alongside Maine — and finally south to Drummond, where they built Saint-Michel, their last church.

Enveloped by the snow's dogged swelling, Drummond now seemed even smaller, if that were possible.

Rose lifts Gaetan from his crib, the same one Alfred made from wood he had chopped down himself 17 years ago, when the first of their children, Camille and Camilla, were born. It was now thick with layers of white paint.

For Alfred, a lumberjack since he was 13, any noise was always just the wind. But put 50 bawling babies in a single room and a mother can always tell which one is hers — matching cries to child as if she were connecting dots. As soon as Rose, a short woman who stands just 4 feet 9 inches tall, lifts Gaetan the baby's tears dry against his softness.

Another crisis averted, she thinks to herself — baby snug against her chest — feeling her way through the darkness in the two-storey home. Most of her children had been good sleepers. Before they were even laid down, their eyes would be shut tight. Just sucking on a bottle would do the trick. But not Gaetan. For him, sleep only comes in fits and snatches as he swims and wrestles against the sides of his crib. Only the warm comfort of his mother's bosom seems to get him back to sleep.

The way the storm had been raging, it sure looked like there wouldn't be church on Sunday and likely no school on Monday. The blizzard would surely see to that.

School days were always welcome. For the kids of Drummond, it meant no outdoor chores. For the women of Drummond, it meant being able to enjoy a few precious hours by foisting their children off for a while. For most of the fathers, though, it just meant another day in the thick woods cutting down trees and hauling them along the often-raging Salmon River.

Rose and Alfred also hoped, though faintly, that school would be a portal out of this part of New Brunswick to something better. Maybe with an education, one child might become a teacher or another even a doctor.

But that wasn't a reality. Here, you were born in the woods, and you would die in the woods. The whole world was nothing but trees. Tamaracks. Jack pines. Red pines. More than likely you would be buried in a casket made of the same trees you had walked beside. Maybe even the trees your husband or one of your sons had chopped down.

For the boys, it was tedious work. When there was no logging, they would pick potatoes in the fall. For the girls, it was pick potatoes, cook, clean, sew or help take care of other children.

Boys toiled hard; girls grew into mamas before they knew what it was like to be a child.

Only Alfred seemed to enjoy his work, relishing a job done well. The Turcottes were poor, but they didn't know it. Poverty hung limp on every clothesline around here, playing no favorites.

The hard truth was that nobody made money going to school. A mother and a father needed their sons and daughters to both help around the farm and go out and get a job to help support a family, which, like Rose and Alfred's brood, was usually very large.

In the Catholic Church, women were born to bear children. The more the better. In these times, in a French Catholic community, it was almost immoral if you didn't birth a child every year. Two of Rose's children died very early. Born prematurely, Joseph died two weeks later; Raymond died of the flu at 11 months.

Rose blinks away a tear.

Doctors from Grand Falls had come to their house several times to help Joseph and Raymond. But there was nothing they could do, nothing anyone could have done. It's God's will, the priest said both times. And that was that.

When the twins, Camille and Camilla, were born in 1940, Rose's mother, Memerie Clavette Devost, came to live with them. Memerie stayed 14 years until, when she was almost 80, she had to be put in a nursing home when she couldn't remember her own name.

After the twins, in order of age, came Ron, Noel, Odette, Aurele, Rudy, Albert, Raymonde, Roger and Gaetan.

"God willing, I've done my part," thinks Rose as she pulls back the leek-green drapes, rubs a hole through frost on the bedroom window and looks out into swirling, chalky white. Their property was now invisible.

Along with farming vegetables, the Turcottes also got eggs from their chickens, milk from their two cows, and fish from a nearby trout stream they called Turcotte Brook. And then there was plenty of wild meat from the animals that Alfred, Camille, Ron and Noel would hunt and skin. Rabbits they had snared hung frozen in the shed. There was always plenty to eat.

The Turcottes' two-storey home was spartan. There were two bedrooms on the main floor, and three more upstairs where the children would sleep — two, three or even four crammed tightly in each bed. What they called a sitting room — mostly because of the faded burgundy couch, which sagged in the middle — was just an extension of the kitchen. There was no running water, just an outhouse and then a heavy metal tub for fetching creek water, which would be heated on the wood stove.

But everything was tidy. Everything in its place. The glass mason jars were lined up like toy soldiers filled with flour, sugar, salt and other spices. The coats and overalls hung from wooden pegs near the front door. The black Bible, with its pages curled like dried flower petals, on the nightstand; the crucifix on the far wall; the iron dipper that leaned against the brim of the tub; the black-foot treadle Singer sewing machine, which had stitched together just about every piece of clothing the family owned.

There was a radio, tuned to French channels. Just the previous month, the radio told how the Soviet Union had launched its second satellite, *Sputnik 2*, into space — this one carrying a dog named Laika. The announcers called it "Muttnik" and laughed when they said it. But Rose and Alfred didn't think this was anything to joke about. It was the Cold War, after all. If they could put a dog into a satellite, who was to say they couldn't send up a bomb?

Comfort, though, could also be heard from the French songs of David Arugete, who was better known by his stage name of Dario Moreno, and Cristina Gigliotti, professionally known as Dalida. English singing stars like Paul Anka, Perry Como and Pat Boone were also favorites. Elvis Presley and Buddy Holly, the Turcottes could do without.

The radio also told Rose that *The Bridge on the River Kwai* was a wonderful movie that she would long to see. But Rose knew she probably never would.

A cold slice of air slips through a tiny crack, making her shiver. "Life never seems to begin, or end," thinks Rose, who is 42. "It just flows like the rivers, crashing into the rocks and carrying on."

Sometimes the hours torment her. The hands on the clock seem to be stuck — time passing only as marked by the shadows that creep along the walls and the hardwood floors. And then there are moments, like now, when she looks back and finds yesterdays racing by; no matter what you do you can't stop the tick, tick, ticking.

The twins already 17. And Ron just a year younger.

Camille, Camilla and Ron had all left school by Grade 8, rushed out by circumstance rather than their own accord. Camille had been working in the woods with Alfred for what, three years? And Ron had already been there for two years. He was just a child of 14 when he left for the woods for weeks at a time. Camilla had left home completely, working as a live-in nanny — a "gardienne" for Lionel Lavoie's family an hour's drive away in Edmundston, where Maine and Quebec's Gaspé Peninsula left a little bracket of New Brunswick alone to itself.

"I swear, the next time I blink Noel, Odette, and Aurele will be out of school too. Then Rudy, Albert and then even you and Roger," she thinks, looking down at Gaetan's little body snuggled in her arms.

A branch thwacks against the window, startling her.

"Good gracious; look at me. Thinking about all these things on a night like this," Rose chastises herself with the snow swirling. The sky is the color of sour milk.

But then this is what the middle of the night always seemed to do to her. The darkness unlatching the imagination, free to conjure up God knows what.

Echoes, creaks, footfalls and the wind all sounding like fingernails scratching a blackboard. Punishment for not being asleep.

But the next sound isn't her imagination, isn't the naked floorboards, isn't the wind and certainly isn't Gaetan, whom she still cuddles in her arms.

It is something else. But what then?

It sounded like the crackle of twigs being stamped underfoot from outside the bedroom.

But in winter? With a wild storm still raging outside?

Rose takes careful steps into the kitchen.

Then comes the acrid smell of something horribly wrong. For an instant Rose hopes it is only the stink of Alfred's cigarettes, the ones she would steal a puff from when no one was watching. But Alfred is asleep.

Then she looks toward the cellar stairs and straight into the gates of hell.

"God, no!" she shrieks as flames — hissing like a hungry demon — start to claw their way from the basement.

"Get up!" Rose yells to Alfred. "Grab the children! Wrap the young ones in blankets!"

A cobweb of fog stuck to his senses, Alfred spins out of the bed. He is on Rose's heels racing up the stairs to the top floor, where Camille and Ron sleep in one bedroom, Odette and Raymonde in another and the four remaining children — Noel, Rudy, Aurele and Albert — sleep two to a bed in the third bedroom.

"Fire! Fire! Everyone out!" he screams, shooing the children toward the front door.

The smoke is already thick — gasping plumes of white and gray all pushed together as if the blizzard had somehow moved inside.

Looking for water to throw down the cellar stairs but seeing the tub empty, Rose cries out, holding Gaetan in one arm, the other covering her face.

Choking and gasping — their own faces streaked with fear and panic — the children pour down the stairs, out the door and into the frozen night.

Rose starts to count.

One: Gaetan in her arms.

Two: 3-year-old Raymonde, clutching tight to her waist.

Three: Albert, only 6, but already as tall as the older boys.

Four: Rudy.

Five: Odette, barefoot and shivering with cold and fright.

Six, seven: Camille and Noel, four dark eyes staring into the flames.

Eight: Aurele.

Nine: Ronnie.

Ten? For a second Rose's heart stops. Only nine. It can't be. There should be 11. Where are the other two?

Trembling, Rose wills herself to concentrate. In her panic, she has forgotten that Camilla is in Edmundston.

But that still leaves one child missing.

"Oh my God. Roger!" someone cries. "Roger is still inside."

Impulsively, Noel barrels back through the flames to where barefoot 3-year-old Roger is still sleeping in the rocking chair, wrapped in a checkered blanket, oblivious to the horror that surrounds him.

Noel grabs Roger and races out.

With Roger safe, Noel goes back through the flames. His eyes darting through the smoke, he looks for something — anything — else to save. He takes the heavy metal Singer sewing machine.

"My money! I must get my money," yells Camille, remembering his life savings — maybe $30, much of it in coins, in a drawer next to his bed. He starts back through the flames, hands crossed in front of his face.

Odette sees Camille's pajama bottoms catch on fire.

Rose screams.

Alfred tries to grab Camille but misses and goes back inside himself, yelling at Camille to stop.

A moment later comes a crash of glass. Then Alfred and Camille jump from an upstairs window — their falls cushioned by the deep snow.

"Our Father, who art in heaven," Rose begins, only slightly under her breath, while crossing herself several times.

Still in their long johns and nightshirts, a few of the children struggle on one leg to put on the boots and shoes they have gathered from the pile of footwear near the front door. Otherwise, they stand half naked in the storm, tears freezing hard against their faces.

Nothing is saved except their lives and the sewing machine.

No clothes except for what they have on. Left to burn are the dresses, skirts and tops that Odette had bought with the money she had made picking potatoes at Danois Cultivators. Odette had spent weeks selecting the clothes from an Eaton's catalogue. It was the first time she had clothes that were new and not made from remnants. They were the only possessions she owned.

No pots, pans, chairs or tables. No food. Not even any snippets of the past — no family pictures or little souvenirs carefully collected through the years.

The water pitcher that Memerie had brought with her with purple flowers painted on the side. The ceramic bowl that sat next to the pitcher. Rose's rocking chair, where they had almost forgotten Roger and where she used to sit at night hunched over her knitting.

Gone. All gone forever.

Life leaking away from them, for the longest time nobody seems able to speak as they huddle together except for Ron and Camille, who have gone to get the horses out of the barn and ride them two miles to safety at their friends' the Pinettes.

The rest of the family stands in silence listening as the roof groans and splinters in supplication.

Just weeks ago, tight for money, Alfred had canceled their home insurance.

Aurele looks around for the familiar wagging tail that is nowhere in sight and asks where is the white and black mongrel they call Puppy — the same name they had called all their dogs they had owned. With their bills piling up higher than the drifts of snow, to clear his tab with Guay, Alfred had sold Puppy to the storeowner, whose children loved the dog. Guay even threw in a foot-long tube of bologna so thick even Alfred's big hands could barely wrap around it. But even though their homes were 10 miles away Puppy kept finding his way back to the Turcottes.

"Maybe he got away," Alfred lies, still able to see the dog's confused eyes staring helplessly after Alfred and Camille had jumped from the window. "He always comes back."

A family cat is also missing.

Weakly, Rose says, "It's okay. We're all safe. We're all together. The family is together."

One minute Rose was walking with her baby thinking about her mother, Alfred's ancestors, church and school. Then you blink and everything has vanished.

You could curse. But not Rose. Now, not even Alfred can do that. They just stand there dumbstruck, their breath billowing out and then slapping back against their faces as the gusts pick it up and swat it away. What is left of the house falls away in shreds, while crackling embers dance and twinkle, spirited away by the whims of the scolding wind. There are muted thuds and hissing as the burning timbers fall into the cushioning heavy snow.

Rose and Alfred tell the younger kids to go with Odette up the hill to their closest neighbors, the Mocklers. They and Gaetan will be right behind.

"It'll be alright. Go ahead now," says Rose.

None of the children want to go but Rose insists.

"If you don't go, you'll freeze to death."

At once, the children trudge single file, as if in a funeral procession, the roiling snow burying their footprints behind them. Halfway up, Odette looks back against an orange-flamed sky as the last timbers fall flickering to the ground like matchsticks.

No one says anything now. Just sobs and tears as they stumble forward, heads and backs bowed as if being pushed down by both the weight of the squall and the much heavier load of their sadness.

In the distance, they hear the ringing bells and the shriek of the sirens echoing the too-late arrival of firetrucks, which had to crawl behind a snowplow that tried to clear a path.

Weeping, Raymonde keeps stopping to look behind.

"Come, Raymonde," Odette says in the best calm voice a 12-year-old can muster. "We're almost there."

But when they arrive at the Mocklers' door and knock gingerly, there is no answer.

"Let's go to the Cotes'," says Odette, her teeth quivering. "Surely, they'll be home."

It means another frigid climb up another hill. When they arrive at the Cotes' the door is open. Rose, who is already there with Alfred and Gaetan, rushes out arms spread wide and wraps them around each of the children. Rose desperately wants to close her eyes and lie down then and there in one of the endless banks of white — just bury her head and cry.

Maybe then it would have only been one very horrifying dream. Gaetan would still be in his crib; Alfred would still be snoring beside her. Instead, sobbing, they retreat inside, where there is an uneasy silence with the Cotes not knowing what to say and the Turcottes still engulfed in disbelief and terror.

"Thank God nobody was killed," Antoine finally says. "You could have all been burned to death."

Another uncomfortable pause follows.

"Gaetan," Rose says suddenly, hugging the baby even closer. "He woke me with his cries. It was Gaetan who saved us. God must have woken us."

Not knowing what else to do or say, Antoine's wife, Jeanne, hurries to start boiling some water for cocoa and coffee.

"How in the world did the fire start?" she calls from the kitchen.

"The wood stove must have overheated," replies Alfred of the two 45-gallon oil drums that had been welded together and dug into a hole in the basement to provide heat for the home. "Maybe the grate hadn't been properly closed. Maybe it had popped open. Maybe a spark. I really don't know."

All he did know was that they were back to starting from zero.

"We're all safe," Rose says again. "That's the only thing that matters."

In a shaken, hushed voice Rudy pulls Noel aside and asks, "Do you think we started the fire? We were shaving wood to make bows and arrows. Do you think the shavings were too close to the stove? The grate may have opened, and a spark may have landed on the shavings."

Rudy and Noel never talk about it again.

The snow quits the next morning.

Chapter 2

The sun has barely started its ascent through the mottled sky and up and over the frosted pines. Rose goes to a neighbor and phones the Lavoies' house, where Camilla, 17, is working as a nanny for Lionel, a baker who has his own shop in Edmundston, and his wife.

Rose dreads making the call. She doesn't know what she is going to say and worries how Camilla will take the news.

On the fifth ring, Camilla picks up.

Rose begins, "Don't worry. We're all safe, but I just wanted you to know ... "

She doesn't get to finish.

"Mama," interrupts Camilla. "What's wrong?"

"There was a fire and ... "

Camilla's legs turn rubbery. The floor seems to fall away; the walls spin.

"We're safe," Rose says again. "No one got hurt."

But Camilla isn't listening. Can't listen. She is kneeling on the floor.

"Tell me what happened. Is the house gone?"

Rose confirms with a throat-jammed affirmation.

Camilla's cries jar the Lavoie family to attention. Lionel and his wife huddle around her in a tight circle.

"I'll come as soon as I can," Camilla says.

"No, dear, stay there. There's nothing you can do," replies Rose, who, like everyone except the youngest children, has not slept.

After a long pause, Camilla tells her mother goodbye, tells her she loves her and slowly puts the phone in its cradle. Trying to rise, Camilla wobbles. She puts out her right hand to lean against the refrigerator, misses, and starts to fall again. Lionel grabs her elbow, but she shakes it loose.

"Camilla? What's happened?" Lionel asks, knowing all too well that whatever it was he didn't want to hear.

Camilla's chest is shuddering and heaving; her stomach climbs into her throat and just sits there, dry as crackers. She can hardly breathe, but she tells him.

Lionel grabs a glass of water and holds it to Camilla's lips. She sips but is unable to swallow. Madame Lavoie pushes a chair underneath Camilla; Lionel puts a clumsy arm around her shoulder. One of them hands her a tissue.

Camilla quietly says, "I need to go home." Home? Camilla catches herself. There is no home.

An hour later, driven by Lionel, Camilla is on her way to Drummond, hugging south along the Saint John River and the eastern border of Maine.

Camilla has put together a cardboard box tied with a piece of twine. It is full of things she has been gathering for her dowry: white sheets and pillowcases she had embroidered with green, yellow and blue flowers (three in every corner), two canary-yellow serving pots with matching spoons and forks and half a dozen porcelain cups and plates.

Before they left, Lionel had also pressed an envelope into her shaking hands. Three $20 bills — a month's wages in advance. Lionel also filled a paper bag with two croissants and two chocolate bran muffins, as well as some other pastries from his bakery, and a thermos of hot coffee. But Camilla is too upset to eat. She does, however, sip on the coffee.

Passing by the evergreen forests, Camilla tries to make sense of any of this during the one-hour's drive.

What would she possibly say when she arrived?

Her mother and father with no money, now without even a roof over their heads. Ten brothers and sisters. All homeless in the middle of another cold winter. A nightmare.

In two more weeks, Camilla would have been journeying home with thoughts of Christmas on her mind. A ham or turkey for dinner. A tree — a big one they would cut down themselves — decorated with strings of popcorn and tinsel. Midnight mass. Carols.

Every Christmas each child would get an orange and one — maybe two if they were really lucky — article of clothing Rose had sewn. Camilla wondered what Mama made for her this year. Probably a sweater. That's what she had told Rose she wanted, and her mother never let her down.

"How quickly your world can change," she thinks. "Even if you could presage the future, there wasn't anything you could do about it." She tries another sip of coffee.

"At least no one got hurt," Camilla tells herself. "It could have been worse. Be thankful it wasn't."

Once a month, Camilla would take a bus and come home. Only two weeks ago she had made the trip, but now, somehow, it felt like it had been 50 years. Each time Camilla came back to Drummond, she would bring some of her wages to give to her parents, as well as clothes and some Dentyne cinnamon-flavored gum for her brothers and sisters. Her siblings would yell and gather around her like little birds, mouths agape, waiting for her to pull the gum out of her pocket.

There will be no shouts of joy this time. Even so, she has brought the gum anyway.

Just before 10 a.m., the car pulls up at the Cotes' front door.

"Mama," cries Camilla, throwing herself into Rose's arms, still able to smell the damp smoke on her mother's clothes.

Running from all parts of the house, the children throw their arms around Camilla. Hot tears run.

"Where will you stay?" asks Camilla.

At this point, there is no answer. Over the next three days, the Turcottes scatter like the ashes of their former home. Ron, Noel and Camille stay with their friends the Pinettes, a little farther up the road from the Mocklers. Rudy, Albert and Aurele live with Guay. Odette, Raymonde, Roger, Gaetan, Rose and Alfred all remain with the Cotes.

Ron, Noel and Camille figure they are the lucky ones; the Pinettes own a television set. Together they watch westerns like *The Lone Ranger* and *Hopalong Cassidy* on the fuzzy black-and-white screen.

Monsignor Alfred Lang, who has baptized all of the Turcotte children, comes to the Cotes' every day, leading the family in prayer.

"The Lord helps those who help themselves," says the priest. "He is always testing us. It is how we meet the challenges that defines us."

"Then the Lord must be family because it is family that have come together to help us," Rose answers to herself. "Family and good friends that are just like family." She finds comfort in that.

A day doesn't pass without someone asking if there is anything they can do. The Turcottes receive armloads of baked casseroles and pots of soup and stew. Some people bring bedding and clothes. But most of what they receive comes from the Red Cross, where a friendly woman lifts big cardboard boxes over an unfinished counter and hands them to a sheepish Odette, a second version of her mother. Grateful for the gifts, Odette, who works in the church rectory, feels ashamed having to stand there with her arms open.

A bell rings above her when she opens the door to leave. In one box, Odette sees a bright red dress — satin with white embroidery along the edges — that she hopes will fit her.

Despite the tragedy, some of the children at the Drummond school revel in the Turcottes' plight.

"Hey, Aurele; that's my shirt you've got on," says one kid.

"And my pants," says another.

Odette hears it too. "Are you wearing my underwear?" someone chides, starting off a flood of giggles. Odette buries her head and runs away weeping.

Within just three days of the fire, the Turcottes are together again. A neighbor, Jos Ouellette, moved in with his recently widowed son, Armand, whose wife died giving birth. For a small stipend, Ouellette rents his house to the Turcottes.

Not much larger than the home they lost, this house at least has an inside pump for water. At their old house, water had to be brought in from a creek, even in winter when ice needed to be chipped until there was a hole wide enough to dip in a bucket. The freezing water would then be warmed on the wood stove for Saturday baths in the kitchen sink or to wash clothes and dishes.

From outside the family looking in, it is as if nothing has changed. One day ends. The next one begins. It didn't seem to matter which way you looked at it. Maybe, just maybe, if you went to church and prayed hard, not too much more damnable misery would come your way.

Albert, Rudy, Odette, Aurele and Noel are back in school. Camilla is back in Edmundston. Soon Camille leaves for Toronto, where he finds work as a roofer.

Saturday mornings, while the younger kids are at the Pinettes' watching television, Rose and Odette do the laundry, pressing the freshly washed clothes with a heavy iron.

Saturdays in the winter, the kids used to sled down the many hills in Grand Falls or skate and play hockey on a neighbor's pond using horse manure as pucks and tree branches for sticks. Not everyone in the village had skates, but they adapted. If a local boy's feet were much too small to fit into any of his family's skates, he'd wear his winter boots inside to fill them out. For the Turcottes, strap-on skates were nothing more than hand-me-downs originally made from blocks of wood with a sharpened piece of metal for blades.

Sundays for the Turcottes were pancakes for breakfast and then church at Saint-Michel, followed by boiled wieners for lunch. A ritual. All of the Turcottes would attend Sunday mass except for Alfred, who had stopped going when the parish priest told him he couldn't eat meat on Fridays.

"To hell with you then," Alfred had said. "I'm going to eat meat when I damn well want to eat meat. If that means I'm not welcome in your church, then so be it."

Instead, Alfred would drive Rose and the kids to Saint-Michel every Sunday and wait outside, smoking one cigarette after another, often forgetting he had one cigarette already on the go.

Alfred would make a few reluctant concessions. He did go to Saint-Michel for baptisms, first Communions and Christmas mass. But even then, he protested all the way.

June brought the annual Potato Festival in Grand Falls: a parade with marching bands, with potatoes strung together like a Christmas tree garland hanging from the floats, and a fairground with carnival rides like a Ferris wheel and merry-go-round.

On Halloween, instead of the children dressing up and collecting candy in bags, one of the farmers would put on a costume and come to them, delivering sweets and apples.

Sometimes there were even games, like hide-and-go-seek, cowboys and Indians, and plenty of clinking games of horseshoes. You didn't need money to have fun.

There was also a lot of fishing with long, whippy branches whittled down to a smooth finish, hooks fashioned from bent wire, worms for bait and fishing lines — usually nothing more than string.

"Now don't tell anyone else," Noel always said to Odette when they got to his favorite spot, where trout practically leaped out of the water and onto their lines. "No one. It's our little secret."

Because those crude fishing poles couldn't cast the string lines very far, Ron made a boat so that he could get closer to the beaver dams, where the fish would gather in large schools. When the primitive boat sank, Ron turned it into a raft.

When they weren't fishing, the kids hunted. They all learned how to shoot when they were young.

Once, when some hunters killed a mother bear near the logging camp, Alfred, cutting wood, spotted the baby cub. Using all his guile, he caught the cub and brought it all the way home to show his kids, who then gave it food and milk.

But television remained the center of activity. It was on TV — at the Pinettes' or at Uncle Sam Turcotte's house on the top of a hill — where they watched *Hockey Night in Canada* on Saturdays — the only game of the week that was broadcast.

When the kids were at the Pinettes', before they watched any TV, they had to get down on their knees and pray one full rosary, which would take about an hour.

Usually, the weekly game was another instalment of the Toronto Maple Leafs against the Montreal Canadiens. You loved one of those teams, hated the other. The Turcottes, of course, cheered for the dynastic Habs, which in the spring of 1958 — led by Jacques Plante in goal, Jean Beliveau, Doug Harvey, Bernie Geoffrion, Dickie Moore and, of course, Henri and Maurice Richard — had defeated the Boston Bruins for their third of what would be five straight Stanley Cups.

On Fridays, there was wrestling and boxing that riveted the attention of the Turcottes and the rest of the nation's French Canadians. Wrestling had Canadians Édouard Carpentier and Killer Kowalski; boxing had Yvon Durelle.

Carpentier — born in France to a Russian father and a Polish mother — moved to Quebec in 1956. A crowd favorite, whose real name was Edouard Wiecz, Carpentier — known for his acrobatic leaps from the turnbuckles — was Alfred's idol too. Alfred roared when Carpentier defeated world champion Lou Thesz on June 14, 1957, and then cursed even louder when Thesz took the title back, as often happened in wrestling's orchestrations, on a disqualification a month later in Montreal.

As worshipped as Carpentier was, Durelle, the "Fighting Fisherman" from Baie Ste. Anne, on the east coast of New Brunswick, was even more revered for Alfred. Watching Gillette's Friday night boxing on December 10, 1958, when Durelle went into the ring in Montreal against Archie Moore, Alfred has gathered with many other men from the village in the Pinettes' front room, which is standing-room only for the world light-heavyweight title fight.

Twelve thousand Maritime fans had signed a telegram wishing Durelle a victory.

Three times in the first round alone, Durelle knocks Moore, the 4-1 favorite, puddling to the canvas. On two of those occasions, the referee counts to nine — Moore barely beating the count. The men scream themselves hoarse. But Moore's will is limitless. Six rounds later, after an absurd comeback, it is Durelle on his back and Moore with his hands raised in triumph.

Even with his hero fallen in defeat, nights like these let Alfred forget the fire that burned down his home just two days ago.

Chapter 3

A year after the fire, Ron, now 17, and Alfred are back in the woods of New Brunswick or Maine, depending on where they are needed. They have been in camp for two weeks with no idea how long they will be there. It could be months.

Forests and rivers. Those were Alfred's and Ron's real homes anyway. Aspen, spruce, fir, yellow birch, maple, ash and tamarack were their roofs and walls, with the varicose veins of the Salmon and Suppertime rivers the borders of their existence.

A fireplug of a man, Alfred is nearly as wide as he his tall. He packs 170 pounds onto his 5-foot 4-inch frame. Strong as moonshine, Alfred has corded, sinewy arms and a neck that seems like it's welded to his broad shoulders.

Three inches shorter and 50 pounds lighter than his father, Ron's bulk is all thick, hard muscle; he is a splintered, slender version of Alfred. Working 16 hours a day lifting, pulling, chopping, sawing, prying and sorting the logs by length will do that to you, especially when you are cutting an average of 100 trees a day.

Spring, summer, fall or winter, it was all the same hard work. The thud of the axes meeting bark, the shrill whirr of power saws, the rasping snores of crosscut saws being pulled back and forth. Every day it seemed like it was raining green and rusty brown with sheets of evergreen needles falling in thick torrents. Needles got stuck in the lumberjacks' hair and latched onto their clothing like leeches. You could always tell those new to the woods by how they frantically kept brushing and picking and plucking the needles.

Alfred and Ron would laugh. Give them a few more weeks. Soon they'd stop caring.

In some camps, loggers lopped off the branches as they scaled the trees. However, in Alfred's camp, the men were instructed to limb the trees only when they were already nestled on the ground. It took longer, but it was safer. Everyone had heard stories of safety lines and harnesses accidentally getting cut or breaking — lumberjacks plummeting to their deaths, their hips compressing into their shoulders when they hit the ground.

Trees have no conscience. Cut trees take everything in their fall. Limbs break, scattering and slicing in a hundred different directions. Chains snap. Power saws kick back like recoiling cannons.

Once on the ground, the fallen trees would be cut into 20-foot logs. Then, with cables hooked around their girth, they would be hauled away by horses.

On top of all his other duties, Ron is in charge of the horses that pull the cut logs to the river or onto the mill. Each day, he rises at 4 a.m. to feed the horses and have breakfast, usually salted pork and baked beans washed down by dishwater coffee. Then he returns to his logging work until 6 p.m. Still not done, Ron then takes the harnesses off the horses, brushes their manes and coats, painstakingly picks the wood shavings and sawdust out of their hooves and then feeds and waters them.

As hard as the men work, the horses do 10 times as much. A good horse, Alfred always said, was everything. A stubborn horse was no better than a stubborn logger. Neither would get much accomplished. The more a man and a horse got along the better off you both were. There were horses you could trust and horses you wouldn't dare turn your backside on.

Two of the camp's horses belonged to Alfred. Small by draft horse standards, they still weighed 1,400 pounds. For reasons unknown, Alfred called them both Bess, but they couldn't have been more different if one were a bear and the other a mouse.

Good Bess had the stoic disposition of someone who knew its lot in life and simply decided to make the best of it. Good Bess never complained, never balked. She worked the lumber as well as any man — positioning herself just right so that she wouldn't get hit when a tree came falling out of the sky. Then she'd wait, patient as a preacher, until the chain was wrapped around the log and then fixed to her harness. If a log got stuck between stumps or between still-standing trees, she would work it free herself.

At the boom, Good Bess would stop, back up without Ron having to say a word so that the chain would slacken, and her load could be unhooked. Then she'd move on to the next log that was ready to be hauled away.

Other Bess was skittish as a cat in a room full of rocking chairs. She always wanted to get things over with in a hurry, which usually meant just getting in the way and having to be whacked on her big ass to get pointed in the right direction.

Either way, Ron was proud of both Good Bess and Other Bess.

In the spring and fall, the logs would be rolled onto the frigid rivers. Then the cattle drive of logs — speeding along the liquid highways, weaving through the narrows, climbing rocks and tumbling, end over end, down the jagged falls — would begin.

It was one thing to cut down a 60-foot bull tree, another to cut it into 20-foot sections, stacked like beaver dam condominiums. It was quite another to ride those bucking logs on rivers down to the smoking mills. The bigger drives, often employing more than 100 men, could take months to complete.

Alfred, a log driver or "river pig," whose job was to ensure the logs drifted freely along the river, couldn't swim a lick. But it didn't stop him from riding the logs. First digging in his inch-long spikes on his boots, he would then drive the point of a cant hook or log peavey into the flesh of the logs.

Keeping the logs moving, guiding them through open water, was what the drives were all about. Otherwise, the logs would jam together — one log piling up on another. Jams were inevitable, like opinions, and every log drive had them. Almost always there were a few infernal logs that caused all the trouble — turning themselves sideways and losing their way. Sometimes just one recalcitrant key log would cause the entire problem — one last snowflake to start an avalanche. A log driver would then have to dislodge the log and then roll it back into the middle of the river.

The first unnerving sign of a logjam is silence. The crashing logs stop; then there is an eerie quiet when suddenly you can hear the birds sing and the rustle of the leaves.

Sometimes when a jam formed, the whole operation would come to a halt and it could take weeks to dislodge. Other times, if the lumberjacks were lucky, their peaveys could be used to birl, prod or poke free the resisting logs. As a last resort, dynamite would be used.

Sometimes a drive took the men hostage. Other times it played judge and executioner.

In the spring of 1948, Rose heard Camilla calling from the front steps: "Mama, come out here. Look over there."

Rose went out to look, as did Camille and Ron. There they saw Treffle Ouellette's children, all 12 of them dressed in black, marching unsteadily in silence.

A jam had formed a mile from the Davis Mill near a covered CN railway bridge. Treffle's peavey had snapped in half, spilling him and half a dozen other men into the raging waters. Everyone was found — shaking, wet and scared. Everyone except Treffle. It would be two months before they found his body washed up near the Turcottes' house, a full mile and a half downstream from where he had fallen.

Rose never could let Treffle's death leave her mind. The image of the Ouellette children walking solemnly in procession assaulted her every time Alfred and Ron left for the woods on a horse-drawn sleigh. One slip and they could wind up the same way — drowned or crushed under the clotting sea of logs.

Treffle's widow told Rose that her husband had smelled the stench of fear the last time they saw each other. Thrice, the widow said, her husband had started to leave for the woods only to have something tell him not to go. Twice he came home. The third time he kept going.

"At least because his body was found we were able to give him a proper burial," Mrs. Ouellette said to Rose.

They both nodded. Often, when lumberjacks died in the woods, they were buried where they were found; their co-workers hanging their spiked boots from tree branches.

A night never passed when Alfred and Ron — and before that Camille — were gone that Rose's vivid imagination didn't spill over with worry, overflowing like the rain barrel on the porch after a week of rain. Since that day, Rose always wondered what she would do when there was a knock on the door and a man from the mill would be standing on the porch staring at the floor. Would she invite him in? Would she turn away and run?

It didn't matter that Alfred had been coming and going to the woods since they were married in September 1939. She never got used to it. The last thing Alfred always did was kiss her on the forehead. Then he would be gone, the door closing behind him and then, soon, the horses' harnesses jangling — the sound meshing with the birds chirping or a dog barking somewhere in the distance.

When Alfred was gone, and the house was quiet, she pictured trees splitting apart in rage — gnarly limbs stretching like the bony fingers of a ghostly apparition. Or she would see a dented, dirty yellow helmet bobbing under more fingers, the frothing hands of waves, and on the shore, a long line of loggers standing silently, their arms at their sides.

Why weren't they helping Alfred? Please. Help him.

Rose never told Alfred or anyone else about these horrible daydreams. He would've just told her not to be so silly, and she would have to lie and agree.

Death and danger were bedfellows of loggers and their families. All they could do was accept it and push it as far as they could into the back of their minds. It wasn't a matter of if someone was going to get hurt; it was when.

Chapter 4

One more winter gnaws on. It is mid-February 1960, and another blizzard's hefty winds blow so much snow that Rose feels everything is burning. She blanches at the thought.

Drummond closes up tighter than a ripening marmalade jar. The logging camps are shut down.

Rose is eight months pregnant with her 14th and last child, Yves.

Without work, Alfred has had more time to pour himself shots of Five Star whiskey. A shot becomes a few fingers. A few fingers become a full glass. A full glass becomes a bottle.

On March 13, 20 years after the birth of Alfred and Rose's first children, Yves is born, and the cold weather finally breaks. The sky turns yellow, and the lumber camps reopen.

But Ron knows he won't last long.

Alfred has just had his third heart attack, and his doctor tells him the work is too hard for a man with his conditions. Instead, Alfred is put in charge of the Grand Falls campsite and fairgrounds.

Ron not only won't have his dad beside him but also won't have his favorite workhorse. Needing money, Alfred sells Good Bess for $400.

Twins Camilla and Camille send money home when they can: Camilla from Edmundston, and Camille from Toronto.

But it isn't nearly enough.

Ron told Camille at Christmas that he wants to come to Toronto. Now he is certain. He would work as a roofer, a carpenter or whatever it takes. Just as long as he doesn't have to stay in Drummond anymore. Five years in the woods was enough.

Ten days later, the stiff winds blow Ron and his best friend, Reggie Pelletier, toward Toronto. They have no idea where they are heading.

Ron and Reggie each have $50 in their pockets. They have a pair of work boots, gloves and two changes of clothes in a gray tattered suitcase.

The furthest Ron went in school was Grade 8. Reggie, stricken with tuberculosis when he was 12 and forced to live in a sanitarium for three years, only made it to Grade 6.

But here they are. Two 18-year-olds out to make their fortunes.

Wilfrid Guay gives the boys a ride to Quebec, where he is headed on business anyway. From there a bus takes the boys to Cobourg, Ontario, where Rose's brother, Aurele Devost, takes them the rest of the way to Toronto.

"You can let us out anywhere," says Ron.

"But where are you going to stay?" asks Aurele.

Through the car window Ron sees a cardboard sign hanging on the window of a boarding house that reads, "Rooms $3 a week."

"There," says Ron, pointing.

On the third floor of their new home, the boys' room is barely large enough to hold a pine table, a couple of chairs, one bed — which they both eye covetously — a hot plate and a clear view of a flashing red neon sign across the street.

"Well, here we are," says Ron.

They shrug their shoulders together.

The boys have Camille's address but when they track him down the next morning, he is picking bottles out of trash cans in his neighborhood.

"I thought you were roofing," says Ron dispiritedly.

Camille explains that a citywide carpenters' strike has paralyzed most of Toronto's construction market. Camille is out of work. When he tried to cross the picket lines, he was pelted with stones.

"Have you told Mom and Dad?" Ron asks.

"Are you kidding?" Camille answers brusquely.

Ron smiles at the way Camille's dark eyes lift into his eyebrows.

"They'd just tell me to come home. I left to get away from the woods. I'm never going back."

"Me either," says Ron in a voice that he realizes doesn't sound as reassuring as it was a couple of days ago.

Spring has prodded Toronto awake but barely. Ron and Reggie — their breaths billowing into the cool, damp days and under skies that are as unsavory as cold porridge — try to find work everywhere, but nothing beckons. A hat shop. Department stores. Lumberyard. Hotels and restaurants. Doors knocked on. Doors closed. Nothing.

When Ron asks if there is any work, the response is always the same. One look at his boyish looks and 5-foot 1-inch height, and the boys are both quickly waved away. "We don't have any jobs for kids," is the common rejoinder. A foot taller and 30 pounds heavier than Ron, Reggie soon becomes the one doing the inquiring.

After three weeks, the best they have been able to do is wash dishes for meals.

"How is it going?" the boarding house landlord asks one day. As little as he sees them and with their weekly rent always coming in on time, the landlord assumes they both must be working.

"No good," says Ron. "We can't find a job anywhere. We're almost broke. I don't know how much longer we will be able to stay." The admission wounds him.

"Well, why didn't you say something before?" says the landlord, who tells the boys that his son owns the Union Bait Company. "I'm sure he can find you work."

"Just tell us when and where," the boys say, never bothering to ask what the work is or how much it will pay.

Rising, the landlord picks up a small red book from a table near the phone. Putting on his glasses he dials a number.

"Tomorrow at 10 p.m.," says the landlord after a brief phone call. "A truck will come by and pick you up at the corner of Bloor and Bathurst."

The first smiles in weeks crease the boys' faces.

"What do you think the job is?" asks Reggie.

"Who cares," Ron answers.

When they show up the next night, a long line of dour faces has already formed. They wait in a broken single file, shuffling their feet back and forth, tracing the cracks in the pavement.

"Must be a big company," Reggie whispers.

At 10 p.m. on the dot, three open-backed vans arrive. But only half of the men are selected to get in. The rest, Ron and Reggie included, are turned away. Hands crunched into their pockets, they watch the red taillights disappear into the darkness.

Rejected one more time, promise and anticipation leak away, like rice trailing from a rip in a burlap sack. But if growing up in New Brunswick has taught them anything, it is perseverance. The next night, they show up at 8 p.m. and claim a spot close to the front of the line. Then squeezed between 30 or 40 men, Reggie and Ron feel every bump as the large truck drives through the night air.

No one speaks until Reggie breaks the silence.

"So, what kind of work are we going to do?"

A couple of men snicker. Finally, one of them says, "Worms, boy. You pick worms."

Reggie turns to Ron, his eyes like a wound-up jack-in-the-box ready to jump out of his head.

"We do what?" Reggie whispers into Ron's ear.

Ron shrinks, lowers his head.

A few minutes later, the truck jolts to a stop, and the men are let out at a golf course. Someone hands them a miner's headlamp, four tin cans and four thick rubber bands. They are told to strap the cans to their legs. One of the cans is three-quarters full of a sticky hazel paste that Reggie at first thinks is lard.

"Pine resin," corrects Ron. "I guess it's so the worms don't slip away."

Neither sure what to do next, the boys glance around and see the other men dip their fingers into the paste, shine their lights into the grass and then comb the blades with their gummy fingers.

In the eerie quiet night air, they hear worms plop against metal.

Eight hours later, the sun driving the night crawlers underground and the golf course about to open, another truck pulls up, picks up the men and takes them to a tin warehouse, where the worms are counted.

With the sparks of matches flashing and tiny red dots of cigarette ash glowing with sucked-in air, again they line up.

As he waits, Ron closes his eyes and spies his flat dreams. They came to Toronto full of hope, and now here is Camille cashing in empty bottles, and them cashing in worms. Camille gets 2 cents a bottle; Ron and Reggie get $3 for a thousand worms.

At the bottle depot, the empties are packed away into wooden crates. At the Union Bait Company, the worms are packed — 500 to a box — into a mixture of peat moss where they will be bought by commercial fishermen.

Reggie mutters, "Maybe we should go back home."

Ron doesn't reply. His silence says it all. Every time he calls Camille the answer is always the same: the strike drags on even as the calendar rolls into May.

Between the two of them all the boys have left is $4.12.

Chapter 5

On the first Saturday of May 1960, Ron and Reggie hesitantly write letters home, saying they are coming back. They will start hitchhiking on Monday.

Deflated, the fates having conspired to deal another busted straight, Ron descends the stairs of the rooming house. The landlord is sitting in a chair rocking back and forth in front of the television.

"What are you watching?" Ron asks.

"What am I watching?" the landlord responds. "Why it's the greatest horse race in the world: the Kentucky Derby!"

"What's a derby?" says Ron, who has never seen a racehorse, let alone a racetrack.

The horses are about to enter the starting gate.

"Sit down," says the landlord, motioning to an empty chair. "See that horse right there? That's Victoria Park. He's a Canadian horse. I saw him run at Woodbine a few times last year. He broke the track record a couple of times. Won the Coronation and the Cup and Saucer.

"Now he's running in the Kentucky Derby against the best three-year-olds in the world," continues the landlord, whose name, to this day, Ron can't remember.

"E.P. Taylor owns him. You know who E.P. Taylor is, don't you?"

Ron shakes his head no.

"Good gracious. Where have you been living that you don't know E.P. Taylor?" the landlord says, explaining that E.P. Taylor is a Canadian business tycoon, investor and philanthropist.

"There he is again," the landlord says almost in a shout, wagging his finger at the image of Victoria Park on the screen. "Looks good, doesn't he?"

At least Ron can agree with this. Victoria Park is a fine-looking animal. Ron has lived with horses all his life, but never one that was all tucked up and muscled like the ones on the TV screen.

A bell sounds. "They're off," the landlord trills. "Come on, Victoria Park. Run! Oh, why won't that jockey let him run?"

Victoria Park, as usual, languishes during the early going on a dull and cool afternoon at Louisville, Kentucky.

"There. Now he's coming! Come on, boy. Run! Keep going!"

Ron is cheering too, even as the landlord has stopped clapping.

Venetian Way wins. Victoria Park's charge is too late; he finishes third.

"Ah well, that's not so bad," the landlord consoles himself, knowing this is the first time a Canadian-bred horse ever placed in an American Triple Crown event.

There is a pause as the landlord looks at Ron.

"You know," he says, sizing the young man up. "That's what you should be doing. Lose a little weight and you could be a jockey."

"A what?" says Ron, to which the landlord's jowls shake between roars of laughter.

"A jockey. The little boys in the white pants. Those are jockeys," the landlord tells Ron, adding he should go to the track. "I hear they are always looking for help. It's got to be better than picking worms."

Ron hurries to find Reggie.

"We're going to be alright," he says. "We're going to the racetrack tomorrow. The landlord says we are sure to get a job there."

Like Ron, Reggie knows nothing about horse racing, but he too is familiar with horses. Reggie's grandfather owned three teams of draft horses; a few times Reggie had even been given the reins.

"So, tell me again about this thing about jockeys," says Reggie.

The next day they are at Greenwood Raceway — "Old Woodbine" as it is being called — the Toronto trolley car dropping them off at its last stop.

A guard quickly turns them away. Wrong racetrack, he tells them. The thoroughbreds are at the "New Woodbine," which opened four years ago in 1956.

"Head to the other side of the city," the guard says.

Early the next morning, they take another streetcar, this time the right one heading the right way.

The backstretch of any racetrack is a compound hiding its mysteries behind tall, wired fences or concrete walls. Guards are posted at every entrance. If one didn't know any better, a first glance might suggest a prison. To get into the backstretch you need a license, which Ron and Reggie certainly don't have.

But this time, for once, luck is on their side. A trainer driving in to work sees the boys walking up the long, winding, crushstoned road to the backstretch behind the racetrack.

"Need a ride?" asks the man, who tells them he trains a few horses.

"Yeah, we're going to try and get jobs," says Ron. "You wouldn't need any help, would you?"

The man shakes his head.

In a few seconds, a guard is leaning his face into the driver's window. "Everyone got their passes?" he asks, to which the driver flashes his parking sticker and license.

The guard nods, backs away and raises the crossing gate.

The car continues on what is now a dirt road until it stops at the racing secretary's office.

"Go in there and tell them you're looking for work," the trainer says.

For whatever reason, Jimmy Irvine, an assistant for the Horsemen's Benevolent and Protective Association, doesn't ask the two teenagers how they got into the backstretch and doesn't send them back where they have come from. Instead, Irvine rises from his chair and leads them across the road to barn 5A. This is the Windfields' barn: the barn that houses horses owned by E.P. Taylor, the barn that is the Montreal Canadiens of Canadian horse racing and the barn where the great Gordon "Pete" McCann, who started Victoria Park on his way, trains. The very fine-looking Victoria Park that Ron saw race just two days ago in his landlord's living room.

It is a set of circumstances that could never be duplicated. Ron comes down the stairs while the Kentucky Derby is on TV. His landlord happens to love horse racing. A trainer offers Ron and Reggie a lift and gets them into the backstretch. And Ron ends up at E.P. Taylor's barn, of all places. It is a billion-to-one quadfecta.

One day ends. The next one begins. They fall like dominos. On May 9, 1960, the dominos are finally in the right place.

"Got a couple of boys here looking for work," Irvine says to Joe Thomas, the manager of E.P. Taylor's exploding racing operation.

In his hounds tooth jacket, tie and hat, Thomas always looks like he is setting out on a fox hunt.

"Thought maybe you were looking for some help," Irvine adds.

Crooking an eye, Thomas peers over his pipe at the two boys.

A groom is just making his rounds, leading a horse that still has steam curling skyward from its sweat-soaked chestnut hair.

Thomas takes the shank — part of the bridle — out of the groom's hand and gives it to Ron.

"Take him for a walk," says Thomas. "Just keep turning left."

Just like that Ron has a job. He is a hot walker, someone who cools out a horse after a race or a morning breeze by walking the horse for miles. Ron's pay is $35 a week.

Reggie finds his way to the track kitchen. It is just after 10:30 a.m. It is rush hour for the kitchen as most of the day's work at the track is already done: the horses exercised, fed and watered, and the stalls plumped with fresh straw. Impatiently shuffling their feet, trainers and grooms want their eggs, toast, pancakes and coffee.

A lanky man in pressed blue jeans and worn tan boots demands to know what the holdup is.

"Come on, Sharkey," he bellows at a rotund man inside a grease-stained smock. "What's the problem? I'm going to have to order dinner with my eggs this morning if it takes any longer.

"Yeah," chime in a few others. "Move it, Sharkey."

On the other side of the aluminum counter, where burgundy trays slide past glass windows revealing puddings, Jell-O, fruits and sandwiches, Sharkey Bianco, is bent over a grill where bacon pops like rain drumming on an aluminum can. He doesn't look up.

"Yeah, yeah. Can't you see we're going as fast as we can," says Sharkey, scraping a metal spatula under eggs while continuing to bark orders at two other harried cooks.

Sharkey is wearing his white fedora and a pinstriped suit with lapels wide enough to land a 747.

"Damn help. One of the cooks didn't show up this morning."

Reggie's ears perk and he makes his way closer to Sharkey.

"I'm looking for work. You need some help?"

"Ever work in a kitchen before?" asks Sharkey, even now barely lifting his head.

"Sure," says Reggie, as Sharkey grabs two plates of ham and eggs and half throws them onto the counter.

Reggie is about to keep talking, just about to explain how he had worked as a cook's helper in a lumber camp, but Sharkey is already on to the next question.

"Know how to make an omelet, peel potatoes, flip bacon?"

Yup, says Reggie, three times.

"Here then," he says throwing an apron at Reggie.

"Atta boy, Sharkey," claps the tan boots. A few others break into half-hearted applause.

Ron holds a leather shank; Reggie, a potato peeler. Both have work.

Ron's job comes with a cot in a tack room; Reggie stays in a room above the kitchen. It is the first night in months that both boys sleep with smiles on their faces.

Chapter 6

The next morning dawns with a magnificent red sky embracing the Toronto skyline.

Ron has just unclicked one shank and was about to be handed another when Pete McCann approaches his new French-Canadian employee.

"You know something about horses, don't you?" says McCann, a former jockey who has been E.P. Taylor and Windfields Farm's trainer since 1950.

The first horse McCann saddled for Windfields, Major Factor, won the 1951 Queen's Plate, the oldest continuously run race in North America. McCann didn't stop there. Two years later he won the Plate with Canadiana, the first Canadian-bred to win more than $100,000. Keeping the streak alive, Lyford Cay won the 1957 Plate and in 1959 swept the Canadian Triple Crown with New Providence.

"Uh, yes sir," replies Turcotte. "My father taught me how to give horses confidence. He was a real good horseman."

He was going to say something more but McCann, knowingly touching a finger to his hat, is already on his way.

Ron has only been at the track for a day but McCann, who uniquely galloped and exercised most of Windfields' horses himself, already senses something different about his newest employee.

Just before 10 a.m., McCann calls to Ron — motioning him into his stable office.

"What's your story, son?"

Eighteen years swept into one question. Ron tells McCann how he grew up in a family with 13 brothers and sisters in New Brunswick. His dad was a lumberjack. So was he. He tells McCann how much he liked working with horses and hated just about everything else. He explains that one of his brothers was working as a roofer in Toronto and how he was going to join him but that it didn't work out.

"Now, I'm here," says Ron.

The next weeks easily slip by.

On May 21, 1960, Victoria Park runs second to Bally Ache in the Preakness Stakes, the second leg of North America's Triple Crown. Instead of running in the third leg, the Belmont, Victoria Park is sent to Delaware, where he wins the June 18 Leonard Richard Stakes, setting a track record of 1:47 4/5 for a mile and an eighth.

Now the horse has been returned to Toronto to get ready for the Queen's Plate, which Victoria Park goes on to win in a race record 2:02 — a time that would stand for more than 40 years.

It has only been three months since Ron, broke and about to return to New Brunswick, watched Victoria Park run in the Kentucky Derby on a television set. Ron smiles at the thought.

McCann, who includes being a former top amateur flyweight boxer in his list of accomplishments, gives Ron a couple of ponies and two racehorses to look after.

Around a racetrack, every horse that isn't running in races is a pony. A pony can be a retired thoroughbred, an Arabian, a Paint or an Appaloosa. These horses' jobs are simply custodial; mounted babysitters, escorting the often high-strung thoroughbred racehorses on post parade, into the starting gate or to the track in the mornings for works or gallops. Like the goats, donkeys and even chickens some racehorse trainers keep around, their mere presence is soothing, a balm.

Soon McCann even throws Ron up on a couple of horses. It is the first time Ron has ever been in a saddle — at home he only rode bareback. But you would never know it.

McCann never even asked Ron if he has ridden a horse before. McCann just knows. As much as he knows horses and can judge their ability, McCann has the same knack for people. He knows what beats inside their chests.

Sitting on a thoroughbred, the young man wears a grin as long as the stretch.

Reggie isn't complaining either. He has grown on Sharkey. Reggie never shows up late, never complains. By now Sharkey has even trusted Reggie to run the kitchen bets over to the mutuels in the grandstand.

On the rare days the kitchen hits big, Sharkey never has to worry about Reggie getting tempted to stuff the cash in his jeans and skip town.

The hot summer of 1960 brings more changes to the Turcottes' home in New Brunswick.

In addition to the money he is paid for looking after the campsite and fairgrounds, Alfred borrows and scrapes together enough money to put a down payment on 117 acres of property on Undine Road, five miles from where their first house burnt to the ground.

Still in the parish of Drummond, their new home is in an area called New Denmark, where English, not French, is primarily spoken. It is the oldest Danish community in Canada.

The land includes a rundown farmhouse that Rose is convinced even just a cough from an asthmatic could topple it on its side. Hinges rusted, the front door lets out a shriek when she opens it. The gray floorboards, many of them splintered, wheeze with every step. When she rubs a finger on the wall, it comes back coated like dirty flour. But Alfred assures her that by the time he and the boys are finished with this place it will be more than fine.

Even with Camille, Camilla and Ron on their own, there are still 11 mouths under one roof. Rose thinks of a car crammed with clowns at the circus.

Noel, 17, is the oldest child still living with them. Then Odette, 15; Aurele, 14; Rudy, 10; Albert, 9; Raymonde, 7; Roger, 5; Gaetan, 3; and the new baby, Yves.

Alfred, Noel and Aurele clear the land and then begin building a new house. Old enough, Rudy, Albert, Odette and Raymonde also help. Having taken an electrician's class in Grade 12, Noel rewires the house almost all by himself. When the rewiring is complete, Noel's teacher, Mr. Grodin, comes to inspect the house. When he flips the switch, the house floods itself with light; Noel beams too. Quiet, almost shy, making things work gives him joy.

One season in Toronto is enough for Reggie. When the last race of 1960 slides under the wire at Greenwood, he takes the Greyhound back to New Brunswick with a tidy wad of cash in his pockets.

Ron isn't going anywhere. McCann has made sure of that. He has sent him to Windfields' training center in Oshawa, Ontario, to break yearlings — getting the babies used to the idea of first a saddle and then someone sitting on their backs.

"They can teach you while you're teaching them," McCann tells Ron. "George will show you the ropes."

George is George Thompson, an ex-jockey and Windfields' top exercise rider.

The first yearling Thompson gives Ron bucks him to the hard ground, almost breaking him in two.

Leaning on the outside fence watching the rodeo, Thompson doubles over in laughter. "When you're done with that one, I've got another one for you," he snickers.

That night, all of Ron's muscles scream in constricted agony. He has muscles on muscles from working in the woods, but the horses have found muscles he didn't even know existed.

The next day goes much better. For some reason, the three colts he gets on hardly offer any fuss.

"I guess they figured they didn't know anything and neither did I," Ron says to Thompson. "So, I guess they decided not to fight about it. Maybe this won't be so hard after all."

By the time spring rolls in to Toronto in 1961, Ron is freelancing his services as a gallop rider along with Thompson, who left Windfields the previous fall.

Some farms only have a couple of horses to gallop, others as many as a dozen. Hitting four, sometimes five, farms a day, Ron is anxious to show McCann and Windfields what he has learned.

But before he gets a chance, Joe Thomas summons all six of Windfields' exercise riders for an early morning meeting. Thomas tells the riders he wants to put them all under contract: five years for $50 a month plus $35 a week but with half of that lopped off for room and board. At first blush, Ron thinks it sounds good. A steady job. He would learn how to be a jockey — one step closer to being one of the little boys in white pants.

But he figures he should probably ask Thompson what he thought.

"You better give this some serious thought," Thompson tells Ron. "I've been around the track for a long time. I know how this works. My days of riding are long gone. Yours are just beginning. They're not offering a lot of money. Think about it. And you know who No. 1 is going to be."

Brash, pugnacious and able to back it up, No. 1 is Cuban-born Avelino Gomez. No. 1 with Windfields. No. 1 in Canada.

If there was any doubt, you just had to ask him.

When Benny Sorenson, a jockey who had moved his business from Ontario to New England, was quoted in a racing magazine calling himself Canada's King of Jockeys, Gomez wasted no time in firing off a telegram.

"Benny," it read. "Gomez is King. You're the Queen."

Gomez was right about one thing: he was the King. For four of the past five years, he has been Canada's leading jockey. Fans both loved him and loathed him. They loved him when he carried their money across the wire on top; they hated him when he lost or ran over their money on horses they didn't bet.

One afternoon, Gomez was leading in the deep stretch when his mount took a bad step and stumbled. Gomez was pitched sideways but managed to roll away.

The crowd hushed as they saw Gomez disappear under a torrent of pounding legs and then lay motionless for a few seconds curled up in a ball. But when the last horse went by him, Gomez jumped up and waved to the crowd to show them he wasn't hurt. People stood and cheered. Then reality set in. Gomez's tumble had shredded their tickets. In a heartbeat the ovation turned to boos.

Cocking his head in disbelief Gomez yelled back, "Maybe I kill myself for an encore!"

Ron isn't convinced by Thompson's warning. How bad could it be to be second to Gomez?

"So, you think you'll be Windfields' No. 2 rider?" Thompson says. "Pretty cocky aren't you? In case you've forgotten, you still haven't ridden in a single race. You haven't even worked a horse from the starting gate."

Ron nods. He was getting ahead of himself — something he never did.

"So, what do I do?" Ron asks Thompson.

"Let me call Gordon Huntley," Thompson replies. "I've been working for him. Let me see what he can do for you."

After apprenticing with Reggie Cornell in California and Jim Bentley in Ontario, Huntley had been running a successful public stable for the past decade.

Few horsemen can get horses — especially young horses — ready like Huntley. Whenever Huntley sends a first-timer to the starting gate, the jockey and the bettors know the horse is going to be a factor; Huntley's horses never come up short.

Huntley, who has been Greenwood's leading trainer five times, hires Ron on the spot, giving him $75 a week — considerably more than Windfields was offering.

"Lose a little weight and maybe you will be a jockey," Huntley says, echoing Ron's former landlord. "How much do you weigh?"

"A hundred and twenty-five," answers Ron fudging his weight by at least three pounds. He looks like he could wrestle a bear. A 42-inch chest sits atop a 28-inch waist. His thighs resemble mature tree trunks.

"You need to get down to 105 pounds if anybody is going to put you up on one of their horses. Me included."

"A hundred and five?" Ron thinks he must have misunderstood. He'd have to lose more than 20 pounds — nearly 20 percent of what he weighs.

Huntley watches Ron's face fall. The warm 1961 April morning suddenly turns cold.

"Impossible," he says to himself. "I haven't weighed 105 pounds since I was 12 years old. What do they want me to do? Cut off one of my legs?"

Ron goes off to tell Pat Remillard what Huntley has just told him. At 55 years old, Remillard, the Methuselah of jockeys, befriended Ron the moment the two met. During his career, which began in 1930, Remillard won almost 2,000 races. He led the jockey standings in Louisiana, Maryland and Florida before coming to Canada in 1933, where he would ride in 25 King's and Queen's Plates, winning in 1943 with a maiden filly named Palotia that paid $76 to win but never won another race.

"You can do it," Remillard tells Ron. "It's not like you are six feet tall or anything. It all depends on how much you want to do it."

"I want it more than anything," Ron answers in a blink. "But why so light? How many jockeys ride that light?"

"The bug boys," replies Remillard, "That's what you will be."

A "bug boy" is an apprentice, a learning rider. The term comes from the fact that there is an asterisk next to an apprentice rider's name that looks like a bug on the *Daily Racing Form* pages.

Bug boys get a weight allowance that varies from five to 10 pounds. It is an inducement for trainers to ride novice jockeys. Lighter jockeys are easier on the horse because there is less weight to carry. Simple as that.

But the 10-pound allowance only lasts until a bug boy wins their fifth race. While the rules have since changed, the jockey's contract holder would get a seven-pound break while other trainers would get a five-pound allowance for a calendar year after their fifth win.

"If you can't take advantage of this allowance, then why would anyone ride you?" explains Remillard. "They'll just get somebody else. Another bug boy who can make the weight."

Remillard smirks. "After a year you can be fat like the rest of us."

"Fat? Sure. This is fat," says Ron poking at his skin.

"If you're lucky like me, it won't be so hard," Remillard says. "I only have to pull about five pounds a week. There are lots of riders who have to pull three or four pounds a day. Do the math: that's like a thousand pounds a year. Most jockeys wish they could bottle all their sweat in a jar and then throw it into the river so it will never come back. But it always does. You sweat off the weight, and the next day, it's there again, staring you in the face.

"I can tell you can do it. You're small enough. But you'll need to go on a diet. Forget those sausages, eggs and pieces of toast you eat every morning in the kitchen. And no lunch. Maybe a salad for supper."

"Are you kidding me?" starts Ron. "You've seen me eat. I love my food."

"Then you better learn to hate it," comes back Remillard. "And after a while, you will. The food will look back at you, smiling an evil grin, and you'll think it's the ugliest SOB ever."

So, Ron begins to lose weight. Wearing a rubber suit, he runs for miles. Then, still with the skintight latex clothes on, he gets into his car, cranks up the heater as high as it will go, and sweats profusely. Most days, he eats just one small meal a day, and often, he purges that little bit of food.

He is literally starving himself. But there is no other option.

It works. Two months later, the needle on the scale in the jock's room halts at 105 pounds. Sweating and starving and sweating and starving himself, Ron feels as though the last ounce of water and fat has leaked and oozed away.

He is ready to be a jockey.

Chapter 7

Picking up the June 21, 1961, morning edition of the *Globe and Mail* from the newspaper box outside of the cafeteria, Ron hurriedly throws back the pages until he comes to what he is looking for: the day's racing selections.

For weeks Huntley, who has treated Ron like a son, has penciled in this day for Ron to make his riding debut. Ron knows this. But it will only be real when he sees it in print for himself.

There it is. Race No. 2. Horse: Whispering Wind. Trainer: Gordon Huntley. Jockey: Ron Turcotte.

He reads the last two words again. His eyes dance.

"Yes," he says, pumping his right fist into the air.

Two men in white T-shirts brush past.

"Your lottery numbers come in?" one of them asks.

"Something like that," Ron replies, floating to Huntley's barn.

"Your big day eh, kid?" a groom says from the end of a pitchfork. "How are you feeling?"

"Never better," says Ron.

The morning seems to take forever. Post time for the first race is 1 p.m. Ron arrives in the jockey's room two hours early.

The clerk of the scales smiles hello.

"Turcotte, isn't it?" he says. "Sign here, and I'll show you where your spot in the room is and where you can hang your clothes."

Ron's space is at the far end of one of two long rows of white-painted cubicles that wrap in a semicircle around the jockey's room. Each stall has a shelf and hooks. Toiletries — soap, shampoos, deodorant — line the shelves along with several photographs. Ron notices that many of the pictures are of Jesus Christ. The others seem to be of wives, girlfriends and children.

A ping-pong table is in one corner of the room; a pool table is close by. Two television sets hang from the ceiling. Fluorescent lighting fills the room. One of the tubes flashes and crackles, needing to be replaced.

Three or four copies of the *Daily Racing Form*, the racetrack's bible, are piled on one table; the day's racing programs sit next to them along with a stack of mimeographed yellow entry sheets with the day's workouts printed on the other side.

Against another wall are three rows of bunk beds. All have pressed white sheets with blue blankets folded into rectangles at each end.

Ron hears the shower — he isn't the first jockey to arrive.

Pulling his mock turtleneck over his shoulders, he sits down, pulls off his shoes and removes his socks. Naked except for his white briefs, he steps on the scale. He is happy to see 105 again.

Nerves jangling, he hopes a sauna will relax him. The dry heat slaps his face as he tugs open the thick door. Sitting cross-legged, Hugo Dittfach, 11th in North America the previous year with 201 wins, hastily pulls a towel across his torso and mumbles hello. Dittfach is spooning tomato soup laced with Tabasco sauce into his mouth. Ron doesn't ask why.

"Mind if I throw some more water on?" Ron asks, already having taken the ladling spoon out of the bucket.

He's not sure if it is Dittfach's German accent or the soup spoon in Dittfach's mouth that makes the reply indecipherable, but he goes ahead anyway, sending a rush of steam skyward.

Half an hour later, Dittfach is still in the sauna, now eating ice cream that has turned to white soup; Ron has had enough.

When he gets up, Dittfach politely says, "Talk to you later," even though they haven't said two words to each other.

Showered, Ron reflexively steps back on the scale. A hundred and four and a half.

Half an hour later, Remillard comes in and winks.

Soon the room is full. A tall, thin man approaches. Dressed in purple trousers and a matching jacket, Bill Gilbert will be Ron's valet — the man who will carry Ron's girth and saddle to the paddock, meet him after the race and return the saddle and tack back to the room.

Gilbert asks Ron if he wants his riding boots polished. Ron shakes his head. He has already shined them twice in the past hour.

Whispering Wind, a $2,500 claimer owned by Mrs. J. M. C. Burns, goes into the starting gate in post 10 at odds of 27-1. A claimer is a horse that is put up for sale, and the owner must agree to sell the horse if someone puts in a claiming slip to purchase the horse.

To no one's surprise, there are no claims for Whispering Wind. Even the most optimistic bettor doesn't believe Ron and Whispering Wind have a chance.

Ron's heart thumps. A starting crew worker has climbed into the gate alongside Ron and grabs Whispering Wind's bridle to keep its head straight ahead.

The jockey to his left makes the sign of the cross.

"Just give me a clean break," Ron whispers to himself after he says a quick prayer.

Feeling the green silks with white maple leaves press lightly against his skin, Turcotte hears the clack of the bell. The gates spring open and the other riders yelp.

Ron gets Whispering Wind away mid-pack in the six-furlong race. Then the darnedest thing happens. Whispering Wind responds to Ron's pushing and pumping hands and shoulders and starts passing horses. By rote, Ron feels the horse change leads, switching from leading with his right front foot to the inside left as they round the turn. It is exactly what Ron wants. A horse that hits the turn with its right front leg first will run wide.

Leaving the turn, Whispering Wind switches back to his right leg. Perfect again.

Thompson has told him that it is like someone carrying a heavy water bucket with one arm. If you switch hands, the load feels lighter for a while.

Remarkably, Whispering Wind is in front as they reach the top of the stretch. Ron hears the roar of the crowd and feels a warm breeze that drifts up the lane. He flicks his wrist against the sweat of the horse's neck.

He has dreamed of this: winning his first race. It's magical.

"Keep going. Come on, boy!" Ron shouts.

Even magic, however, has its limitations. In mid-stretch, Whispering Wind goes back to himself, tires and finishes sixth as two even more improbable longshots go past and finish first and second.

Huntley pairs Ron and Whispering Wind eight more times that summer. The results are always the same: unplaced.

But Huntley can see that even if the horse isn't improving, the jockey is. Ron is gaining confidence and poise with every loss.

A week before the 1961 season gallops to a close, Huntley names Ron on Pheasant Lane. An unstarted two-year-old, Pheasant Lane has quietly been working up a storm in the mornings.

Confident the horse will win, Huntley's grooms and exercise riders bet with both fists, anticipating a leg up on some winter money.

The price, they also figure, will be square. Ron, who is 0-13 on the season, won't inspire any confidence in the bettors. And even if it is a first-timer from Huntley's barn with some good workouts, the bettors also think that if young Turcotte is on board instead of one of the leading riders, then Pheasant Lane can't be much stock.

As the race begins, Pheasant Lane quickly opens an eight-length lead and Huntley's stable help are already counting their money.

It is another one-turn race. But it is one turn too many. Pheasant Lane refuses to switch leads on the turn. Instead of switching to its left lead, the horse stays on its right lead and heads straight for the outside fence.

The entire field passes Ron.

In the barn, one of Huntley's grooms, his pockets empty, passes Ron a note. All it says is, "Turn left."

Ron has all winter to think about it.

He finishes 1961 with 14 mounts, no wins, no seconds and no thirds.

Ron flies home for Christmas. It is his first time on a plane. He has never met Yves, who is now 19 months old.

All the children are there. Rose prepares two turkeys. Alfred sits at the head of the dining room table and smiles.

On April 8, 1962, the day before *West Side Story* would sweep the Academy Awards, the racing season glides into Ontario's Fort Erie Race Track, a few furlongs from the Peace Bridge in Buffalo, New York, and a 30-minute drive from the heart of Niagara Falls.

It is a dank afternoon. Ron has three mounts and finishes second on two of them. The next day, he finds himself back — ironically enough — on the Addison-Hall stable's Pheasant Lane.

The rematch isn't without mishap this time either. The track bathed in mud, Pheasant Lane stumbles coming out of the starting gate. Once again Huntley's crew, which is trying to recoup their money, gasps.

"Not again," one of them mumbles.

But Ron doesn't flinch. He rights Pheasant Lane and catches up to the leaders. However, it isn't over. Ron has two horses in front of him blocking his path. Aggressively, Ron finds a tiny seam and splits the two front-runners.

Mud and slop dripping from his goggles, Ron has won his first race. The first of many.

It is remarkable, mind-boggling when you think about it. Just two years removed from watching his first race in his landlord's living room, and one year after he started riding, Ron keeps succeeding, taking 10 of his 42 mounts to the winner's circle at Fort Erie. It is good enough to finish third in the jockey standings.

But even that wasn't enough for some people.

"Ron Turcotte has a nauseating habit of heading for the outside fence turning for home," writes Joe Perlove in the *Toronto Daily Star*. "It seemed as if every time you looked up at Fort Erie, Turcotte was zooming down the outside. But way outside."

If Turcotte just stayed in the park, Perlove concluded, he'd be the leading rider.

Reading this criticism, Ron grows angry, throwing the paper down in the track's cafeteria.

Just then Remillard arrives.

"Let me guess," says Remillard. "You just read Perlove's story."

"Bunch of crap," answers Turcotte.

"Well, not all of it," Remillard says with a smirk.

"Yeah, which part?" says Ron. "That I don't want to be on the rail?"

"No, the part that said you should be the leading rider," answers Remillard. "You've only ridden less than 50 races."

The praise does little to lift Ron's mood.

"Come with me," says Remillard. "I'm going to take you to the movies."

"What?" says Ron. "The movies?"

"Just come with me," says Remillard, motioning with his hand.

In the jockeys' room, the previous day's races replay at 10 a.m. Remillard grabs a quiet corner and pats the empty space next to him.

"See that?"

"See what?" answers Ron.

"That," says Remillard, thrusting a finger toward the television screen. "Once you got to the front, what was the hurry? Why didn't you save him a bit?"

Ron is silent.

A different race now replaying, Remillard says, "Here you do it again. You have three-quarters of a mile to go. So why start going around horses now. Again, what's your hurry?

"And here," says Remillard showing his protégé another race. "That horse ahead of you was tiring. So, when you went in behind him on the rail, you were asking for trouble."

Ron nods.

Patience soon becomes one of Ron's greatest traits. But then again, patience is something Ron learned years ago working with horses in the lumber camps. The horses, especially Good Bess, moved along at their own pace. Trying to hurry them up didn't do anyone any good.

An "up" rider, Ron likes to sit forward over a horse's shoulders and neck, squeezing the animal's sides firmly with his thick calves and thighs. Ferocious with the upper part of his body, he learns that only a jockey's shoulders and arms should move. The rest of his body should be painted on.

Despite Ron making considerable improvement, movie mornings go on for weeks. Same place. Same time.

One time Remillard asks Ron about moving too soon. Another time it is about moving too late. And sometimes it is about getting behind a horse that is tiring.

After a few sessions, Chris Rogers, a veteran jockey almost as old as Remillard, joins in.

"Whaddya think, Chris? Am I telling him right?"

"You bet," Rogers always seems to reply.

One morning Rogers pulls out a bale of hay for Ron in Huntley's shed row. "Grab your whip and sit on the hay," says Rogers, a jockey that the great Eddie Arcaro once said was the only rider he didn't want to hook up against in the stretch.

"You need to be able to use both hands. Hit a horse right-handed and a horse will move to his left to try and get away from the whip. Hit them left-handed and they will move to the right.

"To keep a horse going straight you need to be able to use both hands. Right-handed. Then left-handed.

"Like this," he says, straddling the hay bale, his arms a blur as he passes the whip from one hand to the other.

Right. Left. Right. Left. Chaff from the bale flies like brown sleet.

"Want to know the secret?" says Rogers. "Eat left-handed."

"What?" Ron asks.

"Eat left-handed for the next couple of months. For that matter try to do everything left-handed. Before long you'll be as comfortable with your left hand as you are with your right hand."

That afternoon Ron watches a replay of a race Rogers wins.

"One. Two. Thre." It is the number of times Rogers switches his stick. "Ten. Eleven. Twelve ... Good Lord."

While baseball's New York Mets are well on their way to the all-time record for futility — losing 120 of 160 games in 1962 — Ron is going the other way.

After the Fort Erie spring meet ends, he wins 14 races at the Woodbine summer meeting. Then he really takes off, finishing second in the standings at the Fort Erie summer session. Even that is just a prequel to the real fireworks. At the Woodbine autumn meet, Ron wins with a record 72 of his 278 mounts, which is a staggering 38 more victories than his nearest pursuer.

Most astonishingly, Ron has more wins than the next three riders combined. Jim Fitzsimmons, the second-leading jockey, wins 34 races; Jerry Harrison wins 20 and Harlan Dalton brings home 17 winners. On September 18, Ron also picks up his first stakes win. Never using his whip even once, Ron wins the $25,000 Breeders' Stakes, the third and final jewel of Canada's Triple Crown, in a track record time on Crafty Lace, a horse that had been running for as low as $7,500.

Later that week, with the late afternoon sun pushing his shadow 15 feet in front of him, he gets out of his car and makes his way to the bank, where he deposits a cheque made out to Ronald Joseph Turcotte for $2,642.16.

Almost half of that came from less than two minutes' work on Crafty Lace. This was when the minimum wage was $1.15 an hour. Ron tries to calculate how many days it would take to earn as much in a lumber camp. He estimates at least five months and tries to suppress a smile.

Now he can buy a new car and still have money left over.

He smiles again. It all seems so far-fetched.

The move to Greenwood for the fall Ontario season doesn't change anything. A hat trick on November 14 prompts Perlove to add two short telling sentences at the end of his day's racing wrap in the *Toronto Daily Star*: "Oh yes, Ron Turcotte rode three winners. Ho hum."

Those three wins give Ron 50 at Greenwood.

In just his first full year as a jockey, Ron is Canada's leading rider. All told he wins 180 races in 1962. It is enough to move past Sandy Shields, who is tearing it up in Alberta, and gives him a comfortable lead over Fitzsimmons, his nearest pursuer in Ontario.

All tallied up, Ron's mounts win $396,635. With a jockey getting 10 percent, Turcotte's share is $39,635 and 50 cents.

The new world winks with him.

It is more money than he could ever dream about.

But one thing that never changes is Ron's humility. Despite his unfathomable rapid success, he is always modest. He never forgets growing up poor in New Brunswick.

When Walter Taylor, a longtime friend of Huntley, first agreed to find mounts for Ron and be his agent, he had to beg trainers to give his apprentice rider a chance. Now those same trainers have to make an appointment just to talk to Taylor.

The former lumberjack, who stumbled onto horse racing by accident, circumstance and chance — arriving in Toronto just two years earlier with just $50 in his pockets and not much more hope — keeps winning races in bunches.

It doesn't hurt that Gomez, finally able to obtain a U.S. visa, leaves Ontario for Florida to ride against the best jockeys in North America. Gomez had won four of six Canadian riding titles from 1956 to 1961. With Gomez gone, some people are now calling Ron the French Canadian El Perfecto.

It is remarkable to everyone except those who know Ron. The kid is a natural, born not to be a lumberjack but a jockey. A Canadian champion jockey.

Nothing frightens a horse more than a scared rider. But when Ron is in the saddle, horses immediately sense everything will be just fine. Patting them on the neck, he whispers to them in French, letting them know that he trusts them, and they can trust him. In any language, he cables messages down through the reins, communicating calm and confidence. As strong as Ron is, he is also hailed for his cool, calm confidence. He now sits chilly on a horse. Seemingly never in a hurry anymore, knowing innately just how much horse he has under him, he makes the right moves at the right time just about every time. He is able to get a horse to relax until it is time for the real running to begin.

People outside of horse racing would often tell Ron that horses are the dumbest sons of bitches on Earth. Stupider than cows. Ron knows differently. Good Bess had shown him that.

When he first arrived in Toronto, Ron's uncomfortableness was exacerbated by his hesitancy with English. Retreating into himself, he seemed aloof, even haughty, to some people. Not anymore. As humble and down to earth as they come, Ron would often flash his quick wit.

"Hey, Turcotte! If I was married to you, I'd poison you," a woman, with one foot halfway up the paddock railing and every other body part practically leaning forward in a contorted rage, once bellowed at him.

"Lady," Ron quickly retorts. "If I was your husband, I'd let you."

"Pat helps me plenty," Ron says to *Toronto Daily Star* columnist Jim Proudfoot. "So does Chris Rogers. And every race I ride teaches me something."

Proudfoot goes on to quote Remillard as saying: "(Ron) is a level-headed gentleman who wants to learn and that's why you can go along with him. A couple of things sold me on him. One was that Walter Taylor (Turcotte's agent) and I were able to talk him into putting all his money — he's making plenty — into a trust fund, just keeping out enough to live on. A kid in his position is liable to spend every dime he makes. And he said the smartest thing I ever heard a boy say at the track. He said he's going to go to school this winter, him and Noel, his brother. 'We're not going to wind up walking hots,' he said."

"That's right," Ron confirms to Proudfoot. "We're going to study to be electricians. I figure like this. Today I'm doing okay. Tomorrow maybe I get hurt. Or maybe next summer when I lose my apprentice weight allowance, I won't ride no more winners. Or maybe I'll get big and won't be able to ride. So, if I need a new job, I want it to be a pretty good one."

One afternoon, instead of advice, Rogers approaches Ron with a query: "I hear you've got another brother who might make a jockey."

'Yup. Noel," says Ron. "He'll be here next year. As soon as he finishes high school."

Ron says this proudly. Noel will be the first in his family to graduate. For Christmas Ron buys bicycles for all his younger brothers and sisters.

Chapter 8

It is the last week of June 1963. A month after U.S. astronaut L. Gordon Cooper circled the Earth 22 times aboard the Mercury capsule *Faith 7*, Noel Turcotte arrives in Toronto, finding his brother Ron lifted into his own orbit.

"Hey, brother," says Ron, greeting Noel as he steps off the train at the opulent Union Station with its facade of smooth beige Indiana and Queenstown limestone and its grand Great Hall, constructed with more limestone, bronze, marble and translucent glass. "Trip good?"

Noel nods. He is nervous. Thinks he might throw up.

Noel's friends in New Brunswick kept telling him he should be a jockey like his brother. "Think of the money," they said. "Think of all the girls who will want to go out with you. You're only 5-foot-1. You're the same size as your brother, and you can't weigh more than 120 pounds. Go to Toronto. Go to the racetrack."

Whenever he heard that, Noel would always try to change the subject, crinkling and arching his thick, dark eyebrows. Happy where he was, the collision of opposites tugs him along discordant roads. Electricity he understood. He rewired the Turcottes' new home in New Brunswick. He once built a radio completely out of spare parts. But he had never stepped foot inside a racetrack. For that matter, he had never even seen a horse race. All he had were Ron's letters home, some newspaper clippings and phone calls.

In New Brunswick, he was safe. Here, in Toronto, he is unknown and unsure.

Wearing a white cowboy hat, Ron picks up one of Noel's bags. They are very light. "We better hurry. Aunt Irene will have supper ready."

Noel merely nods his head.

Ron has been boarding in a Toronto suburb with his uncle Aurele Devost (Rose's brother) and Aurele's wife, Irene, for the past few months. For a short time, Noel lives with them as well.

But it won't be long before Ron, Noel and two other jockeys, Eric Walsh and John LeBlanc, who was also from New Brunswick, rent a house not far from Woodbine.

As Ron and Noel begin their 40-minute drive from the train station, the radio comes on with the start of the engine. The boys talk while Johnny Cash sings "Ring of Fire."

"How's Mom?" asks Ron.

"Fine," answers Noel in his typical one-word answers. Shy and reticent, Noel fidgets.

"And Dad?"

"Good. Still working at the fairgrounds. His heart is good. He's even helping out some of the neighbors truck potatoes into town. Still grumpy. Still Dad."

They both laugh.

"Come on," says Ron, a cigar clenched between his teeth. "Tell me something new."

"Nothing new to say. Really. Everything is good."

The radio now plays Bobby Bare's "Detroit City." Ron loves country and western music.

"Well, at least I'll have the time to teach you," continues Ron, laughing. "They have me on a 10-day suspension for careless riding."

"Geez," starts Noel.

"Ah, it's nothing. I've had lots of suspensions."

Has he ever. In 1963, Ron gets a total of 50 days of suspensions, reflecting his aggressiveness.

Another jockey would be worried. Mistakes cost money. A trainer's job is to keep his horses winning and the owners, who pay the bills, happy. When a rider gets disqualified, the purse the owner would have won is taken away. Do that enough and soon the trainer starts looking for another jockey. In a sport as cutthroat as horse racing, there aren't many riders who get as many chances as Ron Turcotte.

But if he keeps coming through, coaxing their horses first across the finish line, the owners and trainers are willing to look the other way.

Noel looks at Ron. He is still laughing.

After dinner Ron, Noel, Aurele and Irene watch *The Beverly Hillbillies* on TV. Noel thinks it is the funniest thing he's ever seen.

Early the next morning the two brothers drive to the track. Through the windshield, Noel follows the rising sun sear through the rooftops and into a cloudless sky as they make their way to Woodbine.

Shuffling two steps behind his brother, Noel, a year younger, an inch taller and as raw as a February morning, walks into Huntley's barn knowing there is no turning back. His life has been decided for him.

"Come on, brother; what are you doing back there?" says Ron. "They're all expecting you. I'll get you introduced. I've got a few horses to gallop and a couple others to work. Then we'll watch today's races together. Like I said, it's not like I have a lot to do this afternoon."

About the only thing Gordon Huntley said when Ron told him Noel was coming to Toronto was, "If he's your brother that's good enough for me. Bring him around. I'll find him work."

Huntley got about 10 feet down the barn's shed row alley when he suddenly wheels around.

"Can he ride?" he thinks to ask.

"Uh, sure," Ron replies, although he really didn't have a clue.

He had seen Noel ride horses on the farm. But Noel's main job in the logging camps had nothing to do with horses. Instead, when he wasn't at school, his task was to peel pulp, taking the bark off the trees with a draw knife.

And that was two years ago.

"Sure. Sure. He can ride," says Ron, who has big plans for Noel. Bigger than what Noel had for himself. That much is certain.

Just as George Thompson had taught him, Ron would teach Noel. The path was set. It seemed all Noel has to do is follow it. His surname alone will be enough to fast-track him.

Other would-be jockeys had to pay their dues on the end of a pitchfork, shoveling out manure and raking in fresh beds of straw. Not Noel. His mission is clear.

In phone calls and a few letters, Ron has kept telling Noel and the rest of his family that he is "doing well." "Pretty good," he even once said.

Noel had no idea just how good "pretty good" was.

Ron is well on his way to being Canada's leading jockey for a second straight year.

The season leader at the Greenwood spring session with 38 wins — 17 more than any other jockey — he also led the standings at Fort Erie, winning 33 of his 109 mounts — 18 more than anyone else. On one afternoon at Fort Erie, he had five mounts and won them all. He goes wire to wire with Michaelena to win the second race. Sitting out the third and fourth races, he goes pillar to post with odds-on favorite Carroll County in the fifth. Then he comes from far back to win the sixth with Mornin's Morning and the seventh with Bianca Mann. He closes out the program with a win on Whip Out.

Scrubbing and pushing on cheap claimers with the same intensity he rides stakes horses, Ron nets his backers $300 on a $2 parlay.

A week later he wins four in a row. Again, from only five mounts. Now, he is off to another hot start at Woodbine.

Three days after his 22nd birthday, July 22, Ron boots home four winners. The first winner, Never Me, a filly, is led to the paddock by Noel.

From just 41 mounts at Woodbine, Ron has 13 wins.

By the end of that meet, Ron boots home 45 horses to victory — 15 more than anyone else.

"What if I don't make it as a jockey?" Noel asks Ron at a roadside diner.

A waitress in a pink skirt and matching blouse has just taken their order. Two pieces of halibut. Poached. No fries. Coffee, black.

"What happens to me then?" asks Noel, shifting nervously in the red Naugahyde vinyl booth.

Ron puts down his 50-cent copy of *Turf and Sport Digest*, which bills itself as "America's finest racing magazine."

For what seems like an eternity, Ron doesn't answer. He just stares straight ahead, which makes Noel uneasy.

"Maybe you won't," Ron says at long last. "Maybe it won't last for me. Who knows? But you can't worry about what you can't control. Didn't Mom say that a hundred times?"

As Ron talks slowly, Noel slides a saltshaker back and forth across the chrome table.

A neon Coca-Cola sign flashes on one wall next to a chalkboard that lists the day's specials: tuna salad sandwich 45 cents; root beer floats 35 cents.

"Who thought we'd even ever be here in Toronto? Who thought we'd ever leave New Brunswick? You want guarantees? I can't give them to you. Nobody can. Certainly not in this business, that's for certain."

Ron had asked himself the same questions many times.

"One of the first things I heard — and I must have heard it a hundred times since — is that there are no sure things in horse racing. Not for the horses. Not for the jockeys. Not for anyone. You can plan all you want. Then boom! You get shut off and the horse stumbles. All I know is, I'm never going back to those woods to work again. Never. And I'm not going to wind up being an exercise rider again either. That's over. All of it. We've been given a gift. It's up to you and me to make the most of it. You've got your schooling behind you. You know how to be an electrician. What have I got? Grade 8. The same as Mom and Dad got. Look. You've got nothing to worry about. You've got the talent. It'll all be fine. I can't tell you any more than that."

Noel is silent as their food arrives.

Ron continues to read his magazine while he eats.

"Hey, look at this story. If a horse fails to win races, it isn't the horse's fault. The trainer and the jockey are the two handiest victims. Or if it isn't them, then it's the racing secretary or even the groom, who spend all their hours looking after the horse."

All Noel sees is the giant footprints his brother is leaving. Some nights Noel is certain he will fall into one of them and that the ground will close and swallow him.

Not so long ago, he and Ron were playing cowboys and Indians, hunting and fishing and swimming together. Horse racing was no more real than fire-breathing dragons.

It seems every time Noel turns on the radio somebody is talking about the stir that his New Brunswick lumberjack brother is creating. Somebody called it a Horatio Alger story. A few days later, Noel asked what that means.

The world has changed. Forever, Noel thinks. He isn't sure what is real and what is an illusion.

"I worked a Windfields' colt this morning," Ron says. "He wasn't much taller than this," he says extending his left hand shoulder height. A chunky little guy. But man can he fly. Runs a hole in the wind. He floats the way good horses do. You know the kind, Noel. The ones that hardly seem to be moving but then they tell you how fast they worked and you shake your head in disbelief. Powerful. Real strong. Big shoulders. A huge ass. Like Jim Brown as they say around the barn. The horse is a bit of an ornery cuss. They told me he was a runner months ago. They weren't kidding."

"What's his name?" Noel asks.

"Northern Dancer," answers Ron.

One day ends. The next one begins.

Almost unbeatable down the stretch, as he pushes and prods his horses for more, Ron seems as though he can pick up a horse and carry it forward in his hands.

But he still can't stay away from the steward's office. No sooner does he return from one 10-day suspension when he is called into the steward's office to watch film of himself squeezing another horse into the rail. He receives 10 more days.

The end of this latest suspension coincides with the August 2 debut of Northern Dancer, who, because of his small stature, passed through the previous year's yearling sale without any takers. He was so meager-looking that *Los Angeles Times* sportswriter Jim Murray would write, "Northern Dancer is the kind of colt who, if you saw him in your living room, you'd send for a trap and put cheese in it. He's so little, a cat would chase him. But he's so plucky there's barely room in him for his heart. His legs are barely long enough to keep his tail off the ground. He probably takes a hundred more strides than anyone else, but he's harder to pass than a third martini."

Ron slides Northern Dancer, a late foal from the first crop of Canadian champion Nearctic with three white feet and a big crooked blaze, into the starting gate at Fort Erie.

Instructed not to use the whip by Northern Dancer's flamboyant and dapper trainer, Horatio Luro, who won the 1962 Kentucky Derby with Decidedly, Ron lightly taps the colt at the sixteenth pole anyway. Northern Dancer explodes, winning the five-and-a-half-furlong sprint by six and three-quarter lengths.

Still an apprentice rider, Ron's five-pound allowance means Northern Dancer gets in with just 113 pounds.

Two days later, Ron's apprentice extension ends. For most apprentices, it is a day they dread. The five-pound weight break no longer an enticement for trainers, they are on their own, left on their own merits.

But no one bats an eye when it ends for Ron. The weight break was just a bonus. It is Ron they want. Nothing can slow him down.

Back in Drummond, a few steps from his shed, Alfred crumples to his knees and puts a hand over his heart. Struggling to breathe, he feels like a band of wire is wrapping around his chest, pulling itself tighter. The morning dew touches the bare spot between his pant legs and his socks. Still, he feels hot.

For several moments, Alfred doesn't move, wishing the pain away. When he thinks it has passed, he reaches for the shed's door latch and tries to pull himself up. But the excruciating pain returns — this time like a terrible stabbing. He falls to his back.

Clearing away the breakfast dishes, Rose walks to the sink. Through the window she can see Alfred motionless on the grass. A plate shatters on the floor.

Doctors tell Alfred it is only a mild heart attack. A warning sign, they say. He just needs some rest.

Racetracks bustle in the mornings. Dozens and dozens of horses on the track all at once. Each horse, each rider, each barn with its own agenda. Some horses are merely there to limber up. Some take long, stamina-building gallops. Others are asked to do speed drill workouts for an approaching race.

When Ron and Noel are on the track together it is immediately apparent that they share more than just a last name.

Walter Smith, Huntley's foreman, leads an unstarted two-year-old horse with Ron on its back as it climbs up the training track's incline.

Just then Noel rolls by, finishing a five-furlong workout along the rail.

"Hey, how can you be here and out there at the same time?" Smith snickers, one hand still firm on the two-year-old's bridle.

Noel, careful to copy almost everything Ron does, also sits a horse perfectly. Instead of sitting back in the saddle, they both balance themselves just slightly over a horse's shoulders. The jockeys' backs are flat as ironing boards; a glass of water could balance there and not a drop would be spilled. There is just enough room to squeeze a pound of butter under their butts. Jockeys distribute their weight so evenly, horses hardly even realize anyone is aboard.

Ron showed that one more time with Northern Dancer on October 7, winning the Bloordale Purse. Carrying top weight of 122 pounds, Northern Dancer gets away third while Northern Flight opens a commanding lead. Halfway through the mile and 70-yard race, Northern Dancer trails Northern Flight by 15 lengths.

But Ron isn't worried. He knows how much horse he has left and narrows the gap with every huge stride. He draws even with Northern Flight down the stretch before pulling away to win by a length and a half.

It is 25 lengths back to the third-place finisher.

"It looks like you're ready," Huntley tells Noel when he comes back with his last worker of the early October morning, getting a cranky three-furlong workout with Hannibal Miss, a maiden that hasn't shown much indication she will ever win a race. "You ride this one next Thursday."

Noel's stomach instantly kinks.

"You hear me?" Huntley says.

"Yeah. Great. Great," answers Noel, who rushes off to find Ron in front of Windfields' barn.

"Ronnie. Ronnie. I'm riding. Mr. Huntley has me up next week. It's not much of a horse. But I'm riding.

"Good," says Ron. But Ron's enthusiasm seems muted.

"Ron. Did you hear me? Next Thursday. Mr. Huntley ... I'm riding. I'm really riding in a real race."

"I heard," Ron says evenly.

"Do you think I'm ready? Mr. Huntley says I am."

"And what do you think?"

"I think Mr. Huntley is right. I'm ready."

"Then that's all that counts," answers Ron.

"You think it's too soon?" inquires Noel. "You rode your first race just over a year after you came to Toronto."

"But you've only been here just over three months," Ron answers quickly.

Stung, Noel feels his stomach rolling away. He can think of nothing else but to turn away.

October 10, four days before Thanksgiving, dawns gray. In only a few hours, Noel will go to the gate at Woodbine with Hannibal Miss. He is both nervous and excited.

As expected, Hannibal Miss, owned by Mrs. G.C. McMacken and sent away as a 31-1 longshot, shows little and finishes eighth.

Noel is disappointed but Ron placates him.

"I didn't win my first race either. Remember?" Ron says. "I rode in 14 races in 1960 and never won any of them. You weren't exactly riding a horse with much of a chance.

"I've also got some news for you. I'm leaving for Laurel, Maryland, in a couple of days."

"What?" says Noel incredulously.

"I'm leaving on Tuesday. Chris Rogers convinced me. He told me that if I want to be the leading jock in North America I have to leave here. He said I've done all I can here and that if I don't do any good or if I don't like it there, I can always come back here."

Ron knows Rogers is right. He has led the jockey standings at all five Ontario Jockey Club meets: Fort Erie and Greenwood in the spring, Woodbine and Fort Erie again in the summer. Now, at Woodbine for the autumn meet, he is far and away the leading rider again with 47 wins from 211 mounts.

There is nothing left to prove in Canada for Ron, who is almost 100 wins ahead of Jim Fitzsimmons for his second Canadian title in a row.

"They can't catch you. You'll leave here with two Canadian jockey championships," Rogers advises Ron.

Just two days after Noel's debut and just five days after winning the Bloordale Purse, Northern Dancer is entered in the Coronation Stakes, the richest race in Canada for two-year-olds.

With Ron back in the saddle, Northern Dancer is fourth during the early going. But not for long. Northern Dancer bursts with aplomb again and goes on to win by six and one-quarter lengths.

It is the last time Ron would ride Northern Dancer, whom Luro moves to his home base in New York, where he oversaw the careers of 43 stakes winners — three of them voted Champions — and three Queen's Plates.

"Luro wants an American rider," Ron says. "He is a funny guy. He always thought American riders were better than Canadian riders."

The next day Ron heads for the Maryland circuit. To no one's surprise, he continues to win races. Longshots. Favorites. Front-runners. Horses that come from the clouds. Ron gets them all home.

Ron assumed all the live mounts he has been getting are still because of Walter Taylor, the only agent he has ever had. But when he answers the Valencia Motel room door he finds a strange man standing outside.

"Ron, I'm your agent, Joe Shea," the man says.

Ron's forehead furrows.

"I thought Walter Taylor was my agent," he says.

"No. I am. Walter set it up a couple of weeks ago."

"Okay, what do I owe you?"

"Pay me at Christmas," answers Shea, who has shortened his name from Schiavone. Shea first read about the jockey sensation in the *Daily Racing Form*. On his way south to Florida, Shea has stopped in Maryland to see Ron in action.

He is very impressed.

The Woodbine meet over, two weeks later, Noel gets another chance at Greenwood. This time it is with Whispering Wind, the first horse Ron ever rode in a race.

Little changes. Whispering Wind finishes last in 12th.

Noel grimaces.

Four hundred miles away, Ron is nothing but smiles.

With Shea now his agent, Ron tops the jockey standings at Laurel, including two hat tricks in just three days.

Noel, who now has Taylor as his agent, will get one more chance in 1963. Partnered again with Whispering Wind on November 3 he finishes eighth at 52-1.

When the Laurel meet ends, the Maryland circuit moves to Baltimore's Pimlico. Again, sorcery in his fingers, Ron dominates the Pimlico jockey standings, capped by a four-win day on November 20 that includes both ends of a staggering $856.80 Daily Double. For A Time pays $112 to win the first half of the Double; Alpenhorn comes home an $11.80 winner in the second.

Two days later, as riders are watching TV in the Pimlico jockeys' room on a Friday afternoon, their chatter stops cold. U.S. president John F. Kennedy, the jockeys hear along with the rest of the stunned world, has just been assassinated in downtown Dallas. A grainy picture shows newscaster Walter Cronkite taking off his glasses and tearing up as he says Kennedy is dead.

Ron rides in 259 more races before 1963 ends. He wins 47 of them, finishing the year with 263 wins, 172 seconds and 141 thirds from 1,135 mounts. Once again, he is Canada's leading rider.

Noel has no wins, no seconds and no thirds from his three mounts.

Ron's purse earnings are $684,000. Noel's horses earn nothing.

Ron finishes as the sixth-leading rider in North America; Noel is in a 1,000-way tie for last.

Chapter 9

At Christmas 1963, Ron drives home to New Brunswick from Maryland in his new green Cadillac convertible.

He has one thing on his mind: Gaetane "Gae" Morin, a pretty, quiet girl he went to school with. Ron was head-over-heels smitten by her, even though they had never gone out on a date.

Ron had phoned Gae asking her to go to a movie before he left Maryland, but she said no; she already had a date. He tried to get her to break it, but she refused. He will try again when he arrives in Drummond, he thinks.

Barely in the house, Ron picks up the phone. "How about just going for a drive on Sunday?"

This time she agrees. Ron exhales and makes a little fist pump.

Ron's plan is to leave the convertible with Aurele. That way he will have a vehicle the next time he comes home. After a few dates with Gae, he is sure he will be back in Drummond soon.

Two years younger than Ron, Gae had always been the smartest girl in school. When Ron was in Grade 6, Gae was in Grade 4. But Gae kept getting accelerated and by the time Ron left school in Grade 8, Gae was already in Grade 9.

From a family of 12, Gae is the sixth child of Alfred and Cecile Morin. Her father died when she was only 10, leaving her mother to raise nine girls and three boys by herself.

After only a few days in New Brunswick, Ron has to go back to work. As 1964 bursts open, wherever Ron rides he wins. He leads the standings again at Laurel and Pimlico. He also wins the riding titles at Bowie, where the WB&A Railroad runs a train every five minutes from downtown Baltimore for a 65-cent round-trip ticket — less than the track's $1 admission price.

Then at Delaware Park, just outside the city of Wilmington and about 30 miles from Philadelphia, Ron wins 67 races in just 55 days despite having to serve yet another 10-day suspension.

All this takes place in the shadow of a boxer named Cassius Clay, who on February 25 in Miami, Florida, shocks the boxing world by dethroning Sonny Liston, who can't answer the seventh-round bell.

The Clay/Liston fight comes two days after the Beatles appear on the Sunday night *Ed Sullivan Show*. The younger Turcotte kids huddle close to the television as John, Paul, George and Ringo sing "Twist and Shout," "Please Please Me" and "I Want to Hold Your Hand."

Girls in the audience swoon and scream hysterically.

Using riding boots and pants that Ron had left behind, Noel — still looking for his first win — is named on the Huntley-trained and Jam Em Stable–owned Cicelia Binder. Because of Noel's 10-pound weight allowance, Cicelia Binder is only asked to carry 105 pounds.

It is 3:47 p.m. April 13, 1964 — the fifth race at Fort Erie for $4,500 claimers. It is also Noel's seventh mount of his career.

The other six horses Noel has ridden were all longshots. But Cicelia Binder is given a real shot by the bettors and goes off as the second favorite at odds of 1.75-1.

A six-horse field, Noel, has just one horse headed after a quarter of a mile. But he is in no hurry; the horse is running easily.

Down the backstretch, Cicelia Binder and Noel move up to be fourth and are still surging when they reach the top of the stretch — Noel pushing his horse's neck and head forward as hard as he can. Fifty yards from the finish line, it is just Cicelia Binder and the slight favorite Mangea Cake, ridden by Avelino Gomez, who has returned to Canada. The wire rapidly approaching, Cicelia Binder and Mangea Cake are heads apart, but it is Noel who gets there first in a photo.

When Noel gets to the jockeys' room he is showered by buckets of water thrown by other jockeys — a ritual when a rider wins his first race.

Soaked, Noel grins.

"I did it," he tells himself. "I'm really a jockey now."

He watches the replay, satiated.

His only mount on the card, the first thing Noel does when he leaves the track is find a pay phone. Dropping a nickel into the slot, he calls Ron first.

"You should have seen me, brother. The finish was coming up; I knew it was going to be close. But I did it. Drove that sucker past Gomez's horse in the final strides. Won by a head. They called a photo. But I knew. I knew I had won it. I was way back early but I did what you told me to do. I stayed cool and patient. I didn't panic. Mr. Huntley had told me to wait on the horse, that he liked to come from off the pace. I was worried early. But I did what he said. Down the stretch I kept whipping and yelling and pushing and driving," Noel said, by now shouting into the phone the same way he had on the track. "I won, Ronnie. I won!"

"Atta boy," says Ron, who is already one of the top riders in North America. "Congratulations. First of many."

Then Noel calls his parents. They speak in French. Everyone is happy.

Some jockeys don't win their first race until they have ridden dozens of horses. At first, trainers usually give apprentice riders horses nobody else wants to ride. Practice horses. Noel had done it in just his seventh trip to the starting gate. It took Ron 18 rides to get his first win.

Noel tells himself that he will buy a hundred copies of the next morning's *Globe and Mail* and mail the chart line of the race to Ron and his parents. His mom will put it into the scrapbook she has started with articles about Ron, carefully taping each one into place. Each story is another escalator step rising, taking the brothers closer to a world that no longer smells of sap, moss and potatoes.

"Mom will need three scrapbooks by the time I'm finished riding," Noel muses.

Noel's thoughts spin like a clothes dryer, orphaned socks tossed around with towels and garments.

Chapter 10

In 1964 Vietnam is ready to explode. Race riots break out in New York, Newark, Chicago and Philadelphia. The average cost of a new car is $3,500 and a loaf of bread costs 21 cents.

Oblivious to any of this, Rudy Turcotte furiously swats rapacious blackflies and mosquitos in the woods of New Brunswick on a stinking hot July afternoon. Peeling bark off of some cut trees with a draw knife and a bark spud, Rudy waves his hands and arms and ducks his head for cover. But it is no use. The insects keep coming, buzzing, whirring and wheeling, baited by the 15-year-old boy's sweat. The mid-afternoon sun burns its way through the treetops.

"Damn it; get away from me!" Rudy shouts.

It should be the start of summer holidays. But not for Rudy. Not for hardly any of the kids in Drummond. Instead, it is merely the start of physical labor.

If it wasn't for Ron and then Noel, Rudy would have gone berserk a long time ago. No way out, he would have been stuck here in the woods slapping at hungry bugs.

Instead, Rudy already knows it is only a matter of time.

Born with a swagger to his step, school never interested him. Instead, whenever anyone asked him what he was going to do when he grew up, Rudy would stare back and roll his eyes as if it was the stupidest question he has ever heard.

"A jockey. I'm going to be a jockey. Like my brothers Ron and Noel. What else would I do?"

Ron may have had no idea where he was headed in life. Horses were for work, like trucks and plows and tractors. Not for pleasure. And betting? Who would be so foolish to gamble hard-earned money on horses? Ron knew none of that until Toronto.

But Rudy knew. Rudy always knew where he was going and what he was going to do. With each passing day he is closer to escaping — forever leaving behind the flies and mosquitos and wandering through stumps of felled trees.

He wedges the draw knife into the meat of another log, pulling the knife toward him. The bark flies. The wood smells particularly sweet.

At first, hockey was what carried Rudy's imagination. Every winter he would pull on his two-sizes-too-big hand-me-down skates and shoot frozen horse turds between two piles of snow that served as goalposts. He was always "Boom Boom" Geoffrion, named for his thunderous slapshot, Rudy's favorite hockey player on his treasured Montreal Canadiens. Picturing himself whirling around Tim Horton or Bobby Baun and going in alone on the unmasked Johnny Bower, deking left, deking right, Rudy would slide the horse turd into the corner and raise his hands high in the frozen air.

That was a dream — a mouse wishing he could be a lion. Even Rudy knew he couldn't conveniently forget that he was a foot shorter and 20 pounds lighter than most of his friends or that the only pieces of equipment he owned were these skates and a worn hockey stick with what was left of a blade.

But horse racing? That was his future, and it was as real as the jagged crack on his bedroom wall that was covered by the 1964 Esso hockey calendar.

The desire for river ice began melting into dirt stretches three years ago, when Ron, nine years older, rode his first race. Even then Rudy, knew he was going to be a jockey too. It was destiny.

Every night Rudy would fold back onto his little bed, cup his hands behind his head and gaze out beyond the bare ceiling straight into the stars.

"And down the stretch they come," Rudy would think — sometimes say out loud.

Imaginary horses floating against the murky darkness of his bedroom, Rudy would conjure up one race after another. Sometimes his dreams would take him to the front, kneading his arms against his horse's neck, a handful of mane and leather reins in his hands. Other times, he would wrap up on the reins, taking his mounts so far back that he could hear the track announcer say he was in danger of being lapped.

But the results were always the same.

"Here comes Rudy Turcotte," he would say to himself. "Rudy Turcotte wins again."

He used the same voice — deep as red earth — as the Derby announcer had intoned on May 2, when the family had gathered around the new black-and-white television — bought with some of the money Ron had sent home — and watched Northern Dancer become the first Canadian-bred horse to win the Kentucky Derby, holding off Hill Rise by a long neck.

Inching as close to the TV as he could get, Rudy had sat there — cross-legged on the floor, his chin in his hands.

All the Turcottes yelped in glee. All except Rudy, who just sat there transfixed. "One day that will be me," he thought.

That night Rudy replayed the Derby over and over. But this time he was the one riding Northern Dancer.

"It's Hill Rise storming up on the outside of Northern Dancer. Northern Dancer in front by a length, now half a length, now a neck. But Rudy Turcotte will not be defeated."

Days after that Derby, the mayor of Toronto awarded Northern Dancer, the first horse to win the Derby in two minutes flat, the key to the city. Billboards of the horse sprung up across Toronto, and at year's end, Northern Dancer was even voted Canada's Athlete of the Year in 1964 ahead of the likes of Bobby Hull and Gordie Howe.

Alfred believed Ron could have ridden Northern Dancer if Ron had wanted. So did Rudy. Neither of them was ready to understand that when it comes to loyalty, horse racing has a very short memory.

Luro wanted a New York rider for Northern Dancer's U.S. races and, with that, Ron had been pushed aside. Just like Manny Ycaza and Bobby Ussery, who had also both ridden Northern Dancer prior to the Derby.

Instead, Luro chose hard-baked, temperamental and suspicious "Don't call me Willie" Bill Hartack as his jockey for the Derby, the Preakness, which he also won, and then the Belmont, where Northern Dancer faltered, finishing third.

Right then Ron vowed to himself that one day he would be a New York rider, too.

Hartack also rode Northern Dancer to victory in the June 20th Queen's Plate, which would be the colt's final start before being retired to stud, where he became the most sought-after sire of his generation, siring 147 stakes winners including champions Nijinsky, Vice Regal, Fanfreluche, Laurie's Dancer and the Minstrel.

The unusually humid summer continues. Unable to sleep, Rudy slips out of his bed, the thin springs squawking in complaint.

Clad only in white boxer shorts, he grabs a wooden spoon and a broom from the kitchen and strides purposefully to the mirror, where he watches himself crouch down and then whip the spoon against the thick air.

Playing out another race in his mind — another win, of course — Rudy strides the broom handle and raises the wooden spoon high in the air in triumph, saluting the sweet gathering roars of the crowd.

Then the most important part: the winning smile. It has to be just right. Not too big. Show too much joy and it gives something away — that the victory was unexpected. That would never do; that would show weakness. No. The smile could only be a sliver. Just a hint of white between his lips and the plump cheeks his aunts loved to squeeze. Staring into the mirror, he knows his smile must be perfect. Almost a smirk. Knowing and cocksure. The way Geoffrion smiles after another goal — he has done the same thing a million times before and he will do it a million more. That's what he had to do too. Act like it is nothing special; winning was just part of the deal.

You think five Stanley Cups in a row is a fluke? Look at that smile again.

"Nothing to it, fellas," Rudy says into the mirror, which is now a pack of reporters and cameras. "I knew I had it won. I just kept pumping my arms and my horse kept pumping his legs. Give all the credit to the horse, guys. I was just the pilot."

Why not? He could do it. He could be just like Ron and Noel. Rudy was going to be as rich as Jed Clampett.

He looks into the mirror one more time and smiles.

Subtlety is an art.

Chapter 11

Destiny has nothing to do with luck. Destiny is the product of talent, of hard work. Destiny sounds like a locomotive rumbling through a brick tunnel right at you. It is also unstoppable. One day ends. The next one begins.

Ron's move to the northeastern United States in 1964 could not have been more seamless. After leading the standings at Bowie, Laurel and Pimlico, Ron moved with the circuit to Delaware.

One of the wins at Delaware was just a maiden race for two-year-olds. But Ron knew his mount was special.

His name is Tom Rolfe. He is owned by Raymond Guest, U.S. ambassador to Ireland. He is named after a son of John Rolfe, husband of Pocahontas.

Pound for pound, Ron isn't sure which horse will turn out better: Tom Rolfe or Northern Dancer.

"Tom Rolfe is that good," thinks Ron. Tom Rolfe is a horse he doesn't want to get too far out of sight.

Like his father, Ron loves boxing and becomes fast friends with two-time world featherweight champion Willie Pep, who loves horse racing.

"I want you to meet someone," Ron tells his brother Aurele, who has come to Maryland to spend the summer working for trainer Joe Nash.

"Jesus!" Aurele says. "Is that who I think it is?"

"Willie Pep. My pleasure," says the boxer, who won his first 63 fights before retiring in 1960.

Pep, now 42, is making a comeback.

Boxing is also Aurele's favorite sport; Aurele knows everything about Pep.

"'Willie the Whisp.' Wow," says Aurele. "They tell me those four fights against Sandy Saddler were really something. Is it true that you once won a round without throwing a punch?"

Pep manages a shy grin.

"What are you doing here?" Aurele asks.

"He's in training," Ron answers for the boxer. "Going to win his third world title. Right, Willie?"

Again, Pep smiles weakly, clearing his throat.

"What about you?" the boxer asks Aurele. "Going to be a jock like your brothers Ron and Noel?"

"Nah. Not me. I'm too big."

Big boned, almost 5 feet 6 inches tall, Aurele weighs 145 pounds.

"I'm just here until the end of August. Then I got to go back to New Brunswick for potato season," he says as if Pep understands. "I'm like Ron's chauffeur. He's got a girl back home he's hot about."

He sees Ron blush.

"Every chance Ron gets, he flies to Bangor or Presque Isle. Those are the closest airports to Drummond. I drive down there, pick him up and bring him home so he can see his sweetie. I sometimes think that's why he gets suspended so often. It's a chance to come back home."

"That true?" Pep says turning to Ron, who has found a seat on a plastic, green-striped chair. "You got the hots, eh?"

His face still red, Ron waves his hand in dismissal, pretending to read the paper.

"Where are you going next, Ron?" asks Delaware steward Warren Mehrtens, a former jockey who had won the Triple Crown with Assault in 1946.

"You've done all you can here," he says, echoing what Huntley had told Ron when he left Canada. "You should go to New York. You can ride with anyone."

Ron has been thinking the same.

The Big Apple. Where all the top jockeys ride. Bill Shoemaker, Bobby Ussery, Bill Hartack, Manny Ycaza, Bill Boland, Braulio Baeza and on and on. If you wanted to compete against the best, you best ride in New York.

Ron has ridden for many top New York trainers in Maryland and Delaware, especially mustachioed Buddy Jacobson, a slightly built son of a Brooklyn hat salesman who becomes New York's perennial leading trainer. He had also ridden for top stables like Calumet and the Dupont and Phipps families. He has all the contacts he needs.

Ron isn't afraid of going to New York. He knows he can make it there. He also has Joe Shea, one of the best agents of all time, who is moving to New York as well.

In August 1964, Ron heads for Saratoga, famous for its mineral baths and its iconic racetrack 160 miles north of New York City. Named one of the world's greatest sporting venues by *Sports Illustrated*, Saratoga houses North America's top jockeys and horses.

Ron fits right in, finishing first, second or third 36 times from 101 mounts.

He is a locomotive, just getting started.

At New York's Aqueduct Racetrack, he wins 19 races in the first six weeks, many of them lighting up the tote board like the Fourth of July. One winner, Mean Cold, paid $119.10. Others like Free World ($41.50), Tenth Night ($35.80) and Monongahela ($42.90) also surprised the bettors as well as many of the trainers and owners.

It is just past noon. Horsetail clouds are feathered across the pale sky back in Drummond.

Roused by another dog named "Puppy," Raymonde comes out first, the screen front door flapping shut behind her.

"Mama," she says. "There is a man with a truck outside."

Wiping pie-crust flour off of her apron, Rose comes out next, pushed along by Albert, Roger, Gaetan and Yves — all scurrying to get a better look at the shiny aluminum horse trailer with New York plates that had rolled to a stop in their yard.

"Maybe he is lost," Rose finally says, moving toward the truck, where the driver has now moved to the trailer's back end.

"Mrs. Turcotte?" the man asks.

Bobbing her head, she sees the man holding a lariat of braided rope.

"Then these are for you," says the driver.

Two paneled metal doors swing wide, and the ramp bangs heavily to the ground. Three horses are led out.

"Wow," shrieks Roger, a holster with a plastic cap gun strapped to his side.

"Wow," agrees Raymonde, bouncing up and down like a jack-in-the-box.

"Wait until Poppa sees. Wait until Rudy sees."

"My word," says Rose, haltingly, putting one hand over her mouth. "There must be some mistake."

"No mistake, ma'am," answers the driver, who hands the first horse to Albert. Thirteen, Albert is already nearly five and a half feet tall and weighs close to 150 pounds.

"Maybe you should wait until my husband comes home," Rose begins. "He should be home soon. Who sent them? Who would send us three horses?"

"Ron Turcotte," the man replies, reading from a slip of paper he steals from his breast pocket. "Your son, I believe. He said it was a gift."

Miles removed from New York, where their journey began, the horses curl their nostrils and sniff the strange air.

Raymonde hurries to fill three pails of water. Roger runs into the house, fetching three apples from a bowl. Puppy bounces between the horses' legs, nosing each one excitedly.

Rose stands silent.

Led into the weathered barn, the three horses suspiciously peer over from their wooden stall doors at the faces curiously looking back at them.

That night Ron calls. Rudy answers.

"Did you get my gift?" asks Ron.

"Yes, yes, yes," gushes Rudy. "Thank you! Thank you! Thank you!"

Ron tells his brother the horses' names: Dolly, Rusty and Ringo. "Are they racehorses? Did you ride them? Did you win races on them? How fast are they?"

"Yes. Yes. No," Ron answers. "They're pretty fast; you better take a good hold." He suppresses a chuckle.

Ponies is what Ron calls them, which has nothing to do with their size. All three are generously built, standing tall on their long, spindly legs.

"This is unbelievable. The best present I've ever received," says Rudy.

Unlike the plodding workhorses in the logging camps, Ron's gift had come straight from the racetrack. No matter what anyone says to him, Rudy believes all three are champion racehorses.

The tallest of the three is Rusty. Thirteen years old and the senior citizen of the trio of horses, Rusty always holds his head high as if he is getting ready for a portrait. His gait is more of a strut even when he is hardly moving. Then again, why not? Rusty was brought into the winner's circle at the 1956 Kentucky Derby, when Needles, coming as was his wont from out of the clouds — at one point 24 lengths back — won. In the whirling pandemonium of victory, the winner's circle picture shows jockey David Erb patting Needles' sweat-soaked neck. There are the owners, Jack Dudley and Bonnie Heath, hugging each other. At the horse's head, there is trainer Hugh Fontaine. And there is Rusty, who seems to have a satisfied smirk on his face.

Ron had bought Rusty from Fontaine. He rode him from stable to stable, hitching him to each barn's corral fences. While Ron worked and breezed horses, Rusty nibbled on the grass. Now Rusty was in New Brunswick bringing New York and Kentucky with him.

Rusty's self-importance is no different from a human's. In an open field, a stall or a starting gate, when the clambering and nervous anticipation spills out into peevish pawing, banging and clanging, horses can tell who belongs and who doesn't.

There is a caste system at work in horse racing. How else can you explain a horse that has been running 10 lengths slower and disgraced against tougher competition suddenly sprinting to the front and never looking back when dropped into cheaper company? For no better explanation in horse racing, it is called class. It has no thesis, nor is it a universal consent. It simply exists. It dictates and decides. It is the sport's foundation — the claiming, allowance and then stakes races are all rungs up its ladder.

The reverse is almost as true. Although there are a few horses that suddenly get good and find themselves rolling off win after win, more often a horse stepping steeply up in class will find the jump in competition too much — even if it had just exited a very fast and easy race. Perhaps self-conscious, the horse tackling better will get a whiff of reality and understand it does not belong.

Dolly is the most docile of the trio. A Paint with a lightning bolt splash of white running from the tip of her nose to her high forehead, Dolly holds no airs in her soulful eyes.

Ringo, half Paint and half Arabian, is the fastest. He belongs to Rudy. Aurele and Albert are too big to be jockeys. His sisters? No chance. There are no women jockeys then (Diane Crump would not come along for another five years). Who knows about Roger, Gaetan or Yves? It is too early to tell. But Rudy knows.

"Ringo is yours because I know you are going to be a jockey," Ron says, to which Rudy, as always, answers, "Of course."

The next morning, on a stretch of ground owned by a neighbor, Bob Brinkmann, the boys ride the three horses bareback. They race for hours, the finish line a crooked crabapple tree.

"Here comes Rudy Turcotte," Rudy yelps as he roars past his brothers. Raising his whip (now a strap of leather) into the air as he passes the crabapple tree, he sings, "Rudy wins another one."

Ron keeps winning too. On his way to leading the 1964 fall meet standings at Aqueduct, Ron wins the Cowdin Stakes with Tom Rolfe on October 4. The win pays $27.60. It is part of a riding triple for Ron — his first in New York, coming after he won both ends of a $95.60 Daily Double.

Tom Rolfe had lost his previous four races, but Ron and the horse's trainer, Frank Whiteley Jr., aren't worried. They both know Tom Rolfe is screaming for more ground. The Cowdin was seven furlongs — still too short — but Ron and Whiteley understand that the colt will get longer races next year as a three-year-old. The year ends with Ron winning 250 races — third best in North America behind only Ussery and Walter Blum. Behind Ron are the likes of Shoemaker, Ycaza and Hartack.

The horses Ron rides win $1.3 million for their owners. Ron's 10 percent cut, before agent and valet expenses, is $130,000 — nearly twice as much as he earned in 1963. He is Canada's leading money-winning athlete. In just three full years of riding, his mounts have won well over $2 million.

Still, Ron lives on a shoestring with almost all his earnings going into the bank or back home to help his parents. In an interview with the *New York Herald Tribune*, he tells reporter

Jack Mann that he often goes sightseeing and has dinner with his agent just about every night.

"Is that all you do?" asks Mann.

"Well," replies Ron matter-of-factly, "I've been having my teeth fixed lately."

From 364 mounts, Noel wins a total of 51. His net is $10,400. A decent start, Noel thinks.

Huntley isn't so sure. When he hears that Noel is paying someone else $1 to clean his tack instead of doing it himself, Huntley sells Noel's contract to Harry Carmichael, the principal client of trainer Baron Manfred Wolfgang von Richthofen.

A director of the Ontario Jockey Club, von Richthofen, who always wears bow ties, is a former German tank-division captain and a cousin to the Red Baron, the First World War flying ace. He prefers to be called Wolf or Baron.

Ron turns every race into an assault. Stubborn as crabgrass and hating to lose — no matter what the odds — Ron is stronger than three-day-old coffee. He is almost universally regarded as one of the strongest riders. Down the stretch he is almost unbeatable as he pushes and prods his horses for more.

Chapter 12

Half of New Brunswick and all of Grand Falls seem to shut down the afternoon of May 1, 1965.

Everywhere, people who don't know the difference between an exactor and a tractor gather around radio and television sets — like the RCA Victor TV that Ron recently bought for his family.

It is Kentucky Derby Day. The Run for the Roses. Kentucky bluegrass. Sugary mint juleps and the annual pilgrimage to the Twin Spires of Churchill Downs.

"Look! There he is. There's Ronnie," Roger squeals, leaving a smudge on the TV screen as he points a finger overtop the image of his brother, who is riding in his first Derby atop Tom Rolfe.

Stiff shouldered, arms folded across his chest, Ron is listening to two men fidgeting in the paddock.

"Move back and maybe we'll all see," Rudy yells at Roger. "Nobody can see a damn thing."

Screwing his 9-year-old face into a mocking grimace, Roger slides backward a couple of inches along the brown paisley carpet.

"Farther!" Rudy bellows. "Get out of the way!"

Roger sticks out his tongue.

"Quiet down. Both of you," Alfred charges, his deep voice rumbling from the worn-thin ruby folds of his favorite chair. A rug with frayed tassels hangs on the wall over his left shoulder. The rug is a picture of a gnarly horned elk. The elk too seems to be watching the Derby.

The camera shifts to an aerial shot of Churchill Downs, the infield thick with pressed bodies — many of the women wearing both elegant and outlandish oversized wild hats and fascinators.

The view, a faceless voice says, is courtesy of the Goodyear Blimp.

"What's a blimp?" asks Raymonde, who just turned 12.

"Mon Dieu," Rose says, yet to comprehend all the excitement.

It is all so unfathomable. Just five years ago, Ron had watched this very race and didn't know what he was looking at. He didn't know where he was headed.

One day ends. The next one begins.

Now there he was on the screen, with millions of people, like Rose, watching him. Watching her son. Involuntarily, she clucks her lips.

Yesterday, the *Grand Falls Cataract* ran a long story about Ron's Derby debut under a "Good Luck, Ron" headline that smiled broadly across the front page. Only a couple other stories managed to make page 1: a headline of "Grand Falls Girl Wins Bake Off," and another that followed underneath the heading "C.T.C. Store to Hold Official Opening."

Inside, under the headline "Derby to Be Televised," another page carried three more stories about the race. There was also a picture of Canadian actor Lorne Greene, star of *Bonanza*, one arm draped over Ron's shoulder.

Roger, a fan of the western, wants to know where Hoss and Little Joe were.

In Toronto, the *Toronto Star Weekly* ran four open pages on Ron in a special section titled "Ron Turcotte. $1,000 a minute jockey."

Sipping black coffee, a reporter from the *Saint John Telegraph-Journal* is with the Turcottes, watching from behind. Every once in a while, she jots something onto a pad of yellow paper.

"Do you think he got our card?" Gaetan asks of an 8-foot telegram signed by 320 people from Drummond.

"I'm sure he did, dear," says Rose.

"Look, there he is again," Roger yips, leaving another smudge on the television screen.

"He looks so small," says Alfred, the horses now on the track as a band plays "My Old Kentucky Home," which brings many to tears as they smile and chorus along, "Weep no more my lady."

"He *is* small, Dad," Raymonde answers.

"Nah, not Ronnie," Alfred answers. "Ron's horse. Tom Rolfe. He looks so small."

"He *is* small," says Rudy of the horse, who stands just 15.2 hands tall and weighs considerably less than 1,000 pounds. "Like Northern Dancer. Two brick shithouses."

"Rudy ... your language," says Rose, embarrassed, looking at the reporter.

The reporter, writing again, chuckles.

Yves, suspendered in jeans pulled up high over his waist, rocks back and forth on a wooden horse, a Christmas present from Ron. Aurele, looking starched and uncomfortable in a white shirt and tie Rose had made him wear in case the reporter wanted to take pictures, sits on one arm of the crowded couch.

Everyone seems to inhale at once, collectively holding their breaths as if they are all bound together on a roller coaster whose car has reached its apex.

And then they are off, the starting gate clamoring until it is swallowed by the crowd's roars.

As is his style, Tom Rolfe lumbers away in seventh.

In the paddock, Raymond Guest had told Ron to lay as close as possible and to save all the ground he could. Ron winced when he heard that advice; he knew it is wrong. A one-run horse, Tom Rolfe preferred to come from far back. Timid, he also didn't like to race along the rail. He was also heavy-headed. When he came out of the gate, he would drop his head, and it was up to the jockey to make sure he kept it up.

He wasn't an easy horse to ride.

But Ron, who had become someone that other trainers ask for advice, wasn't about to argue with Guest. Especially in his first Derby mount. Instead, Ron bit his lip.

Nudging on the reins against his better judgment, Ron urges Tom Rolfe closer.

Confused, Tom Rolfe relents; he settles into fifth.

Down the backstretch he is on the move again. Fourth. Now third. Only Lucky Debonair, ridden by Shoemaker, and Flag Raiser, with Ussery aboard, are in front of him.

"Atta boy, Ronnie. Go on with him," yells Rudy, wearing a cowboy hat.

The family is screaming. So too is the reporter.

Ron tries to take Tom Rolfe inside of the top pair.

Ron hears Shoemaker yelling at Ussery, "Don't let that horse through, Bobby."

"Don't worry," replies Ussery with still more than half a mile to go. "That sucker ain't getting through."

Tom Rolfe doesn't. Forced to check, Tom Rolfe drops back. A second move doesn't get there either.

By the time Flag Raiser gives up the ghost, Lucky Debonair is too far gone. Dapper Dan passing Tom Rolfe late in the stretch, Ron finishes third.

"You can't win them all," says Alfred.

"He's only really been riding four full years," Rose adds. "I think he did well to come in third."

The *Telegram-Journal* reporter takes down their quotes.

Yves gets in a quote too. "I don't want to be a jockey; I want to be a man," the 5-year-old says.

Back in the barn, Whiteley emphatically says Tom Rolfe will not be going to the Preakness, the second leg of horse racing's Triple Crown.

"He's a small horse and he needs some rest," he says, noting that Tom Rolfe had run five times in five weeks.

A few days later, however, Whiteley changes his mind. He tells reporters he is going to work Tom Rolfe at Laurel Park in a few days. Instead, Whiteley sends out a different bay horse with similar markings as a ruse. Meanwhile at Pimlico, without any reporters to interrupt training, the real Tom Rolfe works. Satisfied with the workout, Whiteley enters Tom Rolfe for the 90th Preakness. Ron is named again as his jockey.

Two weeks after the Derby, at exactly 5:48 p.m., the Preakness field sweeps out of the starting gate.

Again, Flag Raiser is first to show, blazing to the lead and opening five lengths before the field reaches the first turn.

Unhurried, Ron settles into fifth place — nine lengths back and farther off the pace than he was in the Derby — as the first quarter split of 22 2/5 seconds flashes on the tote board.

"A quick pace," the announcer says almost direly, as Flag Raiser continues to speed along as if this were a six-furlong sprint and not a mile and three-sixteenths.

"Come on, Ronnie," pleads Roger as the Turcottes gather again, this time without any reporters.

Shoemaker has Lucky Debonair to Ron's right.

"He's fine," says Rudy coolly. "They're going too fast up front. Way too fast." Still just 15 years old Rudy already knows about the nuances of horse racing.

Going into the last turn, Tom Rolfe is still fifth but running easily; Dapper Dan is sixth, 10 lengths behind.

Around the final turn, Ron makes his move, rubbing hard on Tom Rolfe's neck and moving faster than Dapper Dan.

As Rudy predicted, the front-runners are spent, their gas gauges reading empty.

Rolling out of the final turn, Tom Rolfe and Ron are drawing away.

Nine Turcottes get to their feet in a full-throated roar.

"You got them, son!" Alfred yells.

"You got it, Ronnie," Rose softly echoes.

But it is still far from over.

Over his left shoulder, with only a sixteenth of a mile left, Ron sees the head of Dapper Dan coming hard to his inside.

Ron doesn't blink. He snatches the left rein, sending Tom Rolfe that way, crowding Dapper Dan into the rail.

"Hey! Hey! I'm here!" hollers Dapper Dan's jockey, Ismael "Milo" Valenzuela, the regular rider of Kelso, who won 22 graded stakes to become the No. 1 money winner in thoroughbred racing history.

Head down, Ron continues to edge his way closer to Dapper Dan, who, sensing fear and the inside rail, raises his head out of its crouch and jerks skyward. Valenzuela pushes it down, back into stride.

Ron and Tom Rolfe's lead is half a length. A quarter of a length. Now, only a neck. Dapper Dan isn't giving up.

"Go, Ronnie, go!" Raymonde pleads, the room going limp in suspense.

The wire comes up just in time.

"Yes!" yells Alfred, squeezing his arm tightly around Rose's shoulder. In an instant, everyone is hugging and dancing around in a tight little ball.

But then Rudy wails. "Dad! Dad! The announcer says there is an inquiry," he says.

"A what?" Rose asks her husband.

The announcer answers, dryly telling the audience that Valenzuela has claimed interference in the stretch.

The cameras pan to the tote board, where the inquiry light blinks beside the No. 6 of Tom Rolfe and the No. 8 of Dapper Dan.

"What does it mean?" Rose asks again.

"It means nothing," says Rudy. "They won't disqualify him. Not in the Preakness. He didn't do anything wrong. There was lots of room." In the next breath, Rudy adds, "Wasn't there, Dad?"

Fifteen minutes stretch out into eternity. Ron gets off Tom Rolfe. Valenzuela slides off Dapper Dan. Both horses parade around and around. Ron and Valenzuela both talk to the stewards, pleading their cases.

Trying to fill time while the stewards replay the stretch run over and over from different angles, one of the announcers says, "Ron Turcotte did come over. The longer this inquiry takes the more you have to wonder if they are going to take Tom Rolfe down."

The Turcottes' phone rings. It is Noel calling from Toronto, where he is watching the replays in the jockeys' room.

"No way they take him down," Noel says. "Nobody here thinks they will take him down."

On the television screen, the umpteenth replay is shown — this one that head-on view of the stretch.

"See! There's room," says Noel. "Plenty of room. The horses never touch. Sure, Ronnie makes it tight. But that was the smart thing to do. There. See that? Ronnie comes close to Dapper Dan but then he straightens him out."

That was exactly what Ron was doing. Without interfering, he was intimidating Valenzuela and Dapper Dan. It is a move he has used many times.

"The jocks here say Valenzuela is just taking a shot," says Noel.

The words barely out of his mouth, the lights stop flashing. The inquiry sign comes off. In its place comes the word "official."

"Yahoo!" yells Noel. "Got to go. Everything alright up there now?"

Having dismounted 10 minutes earlier, Ron raises a fist weakly, a thin smile on his lips. As he climbs back on Tom Rolfe and heads to the winner's circle, Whiteley pats Ron on the leg.

The picture taken, the euphoria of relief dissipated, Ron is swarmed by the media.

Cameras still rolling, Rudy hears someone ask Ron if Tom Rolfe swerved in on his own accord.

"On his own accord?" Ron repeats after a knowing, lengthy pause. "Yes. Let's say he swerved in a little."

A few of the reporters chuckle.

"I just moved over there to be sure my horse saw him, but when we got close I straightened out my horse," Ron continues.

Back at Barn 1, where all the Preakness horses were stabled, it is discovered that Tom Rolfe lost his left front shoe and had run down slightly.

Ron is surprised. "He must have lost the shoe after the race because I never felt him change stride or anything," he says.

While Tom Rolfe is led away by his groom for an after-race bath, Ron looks up to the trainer and says quietly, "Uh, Mr. Whiteley, I want to thank you for keeping me on this horse after the Derby."

Whiteley grins and brushes a hand through Ron's hair.

The next morning Rose excitedly buys three copies each of the *Grand Falls Cataract* and the *Telegraph-Journal*, where they point out that the 1:56 1/5 time for the Preakness was the third-fastest in history, only a fifth of a second slower than the record jointly held by Nashua and Bold Ruler. She reads each account twice before leaving the papers open on the kitchen table next to a vase of freshly picked chrysanthemums.

Rudy clips out one of the pictures — Ron arched under Tom Rolfe's neck, a blanket of black-eyed Susans in his arms — and tapes it in the scrapbook Rose is keeping.

Over the past two years, Ron has won 513 races. But it is really only now, after the Preakness, that the U.S. racing world wakes and wants to know more about the curly-haired former lumberjack who rides with a crucifix tucked in the mesh inside of his helmet.

New York; New York, indeed.

Still shy around reporters, Ron has little to offer. Trent Frayne in the *Toronto Star Weekly* asks him about women.

"All they want is your money," Ron shoots back. "I've got me a girl back home in New Brunswick, and that's enough for me."

Three weeks later, on June 5, Tom Rolfe and Ron finish second in the mile and a half Belmont. They had the lead deep in the stretch but this time Hail To All, third in the Preakness, did what Dapper Dan couldn't and powered his way to victory, winning by a neck.

Never afraid to tell the truth, Ron blames himself.

"I moved him too soon, sir," he tells Whiteley. "I should have won the race."

For a second, Whiteley is stunned.

"You're the first jockey to come to me and take the blame. Most riders just make excuses."

"Well," said Ron, still wincing from the loss. "I call it like it is. I should have waited. He only has a short run in him."

It is the last time Ron rides Tom Rolfe. The horse is sent to Chicago and wins his next four races, all at odds of less than even money.

Alfred's doctors were right. The mild heart attack he had two years ago was indeed a warning, telling him to slow down. But no one can get Alfred to listen.

"Just gas. A heartburn. That's all," he keeps saying of the constant pain in his chest. He just needs to lie down and then he'll be fine, he pleads.

He calls them episodes. But this latest episode has felled him like a butchered tree. Still clutching his chest, Alfred is taken to the hospital, where doctors confirm what Rose has known all along: another heart attack.

The three or four episodes he didn't tell anyone about but now reluctantly mentions to the doctor were more likely heart attacks as well.

"Stop working so hard or you are going to die," the doctor tells Alfred. "This is no longer a warning. You can rebuild a house, but we can't put your heart back together."

It was that simple. Or so the doctor told him.

All Alfred has known is work. Now they are going to take it away from him. Guilt wracking him, he tells Rose, "I am useless."

"We will make it work," Rose answers. "We always do."

Chapter 13

These are giddy days for Ron and Noel.

Ron has taken Tom Rolfe to victory in the Preakness; Noel, still an apprentice, frequently finds the winner's circle in Ontario.

Noel, named because he was born two days before Christmas of 1942 and baptized at Saint-Michel on Christmas Day, is still skinny as a crayon and able to tack 109 pounds.

"You are so much like your brother," Pat Remillard, 59 and still riding, says to Noel. He is trying to tutor his second Turcotte.

"That's good, I hope," answers Noel.

"In some ways," replies Remillard. "But in some ways no."

"And that means what?" asks Noel, scrunching up his face.

"At first Ron figured every race was a fight he had to win," explains Remillard. "Knock him down, and he'd come back swinging mad as an old hen. But he changed. You need to change too."

"These," Remillard says, clasping Noel's hands hard between his own. "You need to use these. And this too." He taps Noel on his riding helmet.

Not built nearly as powerful as his brother, Noel had quickly become known as a slasher relying on his whip.

"You see the way Ron rides now. He doesn't slash and bang. He thinks. He rates his horses," says Remillard. "You're stick crazy. Put the whip away and hand ride. Relax out there. The horses feel it. You fight them, they fight you. Surely, you have found that out yourself?"

"Yeah, and when they fight me, I give them another couple of whacks and show them who really is the boss," Noel says, pounding on his right leg three times.

"Oh, forget it then," says Remillard, starting to turn away.

"Hey, where are you going?" Noel pleads.

"You don't want to listen; I don't want to talk. Who do you think I am? A rookie? I was riding horses before your mama even thought about having you. Put that whip away. Only use it as a last resort."

A month later, after losing by a scant nose with Grave Pit in the card's opening race, Noel wins four in a row.

The next morning, Remillard picks up the *Toronto Daily Star* and smiles.

"A jockey is no good if he doesn't hand ride," Remillard reads Noel's printed quotes. "I thought all it took to ride a horse was to beat the daylights out of them. I got into the habit from a horse named Now I Wonder. He needed the whip and really responded to it. Other guys told me it was wrong. But I listened to Pat Remillard. Pat showed me you can do as much with most horses just using your hands. Ron told me it was too soon for me to start riding, and he was right. A rider should know about that before he starts. If you don't then you have to find out as you go along."

"And I didn't think he was really listening," Remillard thinks, still grinning.

Something else Noel says in the paper catches Remillard's eyes: "We think the best (Turcotte) is going to be Rudolphe. He's 15. Only weighs 75 pounds. We want to make sure he finishes school first. It's going to be hard though. He's already got the racetrack in his blood."

Remillard quietly closes the paper.

"I don't know if I can wait that long," he says to himself.

Speeding north along Interstate 95, Ron watches from the passenger seat the trees thicken as they flash by the wide fenders of his black Cadillac hardtop. A St. Christopher medal dangles from the rearview mirror.

It is August 25, 1965.

Ron is in a hurry.

"Can't you go any faster?" he calls to Aurele, who is happy to be driving.

Wednesday, a dark day with no racing in New York, the brothers are heading home, a large expectant crowd already starting to gather outside of Saint-Michel. Grand Falls' favorite son is getting married to Gaetane Morin.

"We're going to miss my own wedding," Ron mutters.

"Relax," says Aurele. "We've got lots of time. I know every inch of this highway. You forget how many times I've driven your cars back and forth? We miss the wedding; we'll just do it tomorrow."

Ron's head suddenly jerks sideways to make sure Aurele is only kidding. He feels the car accelerate.

A fresh cigar clenched in his teeth, Ron imagines Gae, his bride-to-be, getting her hair done, everyone fussing over her the way they always do in the movies. He wonders if she is as nervous as he is. Wonders if she is having second thoughts. They've known each other since childhood, but it has only been a year and a half since they started dating.

He had proposed in the spring when Gae and her mother had flown to New York. He laughs when he remembers Gae's mother wouldn't let her come alone. It was the only time either of them had ever seen him ride.

Striking a match, he thinks of Shoemaker, who was forever packing tiny firecrackers into Ron's cigars when he wasn't looking. The cartoon image of a banana-peeled, blown-up cigar makes him snicker.

In a month, he will be 24. It's only been five years since he left home.

"Remember when Dad brought you to the logging camp for the first time? How old were you?" asks Aurele.

"Seven," Ron answers without having to think. "Mom said I was too much of a handful. She wanted me out of the house as soon as possible."

They both snort.

"I don't remember doing much at first," says Aurele. "I know it was always you and Dad working as a team."

"And Camille and Noel working together as another unit," Ron interjects.

"I'd sit at the back of the horses after you and Dad peeled those logs. I'd go with the horses and the logs to the yard. That was kind of fun. I can still see Camille sawing those big logs into four-foot lengths at the mill."

Reeds of smoke crawl up the partly rolled down passenger-side window before leaping out into the bright sunshine. The lone cloud in the sky looks like an elephant.

On a country and western station on the radio, they hear "King of the Road" by Roger Miller, "Flowers on the Wall" by the Statler Brothers and Buck Owens sing "I've Got a Tiger By the Tail." Aurele sings along, tapping his fingers on the steering wheel.

Three hours pass before Aurele stops the car outside of Bangor, Maine.

"I gotta pee," he says.

While the service station attendant gurgles five dollars' worth of premium gas into the tank, Ron follows Aurele inside and grabs another Styrofoam cup. Overfilling it, he slurps back the coffee off its brown plastic cover. The first sip singes his lips.

Leaning in the ashtray, the cigar is still hot. Ron's tuxedo is folded across the back seat.

"Going to the chapel, and we're gonna get married," Ron sings while a commercial tells him how white his shirts should be. "Gee I really love you and we're gonna get ma-a-arried. Going to the chapel of love."

The forests thin, giving way to rolling hills and large expanses of fields teeming with wheat, barley and potatoes. A trestle bridge takes Ron and Aurele over the Saint John River. The thunder of the falls briefly startles Ron, a torrent of water tumbling until it cascades 75 feet below.

Just outside of town, Ron and Aurele pass the sign welcoming them to Grand Falls. It is written twice. Once in English. Once, Grand Sault, in French.

As the brothers pull into a gravel parking lot off Broadway Boulevard, the air smells sweetly of baked goods, cotton candy and caramel apples. They have both forgotten that today is also Grand Falls' annual Fair Day. Pies sit on white table-clothed picnic tables waiting to be judged, along with sheep, goats and cows. A banner, reading "Congratulations Gae and Ron," hangs between two poplars. A Ferris wheel and a Tilt-A-Whirl are just starting up, their gears meshing and surging between the shouts of passengers.

The air is sweet, and everyone smiles.

Someone yells, "He's here!" And a pack breaks away and heads toward the car.

"How are you feeling, son?" asks Alfred.

"Scared," admits Ron, barely out of his car.

"Yeah, Dad," kids Aurele. "He hardly said two words the whole way. And you know how nobody can usually get him to shut up."

Monsignor Alfred Lang performs the ceremony before the reception moves to Georges Bernier Hall.

Shuffling his feet in front of hundreds of clapping hands, Ron says, "Since I was a little boy, this was the girl I was going to marry. And now that I've done it I want you to know how happy I am. And how lucky."

He carries a horseshoe in his right pocket.

Aurele gives the toast. "Ron, you are only barely over 5 feet. But to us you are 10 feet tall."

The hall erupts with applause.

Cardboard signs tacked to trees and power poles read, "No Liquor. No Beer."

"But they don't say anything about the parking lot," Alfred says, emptying another glass to his lips while the Starfires play on a stage.

"Dad, you sure it's okay to be drinking?" Camilla questions. "It's only been a couple of months since your last heart attack. How are you feeling? Really, how do you feel?"

"Never mind, dear, and shush. Don't tell your mother."

"I imagine she already knows," Camilla replies, motioning with her head to where Rose, arms clasped across her chest, frowns.

Only one Turcotte isn't at the wedding: Noel.

Almost precisely at the same moment that Ron and Gae say "I do," Noel rides under the wire at Fort Erie with Jean-Louis Levesque's front-running Ciboulette in the $12,225 Duchess Stakes.

In sweat-lathered blankets, three other horses flash across the finish line to Ciboulette's outside shoulder.

In the stands, nobody is sure who won. But Noel is. Gathering in Ciboulette, Noel's heart pounding wildly, he thrusts his right arm into the air.

Another rider pulls alongside and extends his hand. Noel takes it. Neither says a word.

Yet, five minutes pass before the photo and then the tote board confirm what Noel already knows: Ciboulette by a head; fast-closing Junonia second; Green Goddess, the favorite, third by a nostril.

His first stakes victory, Noel feels the applause rinse around him.

With Levesque winning $7,225, Noel's 10 percent will buy Ronnie a nice wedding present, surmises Perlove in the *Toronto Daily Star*.

Whehen Gae and Ron check in to their motel room, the clerk hands Ron a note.

"What does it say, honey?" Gae asks.

"Phone Joe Shea," replies Ron tersely. "He's left a number."

After putting their suitcases on the bed, Ron dials the phone.

"Joe. What's up?" asks Ron.

"Ronnie, look, I'm sorry. I know you just got married but you have to be at Rockingham Park on Saturday. Lou Cavalaris has a horse he wants you to ride in a prep for the New Hampshire Sweepstakes and, well, you know Lou."

"Geez, Joe."

"Like I said, I'm sorry. It's one of Lou's horses: Victorian Era. They think he's going to be something special," says Shea, of a horse that would be inducted into the Canadian Horse Racing Hall of Fame for owner Allen Case. "I think you better go. You know what kind of horses Lou has," Shea says, referring to the conditioner, who would lead all of North America's trainers in 1966 with 175 winners.

Gae already knows the news isn't good. The way Ron put down the phone confirms it.

"Sorry," says Ron. "We can have a bigger, better honeymoon later."

Gae nods.

Noel finishes the 1965 Fort Erie summer meet as the leading rider with 53 wins, 17 more than runner-up Avelino Gomez. Four of those wins come on the same day, and he misses a fifth by a nose.

Nothing changes as the horses move to Woodbine. On opening day, Noel wins the Yearling Sales Stakes on Holarctic, the previous year's yearling sales topper at $16,000, by four and a half lengths after getting away eighth. Leaping off the horse's back, Noel feels his legs wobble as the winning trainer, Baron von Richthofen shakes his hand.

On September 1, Mike Armstrong writes in the *Toronto Telegram*: "Noel Turcotte is doing his best to make Canadian racing fans forget all about his older brother Ron."

Armstrong goes on to quote the Baron: "I'd have to say (Noel) is a better rider than Ron. He follows instructions perfectly, and he's cold and chilly. He never gets excited." The Baron adds that he is going to Florida at the end of the year and is taking Noel with him.

Ron will be there too.

When Noel loses his apprentice allowance on September 29, Armstrong writes another piece on Noel after a four-win afternoon: "Noel Turcotte had two strikes against him when he came to the track in July 1962. First, he had no experience. Second, his name was Turcotte, and everyone compared him with his older brother Ron."

"Losing my bug certainly won't affect my riding," Noel is quoted in the article. "But I probably won't get as many mounts as I've been getting. Trainers wanting the weight allowance will still use bug riders, but I expect to get my share."

Noel adds that he has his weight under control — he has no trouble doing 110 pounds.

Noel wins a career-best 142 races as an apprentice in 1965; he is the second-leading rider in Canada. Only Hugo Dittfach wins more. Like Ron before him, Noel also credits Remillard, who has taken him aside, watched replays and given him a few tips.

"Pat has been wonderful. I just hope he keeps telling me about things I may be doing wrong."

Chapter 14

Heading home along Highway 7, just outside of Whitby, Ontario, Noel and his best friend, Johnny Waters, watch as the car's headlights catch the snakes of snow that slurp noisily under the tires. It is eight days into December 1965.

The radio plays, but the sound is drowned out by the roar of the car's heater, which is cranked as far to the right as it can go.

Noel and Johnny aren't listening to the radio anyway. They talk and laugh. About nothing and everything: the ducks they have just shot — carcasses wrapped in burlap sacks in the trunk; the Toronto Maple Leafs, who have lost four of their past five; the Buffalo Bills, who are looking to win their second straight American Football League championship. And women.

Noel's car shudders as a sixteen-wheeler, going in the opposite direction, blows past. Loose gravel spits at the door panel. Horses and cattle, huddled with their backs to the wind, flash by along with the twinkling lights of distant farmhouses.

Noel tells Johnny he is thinking of going to Maryland until the races start back again in Ontario.

Walter Taylor, now Noel's agent, says it would be a good idea.

"Can't hurt, can it?" says Noel, whose mounts this year earned $347,000. It is a third as much as what Ron won on horses like

Tom Rolfe and other stakes winners like Cornish Prince, Lady Pitt and Amerivan. But it is very good in Canada.

"It sure didn't hurt Ron. He's in Florida right now. He's leading the standings at Tropical Park."

A struggling apprentice, Johnny nods with a shiver. "So, are you going to go?"

"Probably," says Noel.

"Probably? You gotta go, Noel. What are you worried about? Daphne?"

"A little. I know she won't like it," Noel says of the girl he has just started dating.

"Hell, Noel. You can get lots of girls. But you can't always get lots of horses. Good ones anyway. You gotta do what you gotta do."

"Yeah," Noel says weakly. "Probably."

Johnny hears the click, click, click of the signal light and feels Noel turning the steering wheel to pass a gravel truck, which has suddenly slowed in front of them.

Both heading west, the truck inexplicably makes a left turn directly in front of them onto Coronation Road.

Johnny sees it first, the nose of the truck and its thick, ribbed tires inexplicably coming right at them.

"Christ!" Now Noel sees it. Yanking the steering wheel to the left, he slams on the brakes, but the tires, not listening, don't take hold.

It all takes but a few seconds. The truck's cab hits them first, a giant can opener ripping through the passenger door. The window explodes. A cold rush of air and shards of glass slap Noel in the face. By the time he blinks, Johnny is gone, hurtling through the darkness.

Noel hears a sickening thump. Then nothing.

The next thing Noel remembers is the blur of the flashing lights. Red, blue and white merging through the black of the night, bouncing deliriously through what remains of the windshield.

"Can you hear me?"

It is the voice of Eric Walsh asking stern and loud.

Also a jockey, Walsh had been hunting with Johnny and Noel. Following in his own car, Walsh saw it all nightmarishly unfold.

"Can you hear me? Noel?" Walsh yells again.

His forehead damp, Noel wipes at it, feeling the stickiness of his own blood.

"Try not to move," he hears someone else say, this voice calm and soft. It is a police officer who wasn't far behind.

"What happened?" Noel murmurs. "The truck. The truck pulled right in front of me."

He tries to lift himself upright but can't and slumps his head back onto the seat.

He feels cold. Almost the entire right side of the car is gone.

"Where's Johnny?" he hears himself cry. "Johnny. Johnny!"

Through the opening, Noel sees four silhouettes. Hands in their pockets, nobody in a hurry.

"I'm sorry, son," he hears a soft voice say. "But it looks like you were lucky."

Thin flakes of white float through the darkness. Noel's screams pierce the silence.

The truck driver is sobbing, his head in his hands.

Soon an ambulance arrives. More lights. The siren shrieks. Then goes mute.

"Johnny is dead, isn't he? I killed him. I killed Johnny." It is almost the only thing Noel says.

"It wasn't your fault," Walsh keeps pleading. "You can't blame yourself."

Noel's eyes are moist, and red as the blood flecked on his coat.

The ambulance takes both Noel and Waters' body to a hospital. Walsh follows. When they arrive, Walsh puts both arms around Noel, who, remarkably, is relatively unscathed. They are both crying.

That night with the truck becomes Noel's shadow. It clings to his bootstraps and follows him everywhere. He wakes with wails, jerking him upright off his sweat-soaked pillow. Mornings are no better. It is all black. Everything. When he goes to the store, it follows. He breaks into a trot, but the shadow runs alongside.

Instinctively Noel will put both hands into the air, trying to suppress the vision of the encroaching truck. Can't the driver see? Why doesn't he turn away?

Then the impact. The metal shearing. The glass shattering. Johnny lifted and swept away into the gloom.

"Why did I have to pass? I've killed my best friend. If I had just stayed behind, even for a few more seconds, Johnny would still be alive."

Months pass. Noel feels he deserves this anguish.

Every Sunday, Rose lights a candle in Saint-Michel, praying on her knees. "Please, God. It wasn't his fault. Please let this pass. Don't take another life. Please."

To sleep Noel starts drinking. But even that doesn't work. Come morning, the shadow is still there.

By March 1966, after weeks of hesitation, Noel is riding in Maryland. In Pimlico, he wins an allowance race by 10 lengths.

"Noel is every bit as skilled as Ron," Hall of Fame trainer and Noel's agent Walter Taylor tells a reporter.

The story runs beside an ad for a Spalding five-club set of golf clubs: 3-, 5- and 7-iron, a driver and a putter. The price is $29.95. Another ad lists a 1966 Bel Air sedan for $2,597 — push-button radio, deluxe seat belts and whitewall tires.

Now 66 years old and the oldest active jockey in North America, Remillard finally calls it quits after 38 years as a jockey, having won 1,922 races, and opens a public stable.

"The average racing life of a jockey is six or seven years. I'm an exception," Remillard announces to the media. "I've never had a weight problem, always rode at 104–105 pounds; never been in a hot box steam cabinet in my life. Weight stops most guys after six, seven years."

The first horse he sends out as a trainer is Win-T-Bird. To no one's surprise, Noel gets the mount.

That same morning, in New York, a 12-pound girl is born. The parents, Ron and Gae, name her Lynn.

Two men sawing a log in Victoria County (1941).

A view of cultivated land for potato crops in Victoria county (1946).

The Turcotte family together in 1962. The twins, Camille and Camilla, are not present.

Back row (L-R): Albert, Alfred, Ron, Rose, Noel, Aurele, Odette.

Front row (L-R): Roger, Gaetan, Yves, Raymonde, Rudy

Ron plays guitar for Yves at home (1962).

Woodbine   " NORTHERN DANCER "   October 7, 1963
Owner   Trainer   Jockey
Windfields Farm   H. A. Luro   Ron Turcotte
1 Mile 70 Yds.   1.42

Ron wins with Northern Dancer (1963).

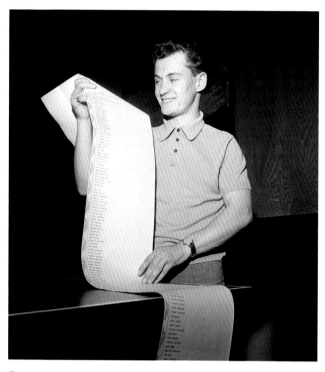

Ron poses with the good luck telegram from people back home in New Brunswick before riding Tom Rolfe in the 91st Kentucky Derby (1965).

Rudy and Ringo in New Brunswick (1965).

Albert rides Rusty (1966).

Ron and Rudy cleaning up in the jockey's room. Rudy, an apprentice, was the leading rider at the Aqueduct; Ron second (1969).

Rudy and Ron at the Aqueduct track (1969).

Queen Elizabeth with Ron after he rode Fanfreliche to victory in the Manitoba Centennial Derby (1970).

Fort Erie   **SYMMETRIC**   July 21, 1973
Owner   "FRIAR ROCK STAKES" Purse $10,000 Added   Jockey
H.A. Grant   Trainer-C.F.Chapman   Noel Turcotte
2nd Shake A Leg   6½ furl   1.16.4   3rd La Prevoyante

Noel wins the Friar Rock Stakes atop Symmetric (1973).

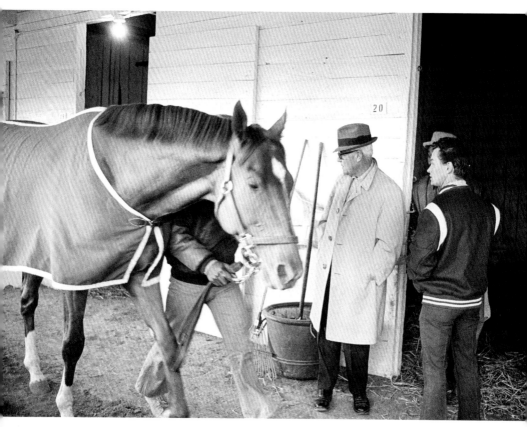

Lucien Laurin and Ron watch as Secretariat parades past them at stables of Churchill Downs in Louisville before the Kentucky Derby (1973).

RIGHT Ron and Secretariat's lead at the Belmont Stakes

Ron and Secretariat as they make the final turn on their way to winning the Triple Crown in the Belmont Stakes horse race at Belmont Park in Elmont, N.Y. (1973).

RIGHT Penny leads Ron and Secretariat to the winner's circle at the Belmont Stakes (1973).

News SPORT Nouvelle

NEW BRUNSWICK   NOUVEAU-BRUNSWI

JULY 1973   FREDERICTON, CANADA   VOL. 1 - NO. 2

RON TURCOTTE	RON TURCOTTE
VOTED INTO HALL OF FAME	AU TEMPLE DE LA RENOMMEE SPORTIVE

Ron Turcotte of Grand Falls, New Brunswick, 31 year-old jockey of Triple Crown winner Secretariat, has been immediately inducted into the New Brunswick Sports Hall of Fame.

Ron Turcotte de Grand-Sault, Nouveau-Brunswick, jockey de 31 ans du cheval Secretariat, vainqueur de la triple couronne, a immédiatement été installé au Temple de la Renommée sportive du Nouveau-Brunswick.

Ron and Secretariat cross the finish line at the Preakness (1973).

LEFT The cover of the July 1973 issue of New Brunswick Sports News, featuring Ron's introduction into the New Brunswick Sports Hall of Fame.

Ron and Secretariat work out before the Belmont (1973).

Chapter 15

Weight is just about every jockey's living nightmare. The Jockeys' Guild estimates that two-thirds of all jockeys have to reduce, but many jockeys believe that is a conservative estimate. Forty percent of all jockeys are bulimic. Many others are anorexic.

Jockeys will do everything to make the weight assigned to each horse. They'll spend hours in sweatboxes, where the temperature can reach 140° F. They'll swallow diuretic pills like Lasix, which are commonly used to remove fluid for heart patients. They'll down laxatives, "rent" food, starve themselves and wear rubber suits while jogging or driving their vehicles with the heat cranked as high as possible.

A jockey who can no longer win the battle of the bulge is out of work. It's that simple.

In steamboxes and saunas, there is no laughter, only quiet consternation, billowing steam and a few buckets of ice the jockeys plunge their heads into when the heat gets intolerable.

Here, there is only one thing that jockeys have on their minds and it isn't winning. It's losing. Every pound critical, the goal for most riders is about 112 pounds, with apprentices asked to ride with even less. For many jockeys, 112 pounds isn't close to their normal body weights of 125 to 130 pounds. When jockeys retire, it isn't unusual for them to "balloon" back to those 130 pounds in just a couple of days.

No matter how hard they reduce, the weight always comes back. Lose four pounds one day, and the next day it is back staring them in the face. It never ends.

Start with one Lasix pill and it isn't uncommon for the body to get immune. Then it's two pills. Then four. You hear of diet programs where people boast about losing six pounds in two weeks. But jockeys have been known to lose six pounds in a few hours.

Sooner or later there's nothing left to come off. There's no fat left and there's not much water in muscles. What comes out then are electrolytes, protein stores and vital minerals like potassium and chloride.

Yet, as they're asked to be lighter and lighter, to control more than half a ton of rampaging horse flesh, jockeys need to be exceptionally strong. It is a dangerous duality. When jockeys reduce, they can't be strong. And when they aren't as strong, they are more susceptible to injuries. Weak, dizzy and drained, some jockeys have passed out in sweatboxes, their bodies going into shock.

Then there are the terrible mood swings. Depression is common too. It is also mentally draining, and when you're tired, your reaction times aren't as quick.

And then there are the long-lasting physical tolls. Jockeys can experience blood disorders, kidney and nerve damage, dental erosion and the wizened thinning bones of osteoporosis.

All horses must carry the weight assigned according to the conditions of a race. Handicap and stakes races, which both have higher purses, are different. In handicap races, heavier weights are assigned to the better horses to try to "even" the field. The goal of every racing secretary is to have every handicap race end in a dead heat. Stakes races are handicap races where part of the prize, or purse, is put up by the owners of the horses.

Unlike claiming races, horses running in handicap and stakes races also cannot be purchased. They run for no tag.

Weight, an adage in horse racing goes, can stop a train. Many trainers believe just a few pounds can make the difference of half a length. Usually, the first couple of pounds melt away fairly easily because it is mostly just water. But it is the last couple of pounds that are stubbornly insolent. Sooner or later, there's nothing left to shed.

On most days, Ron tacked 112 pounds. The 105 pounds that he used to tack when he was an apprentice are a distant memory. Gae put him on a diet of just 800 calories a day, gradually working up to between 1,200 and 1,500. But when the weights came out for the 1966 July 4 running of the Suburban at Belmont, Ron's mount, Buffle, is allowed to carry just 110 pounds.

The favorite, Bold Lad, winner of his past four starts, the champion two-year-old of 1964 and the favorite in the 1965 Kentucky Derby, is assigned a staggering 135 pounds.

For the first time since he started riding, Ron hesitantly pops a tiny 20 mg yellow Lasix pill into his mouth. He knows he won't be able to get too far away from the bathroom; he is going to urinate like a racehorse.

Climbing on the scale the next day he is relieved. He has pissed away three pounds.

On a stifling hot day, Buffle wins by four lengths. It is Ron's first $100,000 stakes victory since Tom Rolfe in the Preakness. Ron's share is $7,208.

Chapter 16

The day after he graduates from high school in 1967, Rudy, 16, takes a bus to Montreal and then a train to Toronto, where Noel and Ron anxiously await his arrival.

Like Noel, Rudy is an inch taller than Ron. But he has always been lighter than both, the needle on the scale barely nudging past 95 pounds.

A natural. That's what people are going to say, believes Rudy. Born to ride racehorses. Going to be better than even Ron. That's what they will say too.

Loquacious, cocky, fearless and baby-faced, when Rudy — nine years younger than Ron — arrives at Woodbine, he starts his racing career the same way as Ron did: with a pitchfork in one hand and a lead shank in the other.

And, just like Ron and Noel, Rudy learns how to gallop with George Thompson and how to ride with Pat Remillard. The basement floor is cemented; Rudy's apprenticeship into the world of horse racing was set as solid as possible.

Now operating a public stable, Remillard takes a special interest in Rudy, who is already being hyped and anointed in the press as the "Next One."

Under the strict labor laws of the time, apprentice riders couldn't just ride for anyone they wanted. Jockeys had to be under contract and Remillard holds Rudy's legal agreement. Again, just as he did with Ron, Remillard doesn't just show Rudy how to race ride; he teaches him how to conduct himself. How to behave and conduct himself with owners and trainers. How to be polite. How to handle money. How to be an athlete. How to be a gentleman.

"Rudy is better at this stage than Ron or Noel," Remillard says to anyone who will listen.

Ron thinks so too. Noel has no doubt.

Invariably a jockey's baptism into racing is a short ceremony. One longshot and usually early in the card, where the cheaper horses get to argue with themselves. Rudy, however, is so highly touted that when he makes his debut on the miserable afternoon of September 5, 1968, he is signed up for four mounts.

Dress Tartan is his first. In thick mud marbled by a steady torrent of rain that makes it almost impossible to see, Rudy pulls down one set of sloppy goggles after another until the fourth and last pair is gone too. Carrying himself and five pounds of lead weight in his saddle, the weights used to make up the difference between Rudy's 95 pounds and the 100-plus pounds the horse is assigned, he gets away seventh. Then he is fifth. At the wire, he finishes third.

Shaking with excitement, he runs back to the jockeys' room splashing and dancing through the relentless rain, looking like a gingerbread man, except for the white icing where his goggles have stopped the kicked-back deep mud.

Rudy finishes last with his next mount, fourth with the one after that and then last again. It doesn't matter. Rudy has become what he knew would happen for many years. A jockey. He is hooked as snuggly as a trout out of the Salmon River back home.

Eight days later, on Friday the 13th, and with the 13th mount of his career, it is unlucky 13 be damned.

Assigned to ride Go Go John, Rudy is sixth going into the final turn. But he shows poise and doesn't panic. Swinging three-wide at the quarter pole, he gradually edges up to third. Then he presses, and Go Go John disappears down the stretch to win by six lengths.

In the winner's circle, posing for the victory photo, Rudy gives that perfect little grin he has been practicing for years.

Rudy is so excited that he begins to strip off his silk riding shirt right there in the winner's circle. He has one arm already pulled through one sleeve when his valet winks and tells him that it would be a better idea if he waited until he gets to the jockeys' room to disrobe.

"I felt quite confident," Rudy tells Laurie Brain of the *Globe and Mail*. "I did everything the way the trainer told me to before the race."

Asked if he can be as good as Ron and Noel, Rudy's arrogance flashes.

"I don't want to be as good as Ron and Noel. I want to be better than they are," he says matter-of-factly.

Loving the limelight, Rudy wants to be a star.

"Ron. Noel. Now we gotta worry about you," says Brian Swatuk, who is the second-leading rider in Canada, as he shakes Rudy's hand.

"He's got everything it takes to be a rider," Remillard tells the *Globe and Mail*. "He's a good judge of pace, he's interested in what he's doing and he's not afraid of horses."

One of the first to greet Rudy with the traditional first-win bucket of water is Noel.

"The first one is the toughest," Noel tells Rudy. "The rest will come easy."

But Noel says it without conviction. While he won races with comfort when he started off, ever since he lost his apprentice allowance, many trainers have stopped using him. Accustomed to riding four and five races a day, he is lucky to find even a couple of mounts a day now. And the ones he does get are usually somebody else's seconds.

Hot new apprentices have arrived; Noel is now an afterthought.

One of those sought-after bug boys is Sandy Hawley, who will have a legendary career, leading all riders in North America in 1970, 1972, 1973 and 1976. Hawley's 1973 season was especially brilliant as he became the first jockey to win 500 races in one year.

Bigger boned than either Ron or Rudy, Noel's hunger is harder to tame.

While 1968 continues to run full speed for Ron, who is the second-leading rider at Aqueduct, as he wins a stakes with the great mare Shuvee, a two-time Eclipse Champion, after winning one with the brilliant Fort Marcy last year, Noel is only walking. When he asks a trainer to give him a chance, the answer always seems the same: Okay, Noel; I'll try to find you something. But they don't seem to be trying very hard. Instead, all they give him is a cold shoulder.

"I'm the same rider I was when I was an apprentice," Noel tells the trainers. "No. I'm better. Just give me a chance."

There is a ledge in every career. Climbing onto it is the first trick. The bigger trick is staying there and not falling. Last year, Noel's 68 wins were almost half of what he won in each of the previous two years. Moreover, his mounts' earnings of $258,000 were also nearly halved. He is counting on much more. So is Daphne, who is now his wife. They have just bought a condominium 10 minutes from Woodbine. The Buick Wildcat he bought wasn't cheap either. That had set him back nearly $4,000.

Rudy, on the other hand, is just getting started.

The next two horses he takes to the winner's circle both come out of Remillard's barn. One is owned by one of Remillard's hot walkers, prompting a big party in the barn that night. The other is owned by one of Remillard's grooms. Again, the beer flows.

After that win, Remillard shuts Rudy down. It is almost the end of the season, and Remillard and Rudy want to keep his 10-pound weight allowance alive for next year.

To celebrate his 1968 season, Rudy buys a new Jaguar V12 luxury car. It is British racing green with a white interior.

On April 13, 1969, a scrawny bay colt with spindly legs, a long neck, a narrow chest and cartoonish floppy ears is born at Claiborne Farm in Paris, Kentucky.

Two and a half months after his birth, the unassuming colt, who still doesn't look any healthier, is vanned 10 hours to his new home: the Meadow Farm in Doswell, Virginia, owned by Christopher Chenery. Despite the land being bare of fertile soil and the property overrun with brambles and brush, Chenery purchased his ancestral farm from his cousins in 1936 — the midst of the Great Depression — and remarkably turned it into one of the leading thoroughbred breeding farms in North America.

By now, however, Chenery, who had found great success in the world of big business, founding utility companies Federal Water Service and Southern Natural Gas Company, is stricken with Alzheimer's and Parkinson's disease. He lives out his final years in New York's New Rochelle Hospital.

As for the unhealthy-looking colt, the Meadow's farm manager, Howard Gentry, gets out his notebook and into his daily report jots down, "Colt looks poor and thin. You could run your fingers along his ribs and play a tune. Looks sick; is sick. Has a temperature of 102.2."

The colt's name will be Riva Ridge.

Chapter 17

Rudy aches for the day he would win a race with Ron watching. Ron had given him his start in horse racing, given him his first horse, his first cowboy hat and his first hunting rifle.

But because Ron is riding in New York, he has never seen Rudy win a race, something Rudy has been doing regularly since the 1969 racing season opened in Ontario.

On May 4, the day the Montreal Canadiens sweep the St. Louis Blues in four straight games to win the Stanley Cup, it happens.

Ron has flown in from New York to contest the Star Shoot Stakes at Fort Erie. It is the first time Rudy, Ron and Noel will ride on the same card together.

Twenty years ago at Edmonton Alberta's Northlands Park, three brothers, Roy, Eddie and Harry Johnson, had done it, even punctuating the historic day with a one-two-three finish in the same race. But it isn't history that Rudy is thinking about; it is simply winning with Ron there to see it.

Just as he had rolled the film in his mind of how he was going to act and smile when he won his first race, Rudy has the scene choreographed when he would win with Ron there to watch it.

The opportunity comes quickly. In the first race, Noel is paired with a front-running longshot named Blondinette; Rudy is on one of the favorites, Matzah Belle.

As expected, Noel whisks Blondinette to the lead while Rudy wraps up with an armload of horse waiting to be unleashed. For five furlongs, their positions remain unchanged. Then, with Noel already in an all-out drive, trying to coax a few more drops of fuel from the gas tank, Rudy starts pumping his arms.

Noel's lead is two lengths. Then one. Rudy smiles knowingly.

"Perfect," Rudy thinks, his mind already 10 steps ahead of him. "I got this one. And Ron is watching my every move."

But Matzah Belle isn't a bottom claimer for nothing. She is spent as well, flying a wet sail.

Tired horses start to wobble. Instead of going straight, they also tend to lug in or lug out, one side of their body unable to keep up with the other.

On marmalade legs, Matzah Belle keeps drifting to the left. Rudy shoves the reins, desperately asking for more. In the final jump, Matzah Belle has just enough left to hold on. Rudy wins.

In the jockeys' room, just as he has dreamed, Ron stands waiting, his arms crossed purposefully. Rudy sticks out his right hand, expecting Ron to embrace it. Instead, Ron takes a firm hold of Rudy's left arm.

"Hey, what are you doing? You're going to break my arm," winces Rudy.

"I thought maybe it was already broken," retorts Ron with a seething glare. "That horse was bearing out all the way down the stretch. You should have switched sticks. Gone to your right hand to keep the horse running straight."

"But. But. I won," says Rudy, his perfect scene now edited all wrong.

"This time," shoots back Ron. "But you won't win in New York riding that way."

One race later, Rudy has another chance with No Success. With a two-length lead at the top of the stretch, Rudy switches the whip back and forth from his right hand to his left eight times and wins by three and a quarter lengths.

"That any better?" winks Rudy when he meets Ron again.

"A little," is all Ron allows himself to say.

By the end of June, Rudy has moved into a tie for the lead in the jockey standings at Fort Erie with another apprentice, Lloyd Duffy.

Two weeks later, it is time for Rudy to make his move. Ron has wanted Rudy to come to New York for weeks. New York has all the best horses, the best jockeys and the best purses. In six years of riding in New York, Ron's mounts have always earned at least $1 million a season. But Rudy has resisted. He wants to make sure he is ready.

"Ten percent of what a horse earns goes to the jock," Ron keeps telling him. "You figure it out. Canada is nice, but you gotta go for the green."

Often, Ron has used a hockey analogy to get across his point, something he knows Rudy will understand: "New York is the NHL. You're in the minors. Until you've tried the NHL you'll never be satisfied."

Then with another wink, he adds, "If, that is, you're any kind of a hockey player."

Rudy doesn't need to hear any more.

Remillard leases Rudy's contract — in exchange for a monthly fee — to Al Scotti, a top New York trainer and former jockey. Rudy had galloped for the soft-spoken Scotti two years earlier at Hialeah, Florida, where Scotti won with an unheard of 50 percent of his starters.

Rudy briefly moves in with Ron on Hook Road in New York's Valley Stream neighborhood. It is a five-minute drive to Belmont, 10 minutes to Aqueduct.

Joe Shea, reluctantly at first but convinced by Ron, agrees to take Rudy's book too.

Everything is set.

July 15, 1969 — the day before Neil Armstrong, Edwin Aldrin and Michael Collins blast into space aboard *Apollo 11* — dawns with syrupy sunshine. It is one of those magical days when everything, even the first sip of coffee, slides down perfectly and the boss greets you with a big smile and a raise.

The boys hum along the freeway toward Aqueduct, where Rudy will make his New York debut with Scotti's Flying Gaucho. Ron is behind the wheel of another new Eldorado Cadillac, this one forest green with whitewall tires and a tan interior. Rudy is beside him looking out the window, seeing everything and nothing whiz past all at once.

One day you're in the New Brunswick woods, swatting flies. The next minute you're on the way to your first race in New York.

Ron has never forgotten where he came from and knows only too well that it took unfathomable happenstance and hard work to introduce him to his horse racing abilities. He knows one slight change in the course of events and he might not be here with his brother, driving this Cadillac with a thick, dark Cuban cigar pressed between his teeth.

Not Rudy. For him this was meant to be, and he laps it in with huge gulps, never questioning what could or could not have been.

For the 20th time, Ron tells Rudy the clubhouse turn at Aqueduct is long and gradual. Like no turn he has ever seen.

"Remember that it doesn't bend like it does at Greenwood. Don't drop in too quick or you'll pile up the field. And remember it's a long stretch. Don't get too anxious. Don't move too soon. Save some horse or you'll never make it to the wire."

"Right, brother," Rudy always nods. "I got it. Don't worry. Gradual first turn; save some horse. Long stretch."

In horse racing, pre-race instructions often prove useless. Ron knows that as well as anyone. He loves to tell the story about one trainer who had plotted every inch of the race for him: sit sixth for the first quarter mile, move up gradually down the backstretch to get within four lengths of the lead, take a breather and then accelerate a little around the final turn. The trainer then told him who would be in front and how that horse would wilt if he moved up to him and looked him in the eye. Then the trainer said he would win going away. But when the starting gate opened, Ron's horse broke last, laid last and finished last.

The trainer was livid. Why didn't you follow my instructions, the trainer yelled? I told you what to do. I told you specifically what to do.

Ron responded: "I would have done just that, sir. But I would have had to call a cab."

Now here he is giving instructions to Rudy.

Horse racing may be a science to many, but it often plays out like a football game. The ball gets snapped, it's supposed to be a screen pass, but the quarterback fumbles the ball and now there are three linebackers the size of mountains in his face.

Flying Gaucho figures to get away close to the early pace. But 10 jumps out of the gate, the ball is fumbled when the horse to Rudy's right slams into him sideways and then the horse to his left bangs him the other way.

Pinched back, Flying Gaucho gets away much farther back than expected.

Rudy, however, never flinches. One thing you can't teach is cool. Rudy simply takes hold of the reins, eases back on the throttle and keeps Flying Gaucho from missing a beat.

Top jockeys feel their way through a race. They react to different situations. If a jockey stops to think, "There's a hole. Maybe I should go through it," it's already too late. The hole would be already closed. Instead, you must anticipate. Move to the hole before it even opens.

Going down the backstretch, Rudy slips his way through one hole of light after another, steering his way through the chestnut, bay and black horse hairs that thunder along with him until Flying Gaucho hits the finish line three lengths in front. Flying Gaucho pays $23.60 to win.

"I don't think I'll tell you anything else," says Ron, whose mount in the race finishes far back.

"Don't worry brother. I've got it," smiles Rudy.

The lumber mill couldn't be farther away.

Neither could Noel. Back in Toronto he is fined $50 for swearing at the starter, Angus McArthur. For the second straight year he wins just 63 races.

Rudy couldn't feel better. Quickly he becomes a big player in a big city. Just as he always knew would happen.

Big lights. Big theater. Nobody likes it better than Rudy, whose big dreams don't include quiet or boredom.

Fast cars. Fast horses. Fast women. That is obdurate Rudy's world — brash and with no place for shadows. He doesn't have a timid or servile bone in his body. He always wants to lead the parade. Being a tuba player is not in his repertoire.

Once, he got to shake hands with former heavyweight boxing champion Joe Louis, the "Brown Bomber."

Another time, at Ron's house, Rudy is awakened by a big man jumping on his bed.

"Who are you? What's going on?" he asks, still half asleep. "Say something."

"Who is he?" laughs Ron. "I thought you knew all the hockey players. Especially a former Montreal Canadiens star."

That's all it takes.

"Boom Boom!" shouts Rudy. "Boom Boom Bernie Geoffrion. Jesus Christ. Is it really you? How the hell are you?" he says, grabbing Geoffrion's hand, pumping it as if he were trying to draw oil.

"Never mind how I am," replies the former Canadiens star who recently had to resign as coach of the New York Rangers due to health problems. "How the hell are you? I'm betting on you this afternoon."

On August 19, 1969, Hurricane Camille, at the time the most intense tropical cyclone to strike the United States, smacks hard into Virginia, where the Meadow stable is based in Doswell. Twenty-seven inches of rain violently pours down, creating floods throughout the state.

Howard Gentry, the Meadow's farm manager, summons all the grooms to round up the horses and take them to higher ground. It is a sage and life saving decision. The next morning, the dike breaks, and within minutes, the torrential downpour fills the entire 354 acres of the Cove, the Meadow's favorite pasture for mares and new foals.

Among the horses saved are Iberia and her foal, Riva Ridge. Hurricane Camille takes 124 lives and results in damages of $1.42 billion.

In October, in the office of Alfred Vanderbilt, chairman of the New York Racing Association, Arthur "Bull" Hancock flips a coin. The coin-toss participants are Ogden Phipps and Helen "Penny" Chenery Tweedy. The daughter of the ailing Christopher, Tweedy has taken over operations of the Meadow since her mother's recent passing.

Under an agreement between the Phipps family's vaunted Wheatley Farm and the Chenery family's Meadow stable that dated back to 1965, the winner of the toss gets the first pick of two foals from the Meadow that are sired by Bold Ruler, the leading sire in North America since 1963.

"Tails," calls Phipps as the coin seems to float in mid-air before landing on the floor.

"Tails it is," says Hancock, serving as witness.

Phipps picks a filly out of a productive mare named Hasty Matelda. Penny is left with a yet-unborn foal out of the mare Somethingroyal.

Chapter 18

It is raining in sheets slamming sideways when Ron and Rudy leave New York to fly into Toronto for the October 26, 1969, Canadian International. With a purse of $75,000, it is the second-richest race of the year in Canada. Only the Queen's Plate has a bigger purse.

Rudy, still an apprentice, will be riding Vent du Nord, who is 4-1 on the morning line. Ron is on a 20-1 longshot named Te Vega, whose connections have promised will run better than his odds.

Avelino Gomez has the favorite: Tradesman.

"How many more Turcottes still to come?" asks Gomez in his strained, thick accent, looking at Ron, Rudy and Noel together in the jockeys' room.

"You better get used to it. There are still three more to come. But you got a few more years before they come," Ron says of Roger, 13, Gaetan, 12, and Yves, 9.

"And then that's it?" says Gomez.

"Yeah. There are three other brothers, but they are all too big,"

"Good," exhales Gomez. "I am glad some Turcottes get too big."

The race breaks with a couple of flyers, Canal and Battling ding-donging on the front end for the first seven furlongs of the mile and five-eighths turf race before quickly giving up the chase down the backstretch. Canal's and Battling's departures leave Rudy in front and alongside the inner hedge. Then Ron ranges up, leaving the Turcottes running one-two and lapped on one another.

That is as close as Te Vega will get. Gomez sweeps up in a flash with his big, gangly son of Swaps. But, in making his move, Tradesman briefly veers sideways directly into Te Vega's path, causing Ron to take up sharply and forcing several others in behind to do the same.

Not knowing what was going on behind, Gomez and Rudy keep going; Gomez now the one pasted to Rudy's outside flank meeting Vent du Nord's progress stride for stride. The torrid battle continues all the way down the stretch. For an instant, Tradesman starts to draw clear, but Rudy keeps willing Vent du Nord for more. At the wire, they are still nostrils apart.

"A guess and a gasp," writes Milt Dunnell in the *Toronto Daily Star*.

"Who won?" asks Rudy as he and Gomez pull up together.

"Me," came the cocksure answer from Gomez.

"You sure?"

"Positive," crows Gomez.

"Damn," says Rudy.

Gomez is right. After several minutes, the numbers on the tote board show Tradesman the winner. When the photo results are announced, Gomez blows kisses to the crowd as he rides his way into the infield winner's circle.

"Damn," says Rudy again.

But then Rudy sees something else. Tradesman's number is flashing along with the inquiry light. Ron has claimed foul for interference.

Blink. Blink. Blink. The numbers continue to flash hypnotically.

Gomez never gets disqualified, Rudy thinks to himself.

Blink. Blink. Blink.

A full 10 minutes pass before the announcement: "For interference around the final turn ... "

That's all Rudy needs to hear. He has won his first stakes race. And it is a big one. His share of the $75,000 total purse is $4,500.

Moments later, Gomez bursts into the jockeys' room. Never saying a word, he marches to his stall, strips and, without even taking a shower, puts on his street clothes.

"Hey, Gomie," shouts Ron.

Gomez doesn't turn.

"Hey, Gomie," Ron shouts again.

Still no reaction from "El Perfecto."

"Aw, don't feel so bad. You didn't get beat by just any rider," says Ron. "You got beat by a New York rider."

"Screw you," yells Gomez. "It took two of you to beat me."

Then, shooting a glare at Rudy, Gomez says, "You only win because of your brother. I feel no bump. You only win because your brother claimed foul."

The stewards had posted the inquiry light themselves, long before Ron made his foul claim. But Gomez doesn't care. He is hot.

Looking at Ron, Rudy knows. He has made his brother proud.

Back in New York, Rudy continues his torrid pace. Two days after the Canadian International, he wins four races. Then on December 2, at Aqueduct, he wins six races, tying the modern New York record first set by Alfred Robertson in 1941 and then equaled by Shoemaker in 1959 and Mike Venezia in 1964.

A week later Rudy rides four more winners on a single card. He is Aqueduct's leading rider with 42 wins. Big brother Ron is second with 32 wins.

"Little brother, you've accomplished something I've never done," says Ron.

"I never thought an athlete could make the kind of money I'm making," answers Rudy.

"I've dreamt of being a rider since I was 14," Rudy is quoted in a story that refers to him as "Baby Faced Rudy" and also includes a big picture of him being hugged by a pretty blonde owner.

"When Ron sent a trio of horses to us in New Brunswick, he gave me the best one, a horse named Ringo. From that day on, becoming a jockey was all I thought about."

Asked for comment Ron is succinct. "Rudy is strong," Ron says. "But he still has a lot to learn."

Hall of Fame jockey Angelo Cordero Jr., who won more than 6,000 races, has something else to say in the story: "Rudy is going to be the best Turcotte. Better than Ron. He looks good on a horse."

Rudy has always credited Ron for his success. "Without Ron, I wouldn't have got the riding breaks so soon," he tells everyone. "Ron taught me everything."

But in one interview, in the *Toronto Daily Star* with Stan Fischler, Rudy adds more: "There have also been big headaches having a big brother like him. There is the name I have to live up to. That can be a disadvantage. The same way it is for Dennis Hull living up to older brother Bobby. In Chicago, everybody expects Dennis to be a superstar too. Right away people expected me to be really good just because my brothers have done so well. No bug boy can ride like a guy who has been going for eight or nine years."

Ron chafes at the story.

"A jockey is only as good as the horse he is on," Ron says to Gae as he reads the article. "I try but my advice doesn't penetrate Rudy's head. He had a mind of his own. Maybe it's just a little bit of a generational gap between us."

Just as Remillard watched race replays with Ron and Noel, Ron has done the same with Rudy, pointing out things he felt Rudy could do better.

The movie sessions work here too.

Rudy doesn't just lead all apprentice riders in New York in 1969, he leads all riders at Aqueduct, with Ron coming in second. Rudy has 52 wins; Ron, 42. Rudy is feted at a big gala at the Waldorf Astoria that honors other New York athletes.

The next day both Rudy and Ron leave for Tropical Park Race Track in Miami. Shea goes with them.

On December 23, in the *Miami News*, Art Grace writes another glowing article on the Turcotte brothers.

Grace quotes veteran rider Hedley Woodhouse: "(Rudy) is awful strong, just like Ron and the other brother, Noel. I remember one race (Rudy) won in particular. Rudy was riding Show Off, a lugging-in filly, and just as she goes to the lead she starts bearing in, Rudy switched the stick to his left hand so fast you could hardly see it. He got her off the inside horse quick enough, so the foul claim wasn't allowed. All them Turcottes are strong as bulls from hauling logs in Canada when they were kids."

As muscular and powerful as he is, with short legs and a long body, Rudy also has an innate sense that can't be taught. He can tell exactly how fast a horse is running.

One morning Rudy works a horse for Bob Bateman of Beasley Stable. Bateman tells Rudy he wants him to go the first quarter in 24 seconds, three-eighths in 37, the half in 48, three quarters in 1:14 and a mile in 1:39.

Rudy hits every pole exactly as asked.

"Never seen anything like it," marvels Bateman.

Chapter 19

Horse racing is the most dangerous sport in the world. It is not whether a jockey will get hurt. It's when and how badly. The roulette wheel never stops spinning.

At many racetracks, an ambulance follows 100 yards behind each field of rampaging, 1,000-pound horses that run on spindly ankles the size of a small boy's wrist. Each piston blow to the ground exerts 5,000 pounds per square inch of pressure on a horse's foot.

Sometimes, something has to give.

Sometimes it is the popping of the suspensory ligament that connects the knees to the ankles. Sometimes it is the shattering of the sesamoid bones at the bottom of the ankle. Sometimes the entire cannon bone, between the fetlock and the knee, can blow apart.

Death tugs on every saddle pad, from the time the gates spring open until the horses are back in their barns.

Race car drivers have roll bars, metal cages and a seat belt to protect them. Jockeys ride virtually naked. It won't be until 20 years later that jockeys even ride with flak jackets.

According to an American Medical Association study, the mortality rate among jockeys is 12.8 per thousand. That compares with 12.3 per 1,000 skydivers, 5.1 for mountain climbers and 1.1 for scuba divers. On top of these magnificently powerful yet fragile creatures ride the jockeys with nothing more than a flimsy helmet to protect them. When a horse goes down, so does the jockey.

Jockeys do not have a pension, and personal disability insurance is, in many cases, prohibitively expensive.

"The only reason more riders don't get hurt seriously is because, pound for pound, they are the fittest athletes in the world," said former Alberta rider Bruce Phelan, who only had three percent body fat before he retired.

On Christmas Eve 1969, another crystal blue afternoon that is begging to darken as the sun begins to slip past the palm trees and into the Atlantic Ocean, Rudy breaks from the starting gate pushing on his horse's neck at Tropical Park, Florida, just as he has done 790 other times in this, his first full year of riding.

It is a race for $12,000, claiming three-year-olds all getting their last chance before celebrating their birthdays on January 1. Two more races and Rudy's day would be over.

Less than three-sixteenths of a mile later, the starting gate bell still echoing in Rudy's ear and the horses just leaving the chute and crossing onto the main track, Rudy's mount, the badly named First Kill, bumps the horse beside him, Verjo. Their heels click like castanets. Both horses stumble, and Rudy is sent flying over his horse's neck. As he has been taught, after he lands heavily on his shoulder, Rudy rolls into a tight ball.

He is unconscious and doesn't awaken until he is halfway to Miami's Baptist Hospital.

"Stay still," the ambulance attendant tells him. "You've just been in an accident."

"A what?" says Rudy. "When?"

"At Tropical Park. You fell off your horse. Try not to move. We're almost there."

"There? Where the hell is there," Rudy says groggily.

Racing accidents almost always happen this way. No time to react. One second you are sitting on half a ton of sweating horseflesh, the next second you are on the ground. Forty miles an hour to zero. Just like that.

Fifteen hundred miles away, listening to the radio, Rose drops to her knees after what she thinks she hears; she has mistaken First Kill with her son's condition.

"Call Mom," says Ron when he gets ahold of Rudy's hospital room after first making sure Rudy is okay. "Mom heard you were dead."

"Nah," replies Rudy, who has a copy of the Christmas Day *New York Times* sports section open on the bedside tray table beside him. In bold letters across the top of the page, the headline screams "Rudy Turcotte Injured Severely When Thrown in Race at Tropical Park; Jockey's Hip Believed Broken."

"I broke my collarbone and one rib. That's all," Rudy says. Then, he realizes what his brother just said. "Dead? Why would Mom think that?"

"Because the horse's name is First Kill," answers Ron. "She just got confused."

Although sidelined two months, Rudy is very lucky it isn't worse. While he recuperates the world continues unabated.

In South Vietnam, 11 children and five women are killed by a group of United States Marines. Four members of the 1st Battalion of the 7th USMC are later court-martialed on charges of murder; two others are convicted in separate trials. The war rages on.

A gallon of gas is 36 cents. Lava lamps are the rage.

It is early February 1970.

At 10 minutes past midnight on March 30, 1970, a humongous colt is born in Northern Virginia. He has three white feet and a white blaze that starts with a diamond on his forehead and trickles down like a teardrop.

"There's a whopper," says Meadow stud farm manager Howard Gentry of the considerable and handsome son of Bold Ruler out of Somethingroyal.

It is Somethingroyal's 14th foal. She has already produced the likes of Sir Gaylord, who won six stakes races and was the favorite for the 1962 Kentucky Derby until injury forced his retirement, as well as stakes winners First Family and Syrian Sea.

In 20 minutes, the wobbly colt staggers to his feet on the dirt floor; 25 minutes after that the foal begins to nurse.

"Big, strong-made foal with plenty of bone, who, with his breeding, could possibly be one of the best horses the Meadow has produced," notes Gentry.

A few days later, Tweedy gets to see the colt. Breathlessly she writes one word into her notebook: "Wow!"

Six names for the colt are submitted to the Jockey Club: Scepter, Royal Line, Something Special, Games of Chance and Do Volente. The sixth and final name — suggested by Christopher Chenery's corporate and personal secretary, Elizabeth Ham, is accepted: Secretariat.

Rudy recovers from his injuries and is back riding in early March. Winning 129 races as an apprentice, Rudy loses his bug on June 2. Like Noel, he also starts losing mounts.

Moreover, when he returns, he is, like his brother Ron, an all-too-regular visitor to the New York steward's offices.

After coming off a 10-day suspension on June 26, Rudy gets another 10 days for trying to go through a hole that wasn't there at Aqueduct on July 14.

The day before the suspension starts, Rudy rides Fred Hooper's Hilo Hop to a $79.20 upset victory. The horse hadn't been close in three starts until Rudy got aboard.

And when his latest sentence ends on July 27, Rudy comes through immediately one more time riding Urgent Message to victory in the Aqueduct opener. Urgent Message pays $31 to win. Ron rides the winner of the second race, Bessie Rice, to complete a $127.40 Turcotte Daily Double.

There certainly are no problems for Ron, who continues to win big races in bunches. He wins the Withers on Hagley; the Manitoba Derby and the Alabama on Fanfreluche; the Jockey Club Gold Cup and the Beldame on two-time Eclipse award winner Shuvee; and the Hialeah Turf Cup and Bougainvillea on Vent du Nord, the latter a track record — equaling performance.

The Manitoba Centennial Derby is especially memorable. On a warm, cloudless July 15 afternoon in Winnipeg, Ron is met in the winner's circle by Queen Elizabeth II.

"That's a nice filly you have," says the Queen, who races a big stable in England, to Ron and Fanfreluche's trainer, Yonnie Starr. "Didn't she just finish second in last month's Queen's Plate?"

"I know all about this filly's sire, Northern Dancer," The Queen continues after watching Fanfreluche come storming through a hole along the rail from a specially constructed royal viewing stand. Watching with Her Majesty are Prince Phillip, Prince Charles and Princess Anne, who are on a 10-day tour of Manitoba and the Northwest Territories celebrating both regions' 100th anniversary.

Still bursting with pride, Ron quickly phones his mother and father to tell them about his brush with royalty. "She gave me a silver plate for winning the race!"

Ron also wins Chicago's Hawthorne Gold Cup on Gladwin, a horse he didn't even want to ride.

"This horse can't do anything," Ron had said to Shea over the phone before the race. "He has absolutely no chance. His best races are behind him."

"I gave them a commitment," Shea persisted.

When Shea doesn't hear from Ron until 10 p.m., he assumes his jockey was right and the horse lost.

"I told you I didn't want to go to Chicago," are Ron's first words.

"Okay. It's over. Forget it," says Shea.

There is a short pause. Then Ron says, "He won by eight. Broke the track record. At even money."

"Ronnie, you do the riding. I'll do the picking," says Shea with a laugh.

While Ron laughs to the bank, there are financial difficulties for the Meadow. The horses aren't winning and the health of its founder, Christopher Chenery, Tweedy's father, is failing. He is stricken with both Alzheimer's and Parkinson's disease.

Tweedy's sister, Miggie, who operates a secretarial and book editing service in Arizona, and her brother, Hollis, chief economist of the World Bank in Washington, want to sell the farm and all their 130 horses — racehorses, broodmares, stallions, foals and yearlings. Everything. Tweedy, however, is resolute. She can't — won't — do it.

"Not while Dad is still alive," she tells them. "It's not your money, yet."

Her dad's dream is to win the Kentucky Derby.

In 1950 his horse Hill Prince, who was the champion two-year-old, winning seven of eight races, ran second in the Derby. In 1959 First Landing ran third and then Sir Gaylord, the favorite leading into the 1962 Derby, broke down just before the race and was retired. After Sir Gaylord was injured, Chenery could have run Cicada in that 1962 Derby but elected to run her in the Kentucky Oaks, which she won easily.

"We're going to win the Derby for you, Dad," Tweedy promises to herself.

Chapter 20

Months chase each other like clouds on a windy afternoon.

Gaining weight and muscles, Riva Ridge is finally growing into his frame at the Meadow. Come September 1970, Gentry writes into his notebook: "A nice colt; has a good way of going."

Born without any markings on his coffee-with-one-cream-colored head and his light bay coat, Riva Ridge has yet to convince Tweedy. "Unprepossessing," she writes.

"He was so quiet you could lead him around on a shoestring," says the Meadow's senior groom and stud manager, Howard Gregory. "He didn't make no hell; he didn't press up against you or try to push you or get away from you or nothing."

While quiescent and timidly serene, Riva Ridge is most certainly intelligent. His deep-brown eyes bear that out. Unlike most horses, Riva Ridge sleeps lying down.

Put into training, Riva Ridge also begins to show something else: speed.

"He's hard to hold back," exercise rider Wayne Mount calls to two other riders, Gene Breeden and Mert Bailes, the son of the Meadow's farm trainer, Bob Bailes, who are jogging three colts together. "He wants to be in front."

"Take a hold," Mert hollers back.

"I'm trying," says Mount. "I'm really trying."

Mert, the Meadow's best exercise rider, decides to try for himself.

"You're right," Mert tells Mount. "You boys are going to read about this horse."

Mount quickly nods in agreement.

Tweedy changes her opinion too. In her stud book, she writes: "Will be a racehorse. Alert; quick to learn. Most promising."

A year younger, Secretariat, whose reddish-gold coat glimmers like copper when sunlight hits it, is weaned from his mother on October 5. The colt doesn't miss his mother's milk. Eating between five and six quarts of grain each day, he quickly puts on weight. Moreover, he is developing a presence and countenance.

While he is still a long way from being a racehorse, head held high and majestic, he looks like something special.

Eight months later, May 1971, the Meadow's trainer, Roger Laurin, ships Riva Ridge to Belmont to begin preparations for the horse's racing career.

Riva Ridge arrives, but a month later, so does bad news.

Laurin tells Tweedy that he is resigning. He has accepted the prestigious role as the trainer for the powerful Wheatley Stable. Outfitting their jockeys in their iconic black silks and a cherry-red cap, Wheatley is the top stable in the U.S. — the Yankees of the 1950s or the Celtics of the 1960s.

Laurin suggests a replacement; his father, Lucien, who is 60 and about to resign as Claiborne Farm's trainer. Reluctantly, thinking that Lucien, who was born just north of Montreal, would work as a stopgap until he retired or she could find someone younger, Tweedy agrees and hires the former jockey.

Lucien will get $25 a day per horse, 10 percent of the stable's purse winnings and 10 percent of any sales he negotiates.

Fate or maybe just plain good luck.

Chuck Baltazar is the Meadow's first-call jockey and is given the ride on Riva Ridge for the two-year-old's first start on June 9. It goes awry early. Bumped at the start, Riva Ridge shrivels and falls far back, finishing fourth, 16 lengths behind the winner.

Riva Ridge and Baltazar atone quickly though. They win the colt's next two starts easily — the first by five and a half lengths, the second by four easy lengths. Both come with Riva Ridge wearing blinkers, which he did not have in his first start.

"Watch when we put the blinkers on him," Laurin tells Baltimore racing writer Clem Florio. "He changes like in a horror movie and turns tiger."

But then Riva Ridge disappoints again and finishes eighth after throwing a shoe and having to be steadied in tight traffic in the Great American Stakes.

Tweedy and Laurin do not give up on Baltazar and name him to ride Riva Ridge in the Flash Stakes on August 2 at Saratoga, New York. Baltazar, however, is set down for a riding infraction, so Laurin needs another rider. After some consternation he decides on Ron, a fellow French Canadian who had ridden for him in the past and with whom he could speak in French. He figures he won't have to worry about anyone stealing their game plans.

Ron, however, has not ridden for Laurin in four years. Laurin had taken him off Tumiga, a horse he had been working with in the mornings in preparation for a 1967 stakes race. Embittered, Ron had steered clear of Laurin. They could both hold a grudge.

But Ron and Shea have seen Riva Ridge's talent and readily accept.

With Ron aboard for the first time, Riva Ridge easily wins the Flash stakes, getting the six furlongs in a snappy 1:09 4/5, just three-fifths of a second off the track record. Baltazar never gets to ride Riva Ridge again. It is like Wally Pipp's famous headache that resulted in Lou Gehrig playing 2,130 consecutive games for the New York Yankees.

In the winner's circle, Ron is giddy.

"Best two-year-old I've ever been on," he enthralls to Laurin, who arches his brow under his tilted fedora.

"Sure. Best ever, eh?" replies Laurin with a smirk. "Better than Northern Dancer? Better than Tom Rolfe? And Riva is better?"

"Dead serious," replies Ron, who goes on to tell Laurin that despite Riva Ridge's fast time, the horse had more to give. "He won but he didn't relax for one inch of the race."

He explains to Laurin that Riva Ridge had fought him almost all the way until he got clear at the top of the stretch.

"Only then did he relax," says Ron.

"Best ever, huh?" repeats Laurin. "You must really want to get in my good books again."

Laurin wants to run Riva Ridge again quickly. Ron has other ideas.

"Let me work with him," Ron says. "He's scared of being close to other horses. He's timid. He needs to be reschooled."

At first Laurin disagrees.

But then Ron flatly says, "You can have a champion or a claimer. A good horse or maybe a Derby winner. It's your call."

Laurin grudgingly gives in.

Ron is already well regarded as an astute judge of horseflesh. Trainers often come to him for advice. With Riva Ridge, Ron is given free rein.

The first thing Ron does is ask the stewards if he can study the films of Riva Ridge's previous races. Even on the stewards' grainy black-and-white tapes, Ron can almost feel Riva Ridge quiver and back off when another horse comes alongside.

"If I could teach him to relax and rid him of his fear of having other horses next to him, he would be a different horse," he tells Laurin after watching Riva Ridge both win handily and lose badly.

Next, Ron gets on Riva Ridge and gallops him in the mornings. The result is the same.

"He jumped all over the track every time a horse went by," he tells Laurin. "I am sure that is his problem; he's scared."

Doing the same thing with timorous Riva Ridge that he had done with horses in the lumber camp, Ron gets Riva Ridge to trust him. Playing therapist to the neurotic racehorse will take a big dose of patience and a bigger dose of kindness.

For four straight weeks Ron rides Riva Ridge while exercise riders Charlie Davis and Paul Feliciano ride two other horses, one on Riva Ridge's right side, the other on his left. At first the other two horses give Riva Ridge a wide berth so that he doesn't tense up and frighten. Then, gradually, they inch in closer. And closer.

When Riva Ridge hardens up, ears twitching nervously and body trembling, Ron calls out, "More space, boys; move away a bit."

Eventually, Riva Ridge loses his fear. Even when the other two horses brush up alongside — their stirrups clinking — the colt in the middle remains composed and doesn't back out of close quarters.

Then Ron gets Riva Ridge to come from behind and move through the tight space between the other pair. Next, he gets Riva Ridge to move past the other horses to their inside. Then to the outside.

Riva Ridge has learned to be a racehorse. A very promising racehorse. Perhaps a beckoning champion.

At the same time Ron finds Riva Ridge, back in Ontario Noel finds his "big" horse: Belle Geste, a gorgeous filly that trainer Carl "Chappy" Chapman calls "Lana Turner," after the vivacious pin-up model and film actress. Belle Geste, an apple-loving filly that William Latimer had given to his wife Bea as a Christmas present, is the first truly magnificent horse that Noel has found and rides her to a couple of nice allowance races. But for the August 14, 1971, Nassau Stakes at Fort Erie, Noel opts to ride Jollysum Dancer.

It is a bad decision. Belle Geste, with Noel's friend, John Bell, in the irons, goes wire to wire, easily holding off Conn Smythe's Not Too Shy for a win that was just two-fifths of a second off the track record; Jollysum Dancer finishes last.

"Belle Geste is a tigress on the grass and that's where she'll stay," says Chapman, who was so nervous before the race that he went to noon mass and couldn't understand why the church was empty. It was a Saturday.

After taking off Belle Geste for one race, Noel frets, hoping desperately that Chapman will let him back on.

Picking up the entries for the following week's International in Fort Erie, Noel is relieved; Chapman stays true and gives him the ride.

Bouncing along, Belle Geste wins the International by a widening five and a half lengths. It is her fourth straight win — all on turf.

Back in the barn there is champagne on ice.

"Just a work for her," Noel tells Chapman. "I didn't touch her; didn't ask her until the quarter pole. Even then I just clucked at her and showed her the stick," continues Noel, who is being called the "King of the Turf."

"This will set her up great for the Prince of Wales."

You can hold all the aces in horse racing. But sometimes you never get to play them. Noel is sitting perfectly in the Prince of Wales Stakes on September 4 at Fort Erie when Queen's Plate winner Kennedy Road and jockey sensation Sandy Hawley suddenly come over on him, forcing Noel and Belle Geste into the inside hedge, sending its leaves cascading like a deep green fountain.

Belle Geste almost comes to a complete standstill yet somehow Noel gets her running again. They pass Kennedy Road, but her last-gasp effort comes a head short of catching 49-1 longshot New Pro Escar, who sets a course record 2:15 1/5 for the mile and three sixteenths.

"I win easily if it wasn't for the interference," Noel chastises Hawley, who leads the jockey standings not just in Canada but in all of North America, knocking off four and five wins a day. Hawley is suspended for 10 days.

After the eventful Prince of Wales, Chapman begins preparing Belle Geste for the third leg of the Canadian Triple Crown, the Breeders' on October 3 at Woodbine. The race is a grueling mile and a half.

Belle Geste is the only filly in the field of 10.

Never threatened, never tested, Noel has Belle Geste on top by five lengths after half a mile. She extends that lead at will. With a quarter of a mile left to run she is now in front by eight lengths. She coasts home by four and a quarter lengths, shattering the course record by a full second when she hits the wire in 2:28.

After the race, Noel is interviewed on national television by a young CBC host. The announcer's name is Alex Trebek.

"This broad, she digs the joint," says the effervescent Chapman.

Riva Ridge's newly discovered fearlessness has an immediate impact. Against a similar field that trounced him in the Great American two months ago, Riva Ridge, in the Meadow's famous blue and white checkered silks, easily wins the futurity on September 18 at Belmont. The victory comes in the slop and gives Laurin a false confidence that his pupil can handle any kind of conditions.

All the work Ron put into reschooling Riva Ridge continues to pay off. On October 9, they win the Champagne Stakes at Belmont by seven lengths. Then it's an 11-length win three weeks later in the Pimlico-Laurel Futurity at Laurel, Maryland, where Rudy is now riding.

"Hey, brother. That's quite the horse you have," Rudy tells Ron. "Triple Crown favorite for next year."

Ron nods heartily.

"I told Lucien after the first time I rode him that he was the best colt I'd ever ridden. Now, I'm sure. It took a lot of work but boy was it worth it. And you are obviously doing well since you left New York."

"Well" doesn't begin to describe how Rudy has been faring.

Before leaving New York, Rudy told reporters, "I kind of got spoiled. I'd been winning a couple of races a day. When I lost my bug, I kept winning but not as much. I've decided to go where I could ride eight or nine every day and win one or two. I'd just as soon try to be a big fish in a small pond."

With that Rudy, a vagabond, went to tracks in Philadelphia, Delaware, New Jersey and Maryland with his agent, Carl Blanc. Opportunities came knocking and Rudy answered them with wins. Everywhere. He was the leading rider at Delaware Park, the second-leading rider at Liberty Bell, Philadelphia, and second as well at Bowie, Maryland.

Now at Laurel, he is tearing up the jockey standings. He has twice as many wins as his closest pursuers. Voted Laurel's fan favorite, Rudy wins a career-high 205 races in 1971 — 50 more than Ron this year.

Five days after Ron and Riva Ridge win the Pimlico-Laurel Futurity by 11 lengths, Rudy wins three races. The next day he rides three more into the winner's circle.

Rudy thinks his success will never end.

After winning the Pimlico-Laurel Futurity, there is just one race left for Riva Ridge in 1971: the Garden State Park Stakes, which, with its purse of $293,000, is the richest race in the sport, offering $100,000 more than the Kentucky Derby.

"I don't expect anybody to beat him," Laurin says on the eve of the November 13 mile and a sixteenth race.

He's right. But the start of the race gives him pause as Riva Ridge gets pinched back away from the gate and gets away last.

While Laurin is anxious, Ron isn't worried one bit. Moving up effortlessly, Riva Ridge shakes loose under Ron's urging at the top of the stretch and wins by two and a half lengths.

"It turned out it was just as well," Ron says of the poor start. "I was a little concerned about getting him to relax."

Still, Ron, who has an unlit Villiger Kiel cigar clenched between his teeth, isn't impressed: "This was the first time I really asked him to run. I tapped him twice, on the shoulder, just as he went to the lead. He started to loaf once he got to the lead. He doesn't do any more than he has to. He wins as he wants. He's a free runner and always performs so good that I don't know if this was his strongest race or not. He doesn't really do more than he has to. He's a helluva horse. As good as any I've ridden."

Asked for his plans for Riva Ridge, Laurin says, "He's going on a long vacation and I'm not going to be far behind him. The colt is going to Hialeah, and I'm going to my farm in South Carolina for a few days and then on to Miami."

Ron is taking a break too. "I always go deer hunting in Canada the third week of November," he says.

With Riva Ridge winning just over half-a-million dollars and receiving the Eclipse Award as 1971's Champion Two-Year-Old, talk about selling the Meadow is muted, for the moment at least.

Chapter 21

The 1972 season dawns with the electric thrill of possibilities for the Meadow. They are days of swelling hope and anticipation.

Secretariat turns two and is about to embark on a racing career still dotted with question marks. Riva Ridge, with his floppy ears and suspect legs, continues to outrun his looks and begins preparations for his three-year-old classic races. Both are sent to Laurin in Florida, where his number one groom, Eddie Sweat, is entrusted to look after them. Now 33, Sweat has been with Laurin since 1957, when he was an 18-year-old and dreamed of being a boxer.

Sweat knows what he has in champion Riva Ridge but is initially unimpressed by Secretariat.

"Too big and fat," says Sweat, a brush in one hand and a rag in the other.

Laurin isn't sure what he has in Secretariat either. "So clumsy too," he concurs. "He's big alright. Very heavy. But I really think there is something there."

Just then Ron arrives and gets his first look at Secretariat, who — as he often does — sticks out his tongue and whinnies.

"Hey, Lucien," says Ron. "Who's the pretty boy here?"

"Take a good look," says Laurin. "I want you to work with this big fella. Like you did with Riva."

Ron flashes a smile.

Over the next few weeks in February, Ron quickly discovers this bulky colt and Riva Ridge are the antithesis of one another. While Riva Ridge was nervous and afraid of other horses as a two-year-old, nothing seems to bother Secretariat, who enjoys contact in the mornings, bumping up hard against the other colts he works with. Ron can even hear Secretariat grunt with delight from the contact.

Secretariat, however, still hasn't flashed the speed the barn has been waiting for. Laurin gallops four two-year-olds together, Secretariat among them, letting them stretch out a little bit. Going a quarter of a mile, the other three horses sprint away from Secretariat, leaving him 15 lengths behind. Twice Bold, Gold Bag and Young Hitter complete the distance in 23 seconds; Secretariat comes home lackadaisically in a tepid 26 seconds.

Spring has come early to Florida. Azaleas in white, orange-red, rose and pink have just started to bloom along with knee-high gerberas, nonstop pentas, fragrant lavender and daisy-shaped coreopsis.

Riva Ridge also continues to blossom, leisurely winning his 1972 debut, the Hibiscus Stakes on March 22 at Hialeah, while conceding seven pounds to the runner-up, New Prospect. It is Riva Ridge's sixth straight win dating back to last summer.

Nine days later, on April 1, north of Miami in the Hialeah morning mud, Secretariat, whom Ron has started calling "Big Red," breezes three furlongs in a much-improved 36 seconds. Hope is rekindled.

Later the same afternoon, Riva Ridge is entered in the Everglades Stakes. The Hialeah track is still sloppy from the spring storm clouds that have rolled in; it looks like chocolate pudding.

Ron worries about the surface. Wide over the shoulders and top heavy, Riva Ridge's body isn't suited to the mud and slop. He had won the Pimlico-Laurel Futurity as a two-year-old on a track listed as sloppy. But that surface was wet-fast, with the six and a half furlongs going in a rapid 1:16 3/5. The Everglades' surface is different; it is deep slop.

Laurin is nonplussed. "Riva Ridge is a superior offtrack horse," he says. "Just like his daddy, First Landing. The track won't be a problem."

Ron, however, is right.

Riva Ridge gets slammed hard at the start of the Everglades, trapped along the rail, and, slipping and sliding in the slop and refusing to stretch out, finishes fourth. It is Ron's first loss aboard the Meadow star.

Ron is chagrined; Laurin, watching from his box seat, is angry. He doesn't confront Ron but instead vents to the *Daily Racing Form*. "It's a damn shame he got beat in the Everglades," Laurin is quoted as saying. "It shouldn't have happened. The colt was trapped in a pocket along the rail and couldn't get room until it was too late. He came back with nicks on his right side; Hold Your Peace rode us close all the way."

Reading the story, Ron cringes but says nothing. He believes — no, he knows — otherwise. It was the track that beat him, he tells anyone who will listen.

The six straight wins Ron has put together with Riva Ridge seemingly forgotten, that night over dinner Laurin and Tweedy talk about making a jockey change.

Rudy, a playboy who has relished the spotlight and the night-life and who has never been short of dates, decides it is time to settle down. He marries Janet Stacey, a dental hygienist, a few days after the cast is removed from the leg he broke in a motorcycle accident.

"Work hard; play hard," remembered Rudy's youngest daughter, Stacey, years later. "That was Rudy's mantra. He was effervescent. He liked to have fun. He liked to jump off the roof of our house into our backyard swimming pool in Baltimore. My mom would just about lose her mind. Here was a jockey with a dangerous career putting himself into more danger.

"He was always singing that country/western song that begins 'Oh, Lord it's hard to be humble when you're perfect in every way.'"

Fully recuperated from his motorcycle crash, six weeks later, Rudy starts riding again and wins 73 times in less than a month at Penn National Race Course in Wyomissing, Pennsylvania.

Riva Ridge has one more race before the Kentucky Derby, the Blue Grass Stakes on April 27 at Keeneland.

"Kentucky is the place to be in the spring of the year with a Derby horse," says Laurin. "The grass and the water and the crisp air are like a tonic and horses do good."

With Ron aboard and over a fast track, Riva Ridge wins by four strong lengths at odds of 30 cents on the dollar. He comes out of the Blue Grass bouncing and hungry. In addition to his regular 4 a.m. feeding, a bale of hay is added to Riva Ridge's breakfast menu.

Chapter 22

It is May 4, 1972, the day before the Kentucky Derby. The Riva Ridge camp has brought a party of 27 people to Louisville, taking up 15 rooms at the Holiday Inn.

Early the morning of the Run for the Roses, Ron arrives at Laurin's barn. He has had a troubled sleep. Although Riva Ridge won the Blue Grass so comfortably, Ron is worried. He keeps thinking of the way Riva Ridge dropped the bit at the quarter pole and started to slow down, looking for company. If the same thing happens in the Derby, Ron worries he could get beat.

He relays those thoughts to Laurin, who doesn't want to listen, especially with the Derby only hours away.

"The three-quarter-cup blinkers he wears only have a small slit. There isn't much speed in the race; he could be on top by himself and if he can't see anything coming ..." Ron trails off, not needing to finish the sentence.

Instead, Ron reaches into his pocket and pulls out a small knife.

"Let me cut the holes in the blinkers larger," he says, opening the blade of his knife.

"What?" says Laurin. "It's way too late to start making changes now. That's the damnedest thing I've ever heard. We're running in a few hours, in the biggest race in North America, and you want to do what?"

"Okay," responds Ron, starting to fold up the knife. "But I sure would hate to lose a Derby that way."

Easily troubled and vexed, Laurin lights a cigarette. "Wait. Are you sure?" he says.

Ron nods with ready assurance.

"Okay. Okay. Do it then. But for the love of God, I hope you're right. You sure it won't hurt our chances?" says Laurin, who is already on edge, having had to answer so many questions about Riva Ridge only running in three prep races. "It has gotten on my nerves hearing that question over and over about whether I think the horse has been raced too lightly. A million times I keep getting asked that. I think three races are enough. I want to show up with a fresh horse, not a dead horse. If this works out badly I'll probably lose my job."

Without another word, Ron unfolds his knife again and begins to saw against the same plastic blinkers Riva Ridge has been wearing since his second start, gradually making the eyeholes larger.

As Ron widens the holes to twice their original size, Laurin can't watch any longer. "You better be right," he says again, turning away.

"I can smell the roses," answers Ron with a wry smile.

Feeling much better, Ron leaves. He goes home and has a quick nap, falling asleep easily.

Sixteen horses line up alongside Riva Ridge as they move into the starting gate. A record crowd of 130,564 people, who bet a world record $7,164,717, roars lustily. Longshots have won a lot of the card's races: the average win payoff for the first eight races averages a healthy $30.05.

Betting Riva Ridge down to 3-2, most bettors are hopeful another longshot doesn't win this one.

The sun crashing through the afternoon sky, Ron intends to sit about third during the early going, but Riva Ridge breaks so well from his ninth post position that Ron lets him go and immediately drumrolls to a length-and-a-half lead.

Although he's in front, Ron keeps Riva Ridge five to six feet off the rail. Having ridden earlier on the card, he has noticed that the rail was a little cuppier than the rest of the track. The rail is not the place to be.

The pace is moderately slow — the first four furlongs going in :47 3/5 and six furlongs in 1:11 4/5.

"Easy, big fella," Ron coos to Riva Ridge, talking to his mount the way he almost always does. "That's it. Nice and easy."

Hold Your Peace is second and after a mile is eight lengths ahead of the rest of the field.

It's a futile chase.

Every time Hold Your Peace's jockey, Carlos Marquez, tries to make a move, Ron simply eases off the brake pedal.

"I make two or three moves at Riva Ridge trying to get to him. He was just loafing on the lead. But every time I'd get close that jock (Turcotte) would let out another notch," says Marquez, who finishes third, with No Le Hace closing up for second. "We tried them, but Riva Ridge is too good a horse — today at least."

With Ron looking through Riva Ridge's funny ears, they win by three and a half lengths to become the first horse since Jet Pilot in 1947 to lead every step of the way in the Derby. A 21 1/2-yard garland of 554 roses that weighs 23 pounds is draped around Riva Ridge's sweaty shoulders.

With very uncharacteristic bluster, Laurin enthuses in the winner's circle that "Riva Ridge is as good as Citation, Man o' War and Whirlaway." He has invoked the names of the most famous thoroughbreds of all time.

"Look at him; he isn't even breathing hard," Sweat says proudly. "He just played with the other horses most of the race then let go in the last eighth of a mile. He'll win the Triple Crown."

Reporters like Joe Dickey of the *Daily Racing Form* believe the same. "Riva Ridge may well be the Triple Crown winner for which we have been waiting so long," he writes.

It has been 24 years since the last Triple Crown champion — Citation in 1948.

Seven hundred and fifty miles away, Riva Ridge's owner, Christopher Chenery, is watching on TV in the New Rochelle Hospital, where he has been since 1968. His private nurse yelps, "Mr. Chenery. Mr. Chenery. Your horse just won the Kentucky Derby."

A warm tear rolls down Chenery's cheek.

Two weeks later, it's the night before the Preakness, the second jewel of thoroughbred racing's Triple Crown. The dark skies open at Pimlico in Baltimore, Maryland.

The splatting of fat raindrops sours Ron. He knows better than anyone how Riva Ridge, a long-striding horse, can't handle wet ground. He has the best horse in the race, but it means nothing if Riva Ridge can't stand up on the slick, sloppy surface. It was the slop in the Everglades that beat his horse; he fears this slop will stymie him again.

He hopes Laurin will scratch Riva Ridge and run stablemate Upper Case, who won the Wood Memorial Stakes in the mud.

But Tweedy and Laurin say they will never forgive themselves if Upper Case wins and Riva Ridge finishes second. So they scratch Upper Case and run Riva Ridge.

It is folly. Breaking awkwardly, Riva Ridge flounders as he slips and slides and finishes fourth, six lengths behind the wire-to-wire winner Bee Bee Bee, a 19-1 outsider, who pays $39.40 to win — the biggest Preakness upset since Display paid $40.70 in 1926. The first-place cheque of $135,300 is more than Bee Bee Bee has won in his sketchy career.

"I knew it," Ron mumbles as he pulls Riva Ridge up in the backstretch, which is pockmarked with puddles from the spitting sky. "He would have romped on a fast track."

What Ron doesn't expect is more of the rage of Laurin.

Again, Laurin doesn't say anything to Ron. But the next morning, Ron unfolds a newspaper and reads Laurin's scathing words: "Turcotte gave him a bad ride. I think Riva Ridge sulked from being restrained too much. Ron didn't ride his race. He was too concerned with another horse, Key To The Mint ... He fought the jockey so hard that he finally spit out the bit and wouldn't respond."

As is his style, Ron doesn't argue. But when he hears rumors that Laurin is going to find another jockey for the Belmont, he asks Laurin point blank: "If you're thinking of taking me off Riva, let me know now."

Laurin merely shakes his head. They are off, together, to New York for the mile and a half Belmont on June 10.

Unlike Pimlico, the New York sky is free of clouds. Called "Big Sandy," the track at Belmont is lightning fast.

In the paddock Laurin tells his jockey, "If no horse beats you to the first turn, go to the front if you want. But whatever you do don't fight this colt if he wants to run. Get position and let him run his own race."

Riva Ridge almost doesn't get that chance. In the saddling enclosure, an overly exuberant fan reaches out over the fence and slaps Riva Ridge on his rear end. Startled, Riva Ridge kicks out, leaving a cut and a swelling lump under the back hock of his left hind leg.

Laurin recoils as he watches Riva Ridge limp. For an instant, Laurin fears that Riva Ridge has broken his leg. He considers pulling the horse out of the race.

But as quickly as the fan had reached out of nowhere, Riva Ridge walks off the incident as if nothing had happened.

Laurin and Ron both sigh in relief.

The first call in the Belmont goes to Smiling Jack, but it is soon all Riva Ridge, who, despite the paddock incident, beats out 12-second eighths, getting to the half-mile post in 48 seconds with a three-length lead.

The race has only just begun, but Ron is already beaming. Before the race, he had told Lucien's son, Roger, that if he saw 48 seconds on the clock after half a mile, to go and cash his tickets.

Running easily, well within himself, Riva Ridge quickly opens a four-length lead. Then five, six and seven lengths.

It is over. With the gas gauges on the other horses all reading empty, Riva Ridge, flattening down like a cat ready to pounce, holds that big lead all the way to the finish. He is the first horse to lead at every pole in the Belmont since Citation in 1948. It is also the largest winning margin since Gallant Man won the Belmont by eight lengths in 1957.

"He did the whole job on his own and I never hit him," says Ron, sipping a glass of champagne in the press box afterward. "Just clucked to him a couple of times at the furlong pole."

The winning time of 2:28 is third-fastest in Belmont history.

"If it wasn't for the slop in the Preakness he wins the Triple Crown," laments Ron.

Chapter 23

Secretariat is coming into his own. He works five furlongs in a brisk :57 3/5. Laurin looks at his stopwatch and shakes his head in disbelief.

"We have a racehorse on our hands," Laurin tells Tweedy.

He chooses a five-and-a-half-furlong race on July 4 for Secretariat's debut.

Ron is despondent; he is committed to ride Summer Guest in the Monmouth Oaks that day — a race he knows he will win.

"Come on, Lucien. There are plenty of other maiden races. Pick another one. Please."

But Laurin's mind is made up. With Secretariat's sizzling work ringing in his ears, he wants to run Secretariat right away and names Paul Feliciano, an apprentice rider who did a lot of the work reschooling Riva Ridge.

Feliciano and Secretariat draw the rail, but it does not go well. Quebec, a horse who starts from post three, ducks in hard at the break and collides with Strike the Line, who has post two. The chain reaction sends Strike the Line to his left, right into Secretariat, who almost hits the inside rail.

Feliciano tugs hard on the reins; just a few strides away from the gate Secretariat is 10th, ahead of just two horses.

It doesn't get any better. Secretariat recovers from the break and moves up along the rail but runs right into a blind switch wall of horses. Again, Feliciano is forced to take a big hold on the big chestnut.

But blocked hopelessly, they end up fourth, defeated by just a length and a quarter despite having nowhere to run for the last 70 yards. The running line on Secretariat in the *Daily Racing Form* reads "finished full of run."

In the box seats with Tweedy, Laurin stands and kicks his chair, which is sent spinning and clattering.

"He should never have been beaten," he says as he storms for the unsaddling area, where he grabs Feliciano's arm hard and holds it all the way to the jockeys' room.

Eleven days later, on July 15, Secretariat runs in another race. But, again, Ron isn't available. This time it's not of his own choosing. On July 6, Ron went down in a spill when his mount, Overproof, had a heart attack. Thrown heavily, Ron was taken by ambulance to the hospital. The force of the fall bent his rib cage, bruising his lungs, heart muscles, back and chest.

With Ron sidelined for three weeks, Laurin decides to give Feliciano another chance.

"Don't do what you did last time," Laurin says sternly to Feliciano. "Just stay out of trouble and let him run. He shouldn't get beat."

He doesn't. Secretariat wins in a romp by six lengths for Feliciano. In bed at his home in Queens, New York, Ron doesn't know what hurts more: his body or another lost opportunity to ride Secretariat.

Two weeks later, Laurin enters Secretariat in a July 31 six-furlong allowance race.

"Are you feeling alright enough to ride him?" he asks Ron. "If I put Feliciano or somebody else on him and he wins like I expect, I might have to ride that jock back in the upcoming stakes races."

"Of course, I'm ready," Ron lies, his body still aching heavily. "Why wouldn't I be?"

Getting away unhurried, as is becoming his style, Secretariat starts last. But willingly and with little coaxing from Ron, Secretariat sweeps past them all to a length-and-a-half victory.

Laurin, nonplussed, isn't impressed but Ron tells him he had a lot of horse left. "I never asked him to run. He just floats; you don't feel like you're going that fast, but then you look up and you're passing horses like they were standing still."

As for the slow start Ron says, "He has a mind of his own — wants to run his own way and that's alright with me. I allowed him to get himself together. I didn't change tactics. He just wants time to settle into stride. Once he starts running, though, there's no horse who can beat him right now."

Given a month off to recover after a taxing neck victory in the Hollywood Derby on July 1 in California, where he toted 129 pounds, Riva Ridge is showing no ill effects. For that matter Laurin raves about just how good Riva Ridge is acting.

Yet, Riva Ridge is vulnerable. He finishes a lethargic fourth in the Monmouth Invitational on August 5.

"After being so full of energy at Saratoga he was so dull in the post parade at Monmouth," says Ron confoundedly.

A blood test taken when Riva Ridge returns to Saratoga reveals the answer: a positive test for a horse tranquilizer and phenothiazine, the latter normally used for worming horses. According to Riva Ridge's veterinarian, Dr. Mark Gerard, Riva Ridge was the victim of tampering.

"Beyond all reasons of doubt," says Gerard.

However, because Riva Ridge wasn't tested at Monmouth, Alfred Vanderbilt, head of the New York Racing Association, tells Tweedy that the chain of evidence had been broken, and there was nothing that could be done.

For Secretariat, it is now on to more rugged competition. For the Sanford Stakes on August 16 at Saratoga, Secretariat isn't even favored. That distinction going to Linda's Chief, who has won all five of his starts. Linda's Chief is sent away at odds of 3-5; Secretariat is 3-2.

Again, Secretariat breaks with the field but then takes himself back. There are only five horses in the race, and Secretariat is last after the first quarter mile and passes only one horse in the second quarter mile.

Then, just as in his debut, Secretariat, full of run but no place to go, is boxed in at the three-sixteenths pole. Fortunately, the leaders, Trevose and Northstar Dancer, drift apart and, in a blink, Ron sends Secretariat through the hole.

It is no contest; Secretariat wins by three. Again, Ron never has to use the whip.

The fractions are dizzying at :23 3/5, :23 1/5 and :23 1/5. Usually, the last quarter of a race is the slowest. Not when Secretariat runs though.

Continuing to grow, Secretariat has become a physical specimen.

"Trying to fault Secretariat's conformation is like dreaming of dry rain," writes veteran turf writer Charlie Hatton of the two-year-old's powerful, well-sloped shoulders, deep chest, huge hind quarter and girth, which is three inches more than his older stablemate star, Riva Ridge.

Two days later, Ron is the first jockey to win five races in a single card at Saratoga.

Going six and a half furlongs, Secretariat romps in Saratoga's Hopeful Stakes on August 26 by five lengths in 1:16 1/5. Flourishing with brisk workouts, Secretariat works five furlongs in 58 seconds flat before the Futurity on September 16 at Belmont, which he wins by a length and three quarters. A month later Secretariat crosses the finish line two lengths on top in the October 14th Champagne, where he runs the second quarter in a brilliant :21 4/5. But as he heads to the winner's circle, Ron sees John Rotz, rider of runner-up Stop the Music, get onto the phone to the stewards. Then he sees the inquiry light flash on the tote board.

"Rotz is just taking a shot," Ron tells Laurin. "It was Linda's Chief that caused the bumping. Linda's Chief drifted out and sent Stop the Music into our horse. Don't worry, Lucien."

Then the stewards ask to talk to Ron, who has grown more and more perplexed.

"Linda's Chief is the horse that came out," he says to the stewards. "My horse did nothing wrong."

But as the delay lingers while the stewards watch the replay over and over, Ron starts to worry too.

"They can't take me down," Ron says to Laurin as the minutes drag on glacier-like.

But they do. Secretariat is placed second.

"Impossible," says Ron, angrily, when he gets back to Barn 5. "The stewards got it wrong. I watched the replay over and over. I defy anybody to view that film and point out to me anything that affected the outcome. A bad call. A really bad call."

The day after the Champagne, Noel wins the Nettie Stakes at Woodbine with Belle Geste. It is her fifth stakes win in her past six starts — all with Noel aboard. She also wins the Canadian Stakes, the Canadian Maturity Stakes, the Nassau Stakes and the Niagara Stakes.

The Maturity win is especially dazzling. Hooking up with Queen's Plate winner Kennedy Road at the outset, the pair run head-to-head for virtually the entire mile and a quarter race.

At the wire, it is Belle Geste and Noel by a neck. The time of 2:01 2/5 is another track record for the brilliant mare.

After each win, Noel and Chappy Chapman drink to celebrate.

On October 28, over a sloppy surface in the Laurel Futurity, Secretariat and Ron win by eight lengths over Stop the Music. Edwin Whittaker's Angle Light finishes third.

Despite the wet track, Secretariat gets the mile and a sixteenth in 1:42 4/5 — just a fifth of a second off the track record.

"His best performance so far," says Ron.

As one Meadow horse soars, the other falters. The same day Secretariat wins the Laurel Futurity, Riva Ridge shows nothing for the second straight time in the two-mile Jockey Club Gold Cup at Aqueduct. With Jorge Velasquez replacing Ron, Riva Ridge finishes third by 18 lengths. Another start with Velasquez is even worse. Riva Ridge finishes sixth by 38 lengths in the International on soft turf at Laurel, Maryland.

Secretariat just gets better. In one of his final prep works for the $298,000 Garden State Stakes on November 18, 1972, in New Jersey, it is Rudy who gallops the chestnut an easy five furlongs.

"Man, now I know personally how good Secretariat is," Rudy enthuses after he dismounts. "He's a machine."

He is exactly that. Maybe more.

The rich Garden State, with $179,199 going to the winner, will be Secretariat's last start as a two-year-old.

Entered in the same race is Angle Light, who is ridden by Rudy.

The entry goes off at just 10 cents on the dollar.

The first quarter goes in a very slow :24 1/5 and a tardy half in :47 2/5; Secretariat is nine and a half lengths behind.

"Jesus," thinks Ron. "I took too much of a hold on him and now they are just walking up front."

Even for the precocious Secretariat, it seems too much to overcome. Secretariat, however, shows why he is so tantalizingly special. Ron lets loose of the reins, buries his head in Secretariat's mane and asks Big Red to run. Immediately Secretariat responds, passing horses around the turn as if they are painted on the inside railing.

There is only one horse in front of them as they turn for home: stablemate Angle Light, who is leading by two lengths.

But it isn't enough. Rudy looks over his right shoulder and sees the big blue and white checkered silks of Secretariat come motoring beside him.

"Damn," curses Rudy.

"How are you making out?" Ron casually says to Rudy as if they were out for a morning gallop and not the richest race of the year.

"I'm alright here," Rudy says. "I got second I think."

"Well, that's fine," Ron answers flatly. "Bye bye. I got to go now. See you later, pal."

"Asshole," Rudy murmurs under his breath.

And go they do. Secretariat draws away to a three-and-a-half length triumph. Angle Light is second.

"Congratulations, Ronnie. What a ride," says Laurin. "What a great ride."

"Mr. Laurin," quickly responds Ron, "that's the worst ride I ever gave a horse in my life."

After his troubled debut, Secretariat has crossed the finish line on top eight times in a row and is named both Two-Year-Old champion and Horse of the Year, winning $456,404 in his 1972 campaign. It is a year where the stock market plunges to its lowest level since the Great Depression. Riva Ridge adds another $395,632 for the Meadow.

Three days into 1973, Christopher Chenery dies at 86. He leaves behind holdings liable for millions of dollars in estate and inheritance taxes.

The Meadow needs money. And fast. Otherwise, as it was prior to Riva Ridge saving the farm in 1971, it seems the Meadow will have to sell its racing stock, broodmare band and possibly even part of the farm itself.

Tweedy opts for another solution. To resolve the financial problems, Secretariat is syndicated for a world record $6,080,000. That's 32 shares at $190,000. This before he even starts his three-year-old season.

Not far behind, Riva Ridge is syndicated for $5,120,000.

Tweedy retains four shares and control over both Secretariat's and Riva Ridge's 1973 campaigns.

Chapter 24

Into the murky quagmire of Watergate and Vietnam, when the United States is longing for something good, strides Secretariat, who is preparing for his 1973 debut.

It is Wednesday, March 14, three days before the Bay Shore Stakes at Aqueduct. A spring snowstorm blankets the Atlantic northeast. By now even Secretariat's workouts have become events, and this last three-furlong blowout before the Bay Shore is certainly one of them.

As Secretariat hits the wire, Laurin clicks his watch. Looking at the dial he is quickly aghast.

"Oh my God," he says out loud.

He has caught Secretariat in a mind-numbing :33 3/5 seconds. Blinking he checks his watch again. Thinking he must have mistimed Secretariat, he phones the clockers.

"How fast did you get him?" he hesitantly says to Jules Watson, one of the clockers.

After a pause, Watson replies, "Thirty-two and three-fifths. Right?"

Watson then reads back the fractions in eighths of a mile: "Eleven and one-fifth, twenty-one and four-fifths, thirty-two and three-fifths."

Laurin gulps. There was indeed something wrong with his clocking. As fast as he had caught Secretariat, the clockers all had him in a full second faster.

Laurin relates the time to Tweedy, who was also watching the workout.

"Well," she says. "That ought to open up his pipes."

Laurin, still in disbelief, doesn't answer.

If there are any doubts about how good Secretariat is, that workout erases them all.

"I've never worked a horse in my life the way I worked Secretariat," Laurin tells the media. "I gallop him from two miles to 2 1/2 miles a day, and the second mile had to be a really good gallop."

Having grown immensely since his final two-year-old race four months ago, Secretariat weighs 1,154 pounds — two hundred pounds more than the average thoroughbred. His shoulders and neck are massive. His girth is a staggering 75.2 inches, almost two full inches more than when measured as a two-year-old. He has also grown an inch and a quarter from the ground to his withers. His chest is enormous.

Charlie Hatton writes, "He has muscles in his eyebrows."

To fuel himself, Secretariat is eating 14 to 15 quarts of oats and 25 pounds of hay a day.

On a March 17 afternoon with dark and angry shadows coming and going, the Bay Shore is riveting. With hard rain falling, the track is sloppy.

Racing through the turn, Secretariat is full of run but has nowhere to go. In front of him are three horses — Close Image, Actuality and Impecunious. To his outside is Champagne Charlie. Ron thinks of taking back and going around the leaders, but when he does Mike Venezia on Champagne Charlie takes back as well, pinning him to the inside. Going around now would probably cost him six lengths.

It's too late, so Ron gambles, stays inside and prays.

Fortuitously a sliver of daylight opens under the dark skies as Impecunious drifts out slightly. But Actuality, ridden along the rail by Bobby Woodhouse, is having none of it and Woodhouse starts whipping left-handed, closing the hole again.

"Bobby! Bobby! Bobby!" yells Ron. "Straighten up. Straighten up."

Woodhouse isn't listening. He continues to make it tight.

"(Turcotte) was in trouble," Woodhouse says after the race. "He yelled my name, but I ain't going to give him no money."

"I was trying to keep the hole closed but Impecunious was trying to get out," says Venezia. "I had been keeping him in until the quarter pole. Then I couldn't keep him in anymore."

There is barely enough room for Secretariat and Ron to squeeze through, but he hits the hole like a linebacker and once clear explodes to a four-and-a-half-length victory.

Sent away at 20 cents on the dollar, Secretariat pays $2.40 to win.

In the box seats, a relieved Laurin shouts, "He's too much horse! They can't stop him! They can't even stop him with a wall of horses!"

But it still isn't over. Jim Moseley, the jockey on Impecunious, claims foul. The stewards, however, dismiss the objection, ruling there was room. Barely.

"I was stupid to take the chance when I was on Secretariat, stupid because he was the same Secretariat I knew as a two-year-old," Ron says to the assembled media. "As it turned out I should have gone around."

Back in Ontario, Noel sets a Woodbine record, winning both ends of a March 28 Daily Double that pays $609.40. He wins the first with Capt'n Roo, who pays $56.60, then the second with Jessie Ann, $34.10.

Two weeks after the Bay Shore, Secretariat wins again. This time in the Gotham Stakes, also at Aqueduct. Not taking any chances this time, Ron sails to the front and wins in a track record — equaling one-mile clocking of 1:33 2/5.

Once again Secretariat has spoken with his quick feet. It takes two lead ponies and an outrider to pull him up.

It looks like nothing can stop Secretariat, who has just one race left before the Kentucky Derby: the Wood Memorial on April 21 at Aqueduct.

While Riva Ridge had used the Florida route to prepare for the Triple Crown races, Laurin has opted to stay in New York with Secretariat even though no winner of the Bay Shore or Gotham has yet to win the Kentucky Derby.

Laurin enters two horses for the Wood: Secretariat and Angle Light. Rudy is supposed to have the mount on Angle Light, whom he rode to a runner-up finish behind Secretariat in the Garden State. Rudy knows Angle Light is a good horse and that a solid performance could get him to the Kentucky Derby, the race every jockey wants to contest.

But his agent convinces him to ride Alma North the same day as the Wood in the $25,000 Trenton Handicap at Garden State. Alma North, a pigeon-toed stall weaver, has been Rudy's go-to horse all year, winning the Conniver Stakes Handicap at Bowie by 10 lengths on March 12 and, just six days later, winning the Betsy Ross at Garden State. The mare also carried Rudy to victory in the Geisha Stakes at Pimlico.

In all Rudy wins five times with Alma North in 1973 alone.

But Rudy worries he has made the wrong choice.

"We finished third on Angle Light in the Louisiana Derby, and he didn't even like the track," Rudy says, trying to make his case for Angle Light. "Angle Light is legit."

"But Rudy, Lucien said that Angle Light might not even run in the Wood," counters his agent. "Then we'll be left with nothing."

Rudy loses his argument and stays in New Jersey.

In the days leading up to the Wood something is clearly amiss with Secretariat. He won't even gallop, exercise rider Jimmy Gaffney having to kick him to get him rolling with any kind of energy.

With the morning just starting to shed its black coat for his final workout, Secretariat lazily goes a mile in 1:42 2/5, about five full seconds slower than Laurin wanted.

Come the afternoon of the Wood, Secretariat won't even open his mouth for Sweat to put a bit in his mouth.

On post parade, Secretariat tosses his head.

"Something is wrong," Ron says to himself. "Something is very, very wrong."

It only gets worse.

At the starting gate, Secretariat throws his head and punches his way through, causing a delay and requiring a gate crew member to manually close it.

When the gate opens for all the horses, Secretariat takes back to seventh while Angle Light heads right for the top and sets slow fractions, with a half mile going in :48 1/5.

Knowing the pace is too tepid, Ron tries to get a response from Secretariat, who has now crossed the finish line in front 10 times in succession.

Instead, Secretariat refuses to pick up the bit.

Not once does Secretariat show his prodigious 25-foot-long stride — a couple of feet longer than most horses — and finishes third, four lengths behind Angle Light, who nips Sham by a head.

When Rudy hears that Angle Light has won — and just as punishing is that Alma North not only loses but finishes out of the money — he is so livid that he books off his final mount of the day at Garden State and has a couple of stiff drinks.

"It hit me pretty hard. Especially when Angle Light would have been my first Derby mount. Not just another Derby mount either, but one of the contenders," he tells the *Philadelphia Daily*

News in a story that runs above an advertisement for a 64-ounce bottle of Hiram Walker's Ten High Straight bourbon whiskey selling for just $11.54. "It kind of hurts, really hurts, though. My mind wasn't straight when I first heard about Angle Light winning. I was upset and angry. But I'm OK now. It was just one of those things. It's a part of racing."

Rudy has been riding hot at Garden State with four wins and two runner-up finishes.

Back in New York, Laurin and Tweedy are angry. Unable to find anyone or anything else to direct their displeasure at, they blame Ron. They point to the slow workout. They say Ron took him too wide on the first turn. They say the pace was too slow. Anything and everything.

Pursing his lips, Ron says little. He knows there was something wrong with Secretariat in the Wood. But what?

A few days later, he gets his answer.

"Hey, Ronnie," says Dr. Manuel A. Gilman, examining veterinarian for the New York Racing Association. "How's the abscess on Secretariat's lip?"

"Abscess? What abscess, Doc?" says Ron, who is bewildered.

"The abscess under his lip," Gilman answers as if Ron should have known. "It was blue. About the size of a quarter. I showed it to Lucien when I looked at Secretariat's tattoo number the morning of the Wood."

"Oh, thank you, Doc. Thank you. I knew it had to be something like that," says Ron, relieved and exhaling heavily. "Every time I pulled on the reins, his head kept flying up.

If Ron had known, he would have ridden Secretariat differently.

"I would never have tried to pick up his head," he says to himself. "I'd have just kept my hands on the reins and chirped to him. By bringing his head up I was aggravating the abscess."

For Ron, the abscess explains everything. But Tweedy and Laurin still have their doubts. Bold Ruler generally didn't pass on endurance to his offspring, and the Derby's mile and a quarter hang like a specter.

Then there are the rumors — mostly propagated by self-promoted Las Vegas oddsmaker Jimmy "the Greek" Snyder, who profoundly announces that Secretariat is lame and has his legs standing in ice.

Amid a swirl of strange innuendos, it is off to the Derby, America's most prestigious horse race.

Chapter 25

A record crowd of 137,476 gathers for the May 5 Derby. Just an hour before post time, Ron awakes from his nap with a startle. He is sweating. He has just dreamed that Secretariat got beat. Shaking his head to unclog his half-awake, half-asleep visions he realizes the television monitors are simply replaying Secretariat's loss in the Wood Memorial.

"Just a dream," Ron realizes happily. "Just a dream."

In the saddling paddock, Ron sidles close to Laurin, who is pacing. Laurin puts a smoldering cigarette down on a stall board and inadvertently brushes against it, burning a hole in his jacket.

"You know the horse, Ronnie," he says. "Just try to keep clear. Don't worry about a thing. Ride the race the way it comes up."

Getting a leg boost into the saddle from Laurin, Ron circles the paddock one last time and heads onto the track, where the throng of shifting fans have already started to sing "My Old Kentucky Home." Ron reaches down and pats Secretariat comfortably on his neck and forehead.

In the starting gate, Ron feels Secretariat's heart thump between his legs. Two stalls down, on the rail, Sham, the Santa Anita Derby winner and second choice in the wagering, is anxious too. He bangs his head on the starting gate and loses two teeth.

At 5:37 they are off. So is the large crowd, which is already standing, buzzing with the impatient thrill of uncertainty.

As the field passes the grandstand for the first time, Secretariat is ahead of just two stragglers.

"My God. Not another one of these," Laurin mutters aloud. "I'm getting out of here."

Tweedy forcefully pulls on one of Laurin's arms.

"You'll stay here and face this with me," she says.

Despite being so far behind, Ron, as opposed to Laurin, has no worries. Unlike in the Wood, he feels Secretariat take the bit and lets him run against it.

They move up to sixth, willingly passing horses and a riot of colorful jockey silks on the outside around the first turn. Down the backstretch, with Shecky Greene setting the pace, they are an unhurried fifth though, still nine lengths behind.

Sham, with jockey Laffit Pincay, is also on the move and flies to the lead turning for home.

But in a flash, Secretariat, still wide, is right there with him. For a hundred yards Secretariat and Sham race head-to-head. But Secretariat is stronger. Ron scrubs harder; the fans yell louder. With Ron waving his whip in front of Secretariat's right eye, Secretariat responds willingly and moves determinedly in front by a head, then half a length, then clear for good, winning by two and a half lengths.

Once again Secretariat has outrun the wind.

Euphoria. Everyone is on their feet, a throat-choking ovation seems to go on forever.

Secretariat has run his first quarter in :25 1/5 seconds, the second in :24 flat, the third in :23 4/5, the fourth in :23 2/5 and then the last quarter in an unbelievable Derby-record :23 flat.

In almost every race, the fractions get slower. When horses come from behind and seem to pick up speed, it is mostly an optical illusion. The leaders are simply passing tired horses.

Not Secretariat. He has just run every quarter faster than the one before, and the last one gives Secretariat a track record 1:59 2/5. He is the first horse to run the Derby in under two minutes. Just as incredible, Secretariat raced the last six furlongs in 1:10 1/5 — two seconds faster than Shecky Greene ran his first six furlongs.

Andrew Beyer of the *Washington Star-News* gives Secretariat a speed figure — the winning time compared to the existing track conditions — of 129, the highest he has ever given out.

The Meadow stable has won its second straight Derby; Ron is the first jockey in 71 years to do the same.

Ron unstraps his helmet and hoists it high into the fading skies.

Laurin and Tweedy embrace.

"This is the most pressure I have ever had on me," says a relieved Laurin, who, for the first time in his life has needed sleeping pills. He is also battling ulcers.

"Sham was rolling, but I was flying," beams Ron. "All I did was fasten the seat belt."

Angle Light, with fellow New Brunswick native John LeBlanc aboard, finishes 10th.

The Nielsen television rating for the Derby is 16.5; half of the national audience was watching.

Two weeks later comes the Preakness at Pimlico, Maryland. Gone are all the question marks surrounding Secretariat.

So are most of his challengers. Only five other horses and just two from the Derby — Sham and Our Native — are entered.

Secretariat shows his stuff and preps for the race with a six-furlong, 1:10 galloping-out work.

A much more jovial Laurin, who has unsuccessfully tried to win the Preakness three times, including with Riva Ridge last year, and Tweedy, who chews on a Rolaid tablet, settle into their seats.

With its tighter turns, which Secretariat loves, Pimlico is a speed-favoring track. Having been the track's leading rider in the fall of 1963, Ron knows that very well.

However, Secretariat gets away last. But not for long. In a majestic and breath-absorbing early move, Ron, sensing the pace is slow, pushes Secretariat early and zips by the field around the first turn. It is an unexpected, surging explosion of power and speed that leaves his rivals gasping for air.

The Preakness is over already.

Almost every thoroughbred has just one move — one burst of speed. Secretariat has several. Riding him is like driving a Ferrari.

Sham gets within two and a half lengths of Secretariat down the backstretch but gets no closer. Ron peaks under his arm twice to make sure no one else is coming and eases Secretariat to an effortless win under a hand ride.

The tele-timer stops the mile and three-sixteenths race in 1:55 — a full second off the track record. The tele-timer, however, has malfunctioned.

Daily Racing Form clockers have Secretariat in 1:53 2/5. Pimlico's official timer, E.T. McClean, has him in 1:54 2/5. The track keeps McClean's clocking, but the *Form* maintains its time — a Preakness record, three-fifths of a second faster than Canonero's winning time in 1971.

With the Belmont still to come, Secretariat is the most famous horse in the world and is pictured on the covers of *Newsweek*, *Sports Illustrated* and *Time*.

"Super Horse," the latter declares.

The Belmont arrives three weeks later.

Secretariat is galloping at least two miles every morning that he doesn't work out. The works are perfect. He works six furlongs in 1:12 1/5. Then, eight days before the Belmont, he works a mile in 1:34 4/5 — when Laurin was hoping for a time of 1:36 — and then, on June 6, a snappy but easy four furlongs in :46 3/5.

He is ready. More than ready.

After a late dinner, Ron, feeling the pressures of trying to win a Triple Crown, which no horse has accomplished since Citation in 1948, tells Laurin, "If we don't win the Belmont, I might as well pack my tack and leave New York."

"You?" replies Laurin. "What about me?"

"He's the greatest horse that ever looked through a bridle," Ron says.

"Do you think so, Ronnie?" asks Laurin, always needing reassurance. "Do you really think so?"

It is the hot morning of the race — temperatures reaching 90° F. From somewhere in the stable area, a chicken clucks noisily. Scooter, the barn's six-toed cat, meanders.

With his teeth, Secretariat grabs the handle of a rake and imitates Eddie Sweat brushing the ground in front of his stall. The other grooms have a good laugh, breaking the uneasy silence.

Ron and Laurin have had three weeks to discuss their strategy for the Belmont. Laurin has pointed out many times how often the mile and a half Belmont has been won on the front end.

But, in the paddock, they go over it again.

"If he wants to run early, let him," says Laurin. "But don't send him. Don't choke him either."

Ron nods knowingly.

It is 5:38 when the gates spring open. Immediately Ron lets Secretariat roll out of post position No. 1 instead of his usual style of falling back early.

Pincay on Sham heads for the front as well, just to the outside of Secretariat. After just a quarter of a mile, Sham sticks his nose out front and soon has a half-length lead. They draw five lengths clear of the rest of the small five-horse field.

It is a match race from the outset. The first eighth of a mile goes in :12 1/5; the second eighth in a mesmerizing :11 2/5.

Pincay knows it is too fast. But he is under instructions to take the lead. So, off they streak together through another blazing quarter in :22 3/5 for a half mile in :46 1/5 and six furlongs in 1:09 4/5, as if running in a sprint race and not a mile and a half.

Laurin's face turns ashen. He thinks that it is too fast. Much too fast.

"If I had a rifle I'd shoot Ronnie," he tells Tweedy. "The way that Ronnie is riding this horse, he's going to drop dead."

Neither Pincay nor Ron say anything to each other. The rest of the field is now 10 lengths behind.

The next eighth of a mile — in :11 3/5 — finishes Sham, whose legs are rubber.

"Secretariat is widening now," says announcer Charles "Chic" Anderson. "He is moving like a tremendous machine."

As Secretariat keeps pouring it on, the fans realize they are witnessing history. They stand on their toes, 70,000 ballet mouths agape.

He widens to three lengths. Then seven.

Reality has been suspended: the preposterous pace must take its toll.

Instead, Secretariat keeps flying. He gets a mile and an eighth in 1:46 1/5 — tying the world record for nine furlongs.

He is all by himself.

Ten lengths. Twenty.

And he is still not done.

Ron looks under his left arm and sees only a vast empty stretch behind him.

He flashes by the mile and three-eighths marker in 2:11 1/5 — three seconds faster than Man o' War's 1920 world record.

"Oh my God, Ronnie, don't fall off. Just don't fall off," says Laurin, almost as startled as anyone else.

"Secretariat! Secretariat! Big Red! Big Red!" the crowd yells.

Ron, who has still not uncocked his whip, now looks over his left shoulder. He can't believe how far he is in front.

Sweat is crying. So are many others.

Still propelling Secretariat forward, Ron looks to his left again and sees 2:20 flash by on the electronic timer. Everyone else is also looking at the clock too. The track record is 2:26 3/5.

A couple blinks later the clock stops in 2:24 flat. Another track record, shattering Gallant Man's mark by two and three-fifths seconds.

"How fast did you go?" outrider Jim Dailey asks Ron.

"Two-twenty-four flat," is the quick answer.

"You're crazy," says Dailey.

"I'm telling you," Ron says.

"Can't be," says Dailey.

But it is.

Up in the press box, the *Daily Racing Form* credits Secretariat with a 31-length victory — the equivalent of a full sixteenth of a mile.

Poor Sham finishes last.

Charlie Hatton, who has been covering horse racing for 60 years, says Secretariat's only point of reference is himself and calls him the greatest horse he has ever seen.

The historic Belmont coronation is the equivalent of Roger Bannister's 1954 mile in 3:59:04 — the first to break the four-minute mile barrier — or Bob Beamon's long jump record by a full 21 2/3 inches in the 1968 Mexico City Olympics.

It is beyond anything ever seen in horse racing. More than 11 million households watch transfixed to their screens.

Saved as souvenirs, thousands of $2 win tickets are never cashed. The memory holds more value.

Secretariat has no limits.

Chapter 26

The Secretariat story doesn't end here.

Twenty-one days after the Belmont, Secretariat wins the June 30 Arlington Invitational Stakes by nine. Secretariat makes five more starts, including two losses that come with huge asterisks. On August 4, at Saratoga, he is sent off at 10 cents on the dollar in the Whitney Stakes. But running with a fever so high that Ron begs Laurin to scratch him, he finishes second to Onion by a length.

After he pulls Secretariat up, Ron is in tears.

"He should never have run," says Ron.

After the race Secretariat's temperature is 104° F.

Ron is angry as he reads the headline "Secretariat Didn't Lose the Race, Turcotte Did," in the next day's *Lexington Herald-Leader*. The article goes on to say Secretariat was the victim of a slow pace, in tight quarters and racing on the rail, which was the slowest part of the track that day. Turcotte was "the victim of a very understandable error in judgment and possibly a bit of overconfidence," the article states.

Ron knows differently.

"I had never had a horse try that hard that was that sick," he says. "How he finished second is beyond me. He wins if he is just 75 percent right. But he wasn't even 75 percent ready to run."

Pitted against older horses, Secretariat wins the September 15 Marlborough Cup Invitational Handicap — beating a stacked field that, besides Riva Ridge, includes Cougar II, Key to the Mint and Kennedy Road by three and a half lengths for another world record. The victory makes Secretariat a millionaire.

Next up is the September 29 Woodward Stakes at Belmont.

Secretariat isn't supposed to run this day. Riva Ridge is. But when the skies over New York open up and it rains in torrents, Riva Ridge, who loathes slop, is scratched and Secretariat, who is being pointed to the October 8 Man o' War Stakes on the grass, takes his place at the last moment.

Not only does Secretariat not have his usual fast blow-out work before the mile and a half Woodward, but he has also only had two casual works and both were on the turf. The Woodward is on the dirt.

The lack of preparation costs him. When Ron takes the lead away from Prove Out with half a mile to go, he thinks the race is over. Instead, Secretariat tires and finished second — four and a half lengths behind Prove Out, who comes back on in the stretch.

Tweedy is furious.

"You've been riding hard all year. Maybe your judgment is off," she huffs. "You should have ridden the horse in the Woodward the way you rode him in the Belmont."

Ron replies, "I didn't have as much horse as I had for the Belmont. He just wasn't ready to go a mile and a half."

Back to being Secretariat — returning to his usual hard training — Secretariat proves a lack of fitness was the reason for the Woodward loss with a startlingly easy five-length triumph in the Man o' War. Running on grass for the first time, he equals the world record.

Then comes Secretariat's swan song — the October 28 Canadian International at Woodbine.

Four days before the Canadian International, Ron is suspended for five days after being disqualified in a race at

Aqueduct. It is Secretariat's final race, and Ron is crushed that he can't be aboard.

Ron does, however, climb on for Secretariat's last workout — five furlongs on the Marshall turf course — at Woodbine three days before the Canadian International, another grass race. On a foggy morning that lingers like a bad toothache, the workout attracts an estimated crowd of 7,000 people, who are given free coffee and doughnuts. Some arrived three hours before the work.

"When word spread that the Big Horse was emerging from his barn to gallop, grooms, hot walkers, exercise boys and trainers lined the pathways just to watch him walk by," said Bruce Walker, the Ontario Jockey Club's publicity director.

Secretariat glides effortlessly.

"You could hear his heavy intake and exhaling of air. Whoosh. Gone," says Walker.

The head clocker, six stories high in the grandstand, however, yells down to John Mooney, the president of the Jockey Club, that Secretariat had worked five furlongs in a pedestrian 1:03.

"He's never worked that slow in his life," says Laurin, disbelievingly.

"There was stunned silence," says Walker.

Trainers Carl Chapman and Frank Merrill, both clocking the work, each got Secretariat in :57 3/5.

"Because the fog was so thick, the clocker had missed Secretariat's starting point," says Walker. "It was a course record."

With Eddie Maple taking over the reins, Secretariat wins the Canadian International by five and a half lengths, simply toying with the field as a cold, drizzling rain patters.

A week later, November 6, Ron, who is North America's leading stakes-winning jockey for the second straight year — winning 14 stakes in 1973 after taking 17 last year — climbs aboard Secretariat's back for the "Farewell to Secretariat Day" at Aqueduct. Held between the track's third and fourth races, despite being an election day in New York State, 32,900 fans line up to sing "Auld Lang Syne" and say their goodbyes to the greatest racehorse in the world. Despite all the festivities and the cheers of the crowd, the afternoon is as poignantly sad as the cold, gray and misty weather.

"It is the last time I will sit on his back," laments Ron, his eyes moist. "He was just getting good. If he had raced as a four-year-old, only God knows what he'd have done. His last two races were unbelievable. They were on the grass and people won't believe me, but Secretariat is 10 to 15 lengths better on turf than dirt. The way Secretariat moved on turf he was a completely different horse. He just skipped over it, carrying himself like a deer."

Ron also knows something else: "Secretariat should never have been beat except for his first race when he got into trouble. He had a painful abscess in the Wood Memorial, he had a fever in the Whitney and he wasn't ready to run a mile and a half in the Woodward. He never failed us. We failed him."

Maybe most telling and lamentable is what Ron says next: "Secretariat hadn't reached his peak. Horses don't reach maturity until they are five, six or even seven years old. God only knows how good he could have been if he wasn't retired as a baby. Nobody saw the true Secretariat."

Five days pass and Secretariat climbs into a van that will take him to New York's Kennedy Airport, where he will be flown to Claiborne Farm in Paris, Kentucky. There he begins a new life as a stallion breeding expensive mares. His stall at Claiborne will be the same one his father, Bold Ruler, resided in.

Following Secretariat to the van, Ron takes hold of his halter, peers deep into his eyes and then kisses him on the nose.

"Goodbye, old friend," he says wistfully.

Laurin, Tweedy and Sweat are similarly moved.

"It's like a funeral," says Laurin, between tears. "I tell ya, when they came to load 'em up at the stable this morning, those vans looked like hearses to me."

When the Overseas National cargo plane carrying both Secretariat and Riva Ridge begins its final descent into Lexington, the airport tower, as the story goes, speaks to the plane's pilot, Dan Neff.

"There's more people out here to meet Secretariat than there was to greet the governor."

"Well," answers Neff, "he's won more races than the governor."

Penny Chenery (right) jockey Ron (second from right) and Lucien Lauren (third from left) in the Winner's Circle at Churchill Downs in Louisville, Kentucky (1973).

Yves posing for a class photo (1973).

RIGHT Roger's first win atop Profit Marge (1974).

Furlongs – 1:14 2/5
...ama Rama, 2nd
...weet Kakki Briar, 3rd
...ecember 30, 1974

Profit Marge

J.J. Paoli,
Owner–Trainer
Roger Turcotte, up
KEYSTONE RACE TRACK
FIRST WINNER

Rudy, sitting down with his daughter Stacey. Roger, Janet and Yves stand (1975).

ROGER TURCOTTE SETS RECORD

D & S STABLE-OWNER		ROGER TURCOTTE - UP
R. E. DUTROW-TR.	**"DON GATO"**	DOUBLE MESA 2ND
6 FURLONGS 1:13		DR. T. MING 3RD
	DELAWARE PARK AUGUST 10,1975	

104th WIN AT DEL. PK. MEET

Roger sets the course record at Delaware Park (1975).

LEFT Rudy and Roger at Keystone (1975).

Noel, Rudy and Roger at Calgary Turotte Day (1980).

LEFT Ron walks with braces for the first time after he and Noel make a leather belt for him to grab if he falls (1978).

A portrait of Noel at Calgary Turcotte Day (1980).

Rudy takes Cure the Blues for a morning gallop (1980).

– OWNER –
S. GREENHOOT FISCHER
R. CARLOS MACHEZ - TR.
DEC. 28, 1981
LAUREL, MD —

"– MAIDEN 2 YR. OLDS –"
"GREENIE'S MISS"

6 FUR. - 1:14 : 3/5 —

– JOCKEY –
YVES TURCOTTE - UP
HAGLEK
DANCER 2ND
UNDERCURRENT - 3RD

– FIRST WINNER FOR JOCKEY YVES TURCOTTE –

Rudy teaches Yves how to read the racing forms in Bowie, Maryland (1982).

LEFT Yve's first win atop Greenie's Miss (1981).

235

Yves with trainer Bernie Bonds (1982)

Roger and Yves in Alberta (1986).

SUNDAY

CALGARY HERALD MAGAZINE

5

ROGER TURCOTTE

A LONG JOURNEY
to the
WINNER'S CIRCLE

RIGHT: Roger takes a few moments in the jockey room to collect his thoughts and don silks for the next race.
BELOW: Turcotte clenches his fists to emphasize a point in a post-race discussion.

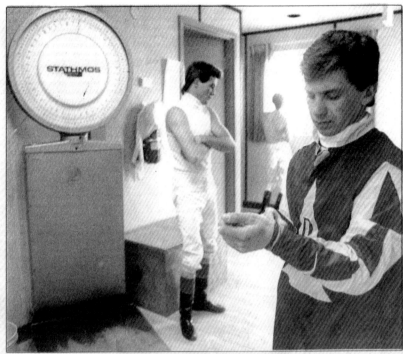

ABOVE: Turcotte and his agent, Ken Deines, heading out of the barn into the early morning light.
LEFT: Ellen Turcotte and children Jessy and Joey were at the track to see dad post his 999th win.

Rose and Alfred Turcotte at their 50th anniversary (1989).

Roger walking a horse at a farm, sometime in the 90s.

PREVIOUS SPREAD The cover story of a 1988 Calgary Herald Sunday edition, featuring Roger's chase for his 1000th career win.

Chapter 27

It is a muggy 86° F at Toronto's Woodbine, the air thick. Two months after impeachment hearings against U.S. president Richard Nixon began, the glow of Secretariat's Triple Crown season still lingers at racetracks everywhere.

Roger, the fourth Turcotte brother to become a jockey, gets ready to ride his first race on July 3, 1974.

It has been a year since Roger quit school in Grade 10 at the age of 16 and came to Ontario working — as Ron, Noel and Rudy all had — for trainer Gordon Huntley.

"I think Roger will be a great one in just a matter of time," says Huntley.

Many others think so too.

Filled with hope and the ebullience of youth, Roger has everything going for him: the name, the style, the confidence and, most assuredly, the talent.

"Nervous?" Noel asks Roger in the jockeys' room.

"A little," Roger answers, lying. He hardly slept last night, and his palms are wet.

"I was nervous too," Noel recalls. "Every jockey gets nervous before their first ride. Get this one over with and you'll be fine. It's not like anybody is expecting anything from this horse you are riding."

That's for sure. A three-year-old with little potential, Stritch is sent off at 24-1. Stritch's chances are so unlikely that the horse is coupled with another longshot, Flying Command, in the mutuel field.

"Just do your best," says Noel, putting his arm around Roger's left shoulder. "Ride him like he is the favorite."

"Sure," says Roger, rolling his eyes. "The favorite, huh?"

Huntley thinks so little of Stritch that he doesn't even bother to show up to saddle the horse, leaving one of his grooms to tighten the girth under the horse's abdomen and then boost Roger into the saddle for the day's first race.

Stritch surprises no one. He gets away last in the crowded 13-horse field, passes three horses even slower than he is and finishes 10th.

It is Wednesday and just another nondescript card. And yet, a cluster of reporters waits for Roger as he dismounts. Roger isn't just another rider making his first start. He is a Turcotte.

"Butterflies?" asks one of them.

"No," he simply replies, lying.

"Did Noel give you any advice?" asks the *Globe and Mail*'s Larry Millson.

"Yes," Roger answers uneasily, his shyness showing. "He gave me a couple of tips."

"Do you know when you will ride again?"

"No. Soon, I hope. Because the only way I'll learn anything more now is by riding in more races."

Huntley has plenty of opportunities for Roger to get more experience, but most of them are on babies. With a stable of 45 horses in training, fully 35 of Huntley's barn are two-year-olds. That isn't good for Roger because, under Ontario's racing rules, the stewards can prevent an apprentice from riding two-year-olds if they believe the jockey lacks the experience to handle a potentially unpredictable raw horse. Roger, the stewards decree, is one of them. He is only allowed to ride three-year-old or older horses.

"It's not fair," Roger bemoans to Noel, reading the stewards' decision about his ban aboard two-year-olds.

"They told me I wasn't experienced enough to ride two-year-olds, and that's what Huntley has. Claude Mugford rode for Huntley. He only rode in about 10 races, and they let him ride two-year-olds. First-time starters too. I think they have something against me."

"Don't worry about it," says Noel. "You'll get your chances."

No one thinks Roger's opportunities will be so scarce. Roger rides 25 more times without a win and decides to leave Toronto for New York, where Ron is riding. It doesn't get any better there. Roger goes winless in 12 more races.

"Sure, some people expect more," Roger says of his name. "But the name I have to make is Roger, not Turcotte."

Again, he is on the move. Leaving New York, he heads for Keystone, a new track in Bensalem, in northeast Pennsylvania, which has replaced Liberty Bell.

On December 13, Rudy, Ron and Roger all ride in the same race at Keystone. The world is almost treated to a four-Turcotte race, but Noel's scheduled mount is scratched.

Roger doesn't win that one — none of the Turcottes do — but he soon gets on a big roll.

In his 38th career mount, he rides his first winner on December 30 at Keystone — almost six full months after he made his debut — pushing home Profit Marge to a $17.40 payoff. The next day he wins again.

It is only just beginning. Living with Rudy, Rudy's wife, Janet, and their baby, Stacey, Roger goes on a furious run to start his first full year of riding in 1975.

He wins three races on February 3 and then four more the following afternoon.

"I could have won five if Rudy hadn't nailed me in the sixth race," says Roger.

He doesn't have to wait long to reach that goal. On February 5, he rides five winners out of six chances.

Rudy was the leading rider at Keystone last year, but Roger is the Turcotte who is now Keystone's top jockey, leading Rudy 34 wins to 19. It took Roger forever to get his first win. Now, they can't keep him out of the winner's circle.

Three days later, Roger gets his first stakes victory. Riding Wicked Park, the longest price in the $33,350 Militia Stakes, Roger sweeps around the final turn and pays $57.80 to win as he glides home by four and a quarter lengths. Because it is a stakes race, Roger doesn't get his usual five-pound apprentice weight allowance. That's fine for trainer Jim Cowden, who had claimed Wicked Park for just $10,000.

"Roger has been riding him, and he's a good rider," says Cowden. "I can't believe he was more than 25-1. I thought he'd be more like 10 or 12 to one."

"I'm just sort of keeping an eye on Roger," Rudy says when asked about his younger brother's future. "I hope to be able to help him avoid making mistakes. But I think you have to learn on your own. You can only say so much."

Asked by Russ Harris of the *Philadelphia Inquirer* if Roger could be the best Turcotte of them all, Rudy, with a grin, says, "Sure."

Then he pauses. "Seriously, it's too early to say. My brothers all hope he is better than all of us. He's looked really good to me. I hope he has continued success."

He does. Roger wins 70 races at Keystone. And they certainly aren't all with favorites. If you bet just $2 on Roger, you would be up $108.20 — tops among all of Keystone's riders.

Ron and Gae hold a housewarming party at their new home on Long Island in Oyster Bay Cove. The Turcottes visit from New Brunswick, and all the big owners and trainers are there. So is Ron's agent, Joe Shea.

Someone asks if there are any more Turcotte jockeys in the making.

"Well, this one will never make a rider," Shea says, pointing to Yves, 13, who already weighs 135 pounds. "The only thing he'll ride is an elephant."

Tearing up, Yves runs upstairs.

Angry, Yves devises a scheme. He is going to turn the dogs, including a full-grown Great Dane, on Shea.

"I'll teach him," Yves says to his brother Gaetan. "Let's see how this Joe Shea likes dogs."

"Don't," says Gaetan. "You'll just make Mom and Dad mad."

"So what? Did you hear what he said to me?" answers Yves, whose face is still red with rage.

"Yeah, I heard it. Just don't do it."

"Okay. But if he says one more thing to me, I'm getting the dogs."

Yves hasn't told anyone, but he too, despite his size, wants to be a jockey.

A few weeks later, another party takes place.

Buoyed by his success, Roger hosts a farewell party for fellow riders, officials, media and friends in the backstretch at Bowie; he is going to try New York again.

It pays off early, as he quickly wins 25 races at Aqueduct. But then, just as quickly, he runs afoul of the stewards and gets three riding suspensions in short order. Suddenly his opportunities diminish. Roger is nervous.

Then his phone rings. One of the United States' top trainers, Buddy Delp, is calling. Delp has horses in both Delaware and New Jersey. He needs a go-to rider. He asks Roger if he is interested. Roger can't say yes fast enough. He can't wait to get out of New York.

"After those suspensions, I wasn't riding that much in New York and although I didn't like to leave, I felt it would be best for my career to come here," says Roger on his arrival in Delaware. "I like working with Mr. Delp. It helps to work the same horses you'll ride. Then you know how they will react. All I do is ride the horses like he tells me and with very few exceptions they run just like he says they would."

Rudy is also riding in Delaware.

"The one thing people don't realize is that Roger is my brother before and after the race. But when we're in the gate and the man says 'go' I don't have any relatives," says Rudy, whose agent, Karl Block, agrees to take on Roger too.

Block and Roger are a lethal combination. Roger wins three races on Delaware's May 24 opening day card. Then five more on June 4. Two days later, he wins the feature. In just nine days, he has 25 wins and leads Delaware's jockey standings.

Roger is happy. So is Delp.

"Roger has probably given us at least 15 extra wins through his riding ability and his weight advantage," says Delp, referring to the five-pound break Roger gets. "Over many races, I'm sure we've had several that we have won by a nose or head only because of the weight advantage."

They both keep rolling. Roger breaks Chris McCarron's seemingly untouchable record of 103 wins for the 62-day meet by one. He does it in style, winning three races on August 10, the final day of the Delaware meet.

By the end of 1975, Roger has won 290 races — the most by any apprentice in North America. He also has 275 seconds and 199 thirds from 1,548 mounts, which earn $1.5 million — all staggering numbers.

Yet, somehow, some way, Roger is not awarded the prestigious Eclipse Award as North America's top apprentice. Instead, the honor goes to Jimmy Edwards, who won one less race than Roger.

Roger is frothed. He needs a stiff drink. Vodka. With water or orange juice.

Noel needs a drink as well. Struggling with his weight, he only won 17 races in all of 1975.

There are no problems for Ron and Rudy this year. Ron wins 171 races for purse earnings of $2,115,991; Rudy has his best year ever, winning 232 races, with his mounts earning $1,268,727.

Expecting to continue his success, Roger loses his apprentice allowance two days into 1976. Then he gets a five-day suspension. To many trainers, getting the weight advantage is huge, and many apprentices struggle to get mounts when they lose the bug.

Roger is one of the victims.

"I came back from my suspension an older rider and every-body quickly forgot about me," he says of the trainers who abandoned him, giving their best horses to established jockeys or the latest hot apprentice.

Unable to accept this, he starts drinking heavily. It catches up to him like a thoroughbred that refuses to quit. He drinks to forget his worries, but the knifing reality of the mornings after only reveal more worries, more reasons to drink.

He is arrested for drinking and driving and winds up in the hospital with a pancreas infection. Doctors tell him if he keeps drinking, he has a year to live. Only 21, but drinking since he was 14, Roger doesn't listen.

Struggling with his weight more than ever, Noel, 32, starts the 1976 season winless in 48 races.

On April 13, exactly 12 years to the day that he won his first race, Noel steps on the scales in the jockeys' room at Woodbine and winces as the needle hits 117 pounds.

He turns to fellow jockey John LeBlanc and hesitantly says, "John, you know what I'm going to do? I'm quitting."

Noel steps off the scale and goes upstairs and tells his valet to pack his tack.

"One hundred and seventeen pounds," he grimaces. "That means I'd be riding at 121 pounds with the tack, and you don't get too many mounts doing that. I'm fighting the weight every day and I'm only getting on a couple of mounts a day. I'm going to gallop horses in the mornings for Carl Chapman and see if I can get my weight down. Maybe if I'm relaxed and not fighting it all the time, the weight will come off easier.

"But for now, that's it. The last two years have been way too difficult."

A few weeks after he retires, Noel weighs 138 pounds.

After an argument, Delp stops using Roger. Then, after another argument, Roger also fires Block, his agent, which sends Roger taking his tack from Keystone to Maryland, then New Jersey, then Delaware, then Chicago and then Toronto. Next, in Detroit, he wins the Grosse Pointe Handicap aboard Sam's Own.

"I've been all over," says Roger.

But he can't find a home.

He does, however, find the winner's circle on August 14 in Edmonton's $75,000 Canadian Derby with Jean-Louis Levesque's one-eyed Laissez Passer.

Realizing there is no speed in the race and confident he has the best horse, Roger sends Laissez Passer, who usually comes from behind, hard from the gate. He forces the pace set by Mike Kaye and overtakes that horse with a half a mile left. He wins by 11 lengths, wiping the hearts off his challenger's hooves.

"Biggest race I've ever won," says Roger, who ends 1976 with 54 wins — a fifth as many as he won last season.

For Ron, 1976 is one of his best years.

He wins 237 races, including six in a row at Aqueduct on March 5, for purse earnings of $2,903,539, thanks in large part to winning 11 lucrative stakes: the Bay Shore, Jennings Handicap, Stymie, American Derby, Hill Prince, Tidal, Diana, Aqueduct Handicap, Busanda, Bowling Green and the Red Smith.

It is the most money Ron has won since his spectacular 1973 season.

Rudy tops 100 wins and $1 million in prizes one more time.

The calendar flips to 1977. Almost as fast as he rose to the top, Roger plummets, winning just 12 races the entire year, all in Toronto. Those mounts earn only $43,154.

Losing the bug was critical, but a much bigger problem is the bottle.

"I didn't need an excuse to drink," he tells the *Edmonton Journal*. "Drinking is a way of life in horse racing. If you are going bad, you drink to feel good. If you're winning you drink to celebrate.

"After a while, I needed more and more booze to start feeling good. And in the end, I was thinking more about drinking after the races than I was about the races themselves.

"Alcoholism is a disease that eats at you. It gets hold of your mind and doesn't want to let go. It's especially hard at a racetrack where just about everybody drinks."

Staying out until very late, he is in no shape to gallop horses in the morning. The more he drinks, the fewer mounts he gets. Used to riding in eight or nine races a day, he is now riding in only one or two. To close out the year he never finishes better than seventh with his last 11 mounts.

Roger's dreams become nightmares. Wray Lawrence, a Toronto trainer and friend, tells him: "You're dead. You've got to go someplace else."

"Yeah, but where?" Roger answers.

"Try Alberta," says Lawrence. "You won the Canadian Derby there. They'll remember that. And everyone knows you were the leading apprentice rider in North America.

"I'm going to Alberta myself. You may as well come with me."

On September 23, after going to acupuncture twice a week, Noel makes a comeback.

"I lost 10 pounds since I got the needles. I'm sorry I didn't start the therapy sooner," he says. "It feels good to be back. It feels like I'm starting all over again."

It is a long road back though. For the 1977 season, Noel only has 37 mounts; he wins five of them, earning just $9,476 in his purses.

While Roger and Noel struggle, Ron wins 155 races, 10 stakes and $2,388,296.

Rudy triumphs 145 times with his mounts, earning $881,806.

Chapter 28

Roger, dispirited and angry, leaves Toronto and brings his tack to Alberta in the summer of 1978. But he keeps the bottle close to his side, and the memory of his 1976 Canadian Derby triumph isn't enough to make people forget about his drinking.

One of the first mounts Roger takes in Alberta is for Lawrence. But Roger is still so drunk from the night before that he almost falls off. With the horse's owners, Dave Carnie and James Saunders witnessing it, Lawrence fires Roger.

"I feel bad," says Lawrence. "But I've got no choice. It's either you or me."

Roger merely shrugs.

"Aw, don't worry about it. I'm working a horse for Alan Payne. He'll win."

As prophesied, the horse wins and pays $27. The barn bets; Roger never bets a dime. He seldom did.

"Roger was the best tout," says his new agent, Ken Deines.

"When he tells you a horse would win, it invariably wins. It doesn't matter what the odds are. He would get out front, suck in the other riders to think he is going too fast and goes wire to wire."

One of the few times he did bet was on Arctic Point, a horse trained by Lee Haynes. Despite the horse's dismal record, Roger bet $20 to win. The horse paid $88 for every $2 and won by seven lengths. The money was gone in a few weeks.

Consumed not only by alcohol but by a talent he feels he has wasted and the financial security and rewards he should have reaped along the way, Roger invests in a condominium and is building a house.

He can't afford either.

May 3, 1978, wallows gray over the Pimlico racetrack in Baltimore, the sun fighting but failing to pierce the pewter clouds.

It is just another race, the second event on the card, at just another track. The field of half-ton racehorses speeding along at 36 miles per hour is just leaving the turn for home; soon they will be in the stretch, making one more drive for one more finish line.

But then, in a heartbeat, it turns sideways.

Rudy is challenging for the lead when, without warning, his horse, Easy Edith, breaks her left front leg just below the knee and crashes to the ground.

It is 1:37 p.m.

Robert Pineda, who is right behind riding Easter Bunny Mine, has no time to react. His mount stumbles over the fallen horse. Pineda is catapulted 10 feet in the air. His head strikes the ground first.

Two other horses can't avoid Pineda or Easter Bunny Mine. Countess G., ridden by James Thornton, and Friendly Emma, with F.W. Kratz aboard, fall as well. Countess G. strikes Pineda in the head with one of its legs, leaving a deep crease in his helmet.

Lying motionless on the ground, Pineda is bleeding through his ears and mouth.

To all in attendance, the gray sky seems to darken even more.

Pineda, Rudy and Thornton are all rushed to Sinai Hospital; Kratz escapes uninjured.

Less than an hour later, Pineda, 25, who has been riding for eight years and has won nearly 2,000 races, is dead of head and multiple internal injuries.

Rudy is lucky. He only breaks his collarbone — for a third time — and dislocates a shoulder.

Thornton also escapes. He is listed in serious condition with a "relatively minor fracture of the second vertebra of the neck, and chest injuries." He is in the intensive-care unit as a precaution.

"How's Pineda?" Rudy keeps asking a nurse while lying on a stretcher. Pineda lies on the other side of a closed blue curtain.

She doesn't reply.

"Somebody please tell me," Rudy pleads.

Still no response.

"Does he have a 50 percent chance?" Rudy asks.

Silence.

"Less than 40?"

At that point, another nurse answers. "Mr. Turcotte, I don't know how to bring this up ... "

"Is Bobby not going to make it?"

The second nurse shakes her head.

"Are you telling me he passed away?"

"Yes," she says solemnly. "I hope you don't blame yourself."

"Why should I?" Rudy says immediately. "A horse broke a leg. I'm not blaming myself. It's not my fault that a horse broke its leg. It's part of racing."

Statistics show that a jockey falls once every 240 rides. Since 1940, on average, once every two years a jockey dies of injuries sustained in a race.

Virtually every day a jockey gets injured somewhere. It is a chilling reminder of why horse racing is the world's most dangerous sport.

Tragedy was no stranger to the Pineda family — Catalina Pineda and her husband, Sixto, and their nine children, including Robert.

Three and a half years earlier, on January 18, 1975, another son, Alvaro, 29, a jockey who won 2,731 races, was also killed when his mount, Austin Mittler, reared up and struck Alvaro's head against the metal starting gate.

"There was so much blood; it was like somebody turned on a hose," said jockey Fernando Toro, who was in the gate just to the outside of Alvaro.

After the ambulance took Alvaro away, Austin Mittler was scratched, the horses were reloaded, and they ran the race.

Another Pineda brother, Tito, died in a house fire. A fourth brother, Jorge, was killed in a robbery at his home in Louisville, Kentucky.

The day he died, Robert Pineda was paid $30 for a losing jock mount. From that, $3.50 was deducted by the Jockeys' Guild to pay for medical and life insurance. The valet got $3, which left $23.50.

The day after, the infield flag flies at half-mast at Pimlico, and the jockeys gather in the winner's circle for a moment of silence.

The races go on. They always do.

One day ends. The next one begins.

Two weeks after Pineda died, Ron is involved in a spill on May 16 at Edmonton's Northlands Park, where he is riding in a special promotional appearance.

With his brother Aurele in the stands watching, Ron's mount, Kid Roque, just leaving the clubhouse turn on a rainy day on the card's seventh race, snaps both his front legs. Ron falls and puddles into the mud. He is taken to the Royal Alexandra Hospital with three broken ribs and a punctured lung.

The previous night, after learning that hard-luck Ron Burrell had broken his collarbone, Ron donated his winning jock mount from Antrim Lad that day to Burrell.

A few years earlier, Burrell shattered his cheekbones, pushed his nose flush against the side of his face, knocked out all but three of his teeth, shattered his jaw and smashed one eye socket.

Burrell is out of action for only two weeks.

"Jeff! Hey! Hey! Jeff! Jeff!" yells Ron. "Hey, Jeff look ... "

Ron never gets to finish.

The cries get lost in the blue skies over Belmont Park on July 13.

Ron is aboard Flag of Leyte Gulf in the day's eighth race — a small five-horse feature for three-year-old fillies.

To his left, jockey Jeff Fell continues to drift directly into his path with Small Raja, who started from post two. To his outside are the heels of Walter Malone, who started from post four. They are three abreast. The field is only about 30 yards out of the gate.

Ron is pulling hard on his reins. But it is to no avail. Small Raja nudges Flag of Leyte Gulf to his right. The next thing anyone hears is the clicking of heels and then the heavy *whomp* of Flag of Leyte Gulf hitting the ground headfirst, hurling Turcotte over its shoulders like a catapult.

Ron lands high on his own shoulders and back, somersaulting twice before he comes to a stop in the fetal position. He can taste the blood from biting his tongue.

The wind knocked out of him, the first thing Ron does is reach for his stomach. It feels like he is pushing in a bag of water. Then he reaches down and touches his legs. They do not feel like his own.

Outrider Bobby Barberra is the first to come to Ron's assistance. After jumping off his pony Barberra bends over Ron's limp body.

"You alright, Ronnie?" says Barberra. "You want me to move you?"

"No," Ron says sternly. "My back is broken. I'm paralyzed."

Ron's 20,281st mount is his last. He'll never add to his 3,032 wins or his career earnings of almost $30 million, which at this time are eighth-highest in racing history.

In a sport that is so dangerous an ambulance is always on-site, the EMTs know immediately this fall is serious. They quickly load Ron onto a stretcher. Sirens wailing, they rush him to the Long Island Jewish Medical Center in New Hyde Park just minutes away. Three hours later, when the severity of the injury is apparent, another ambulance takes him to the New York University Medical Center in Manhattan.

Gae, having received a phone call from the track, is in the back of the second ambulance with her husband, who is drenched in sweat. She wipes away Ron's never-ending perspiration with a towel that she has to keep wringing out. For the first time, Turcotte is in excruciating pain.

"I think I'm paralyzed," Ron says to Gae.

"The feeling will come back," Gae says, trying to reassure.

X-rays confirm the worst. In the mid-thoracic region, approximately opposite the sternum, two vertebrae are crushed. Two others are fractured, including the sixth thoracic vertebra that impinges on his spinal column, which is also fractured and displaced. The broken vertebrae have severed nerves, causing the paralysis.

The clock reads 1:27 a.m. when Ron signs the papers permitting Dr. Vallo Benjamin, a neurosurgeon, and Dr. Gordon Engler, an orthopedic surgeon, to proceed with the operation.

"If there is any chance, we'll give it to you," says Engler as Ron is wheeled into the operating room.

Four hours of surgery fuse the sixth through to the 10th thoracic vertebrae to keep them erect while relieving the pressure on the spinal column. Two 10-inch stainless-steel rods to realign, support and stabilize the spine are inserted. A bone graft from the back of his pelvis is fused onto his spine, where the broken sixth vertebra is exerting pressure on his spinal column and impeding the back-and-forth flow of spinal fluids.

The surgery is a success. But Ron will never walk again.

Remarkably, even though Small Raja wins the race, there is no inquiry into the accident. In virtually every race where an accident occurs, the stewards at least post the inquiry sign and review the race.

Not this time.

Trembling, Gae phones Rose.

"Ron is hurt," Gae says softly between tears. "He was in an accident today in New York."

Rose grabs a chair to sit down.

"How badly?" Rose asks.

"It's bad," Gae answers. "He's paralyzed."

"Lord, Jesus, Mary," Rose says, quivering.

One of her children getting hurt has always been her nightmare. Especially one of the jockeys. She knows only too well the dangers of horse racing. She knows about Rudy getting into the spill that caused the death of Robert Pineda. She knows about Ron's injury in Edmonton.

She prays several times a day, pleading that God keeps them safe.

"Please don't take Ronnie," Rose asks after she limply hangs up the phone.

That night, Yves is working his 12-hour shift at McCain Foods in Grand Falls, where he loads a tractor trailer with 30-pound boxes of french fries for $2.45 an hour. After his shift, he comes home to find his mother weeping at the kitchen table.

"Mom. What's wrong?"

"Ronnie was hurt in New York today," she says. "He's paralyzed."

Shocked, Yves stands still for a few minutes. "What happened?" he finally says.

"I don't know. A horse he was riding fell. So did Ronnie," she says, gathering herself. "Gae is in the hospital with him. He spent four hours in surgery."

Yves lets the horror sink in.

"It'll be okay, Mama," he says, putting his arms around his mother's shuddering shoulders. "Ron is strong. He'll pull through."

Then Yves tells his mother the secret he has kept tightly bottled up inside.

"Mama, I'm going to take his place. I want to be a jockey too. It's what I've wanted for a long time. One Turcotte is gone. Another has to take his place."

"No, Yves. No," says Rose, raising her voice. "Did you not just hear what I told you about Ronnie? It's too dangerous. You told me you were going to go to college next year and learn to be an accountant."

"I did, Mama. But deep down, I've always wanted to be a jockey. I think about it every day. I've thought about it for years. You're the first person I've told. I didn't want anybody else to know. Now my mind is made up for good."

"But you're too heavy to be a jockey," his mother implores. "You weigh 140 pounds. I don't know much about horse racing, but I know jockeys have to be skinny. Look at your shoulders and your chest. You're too heavy."

"I can lose the weight. I've been reading about jockeys losing weight. They do it all the time. I'll just stop eating as much. I'll exercise. Ronnie weighed 130 pounds when he decided to be a jockey."

"No, Yves. Please don't. Anyway, I can't talk to you about that now. I'm too frightened. This is all too much right now. Come. Let's pray for Ronnie."

Yves prays, but he continues to dream.

On July 22, Ron's 37th birthday, his condition worsens. Meningitis, an inflammation of the fluid and membranes surrounding the brain and spinal cord, sets in. Twenty to 50 percent of meningitis cases are fatal. Even those who survive are left with brain damage.

Even though ice is packed around him, Ron begins to sweat heavily again, soaking his pillow. The excruciating pain returns as well, shattering his sleep. Even shots of Demerol and Codeine have little effect.

Next, a swelling of blood oozes and weeps through the stitches. He becomes delirious.

"What do I do now?" he suddenly murmurs.

"Nothing," answers Gae. "Just rest."

"Get a hot walker and blow the horse out," he says, believing he is back at the track.

"Okay," says Gae, who laughs for the first time in a long while. "Go back to sleep."

"I've got a wife and four kids; I can't give up."

"Hang in there," says Gae. She has been with Ron almost every hour of every day since the accident.

Edward Cooperman, his tenacious lawyer and friend, calls Gae an angel sent from God to minister to Ron.

Joe Shea, who continues to work as an agent for other jockeys, says of Gae: "If sainthood were measured by attitude, she'd be canonized."

Noel is there almost all of the time. Still struggling with his weight, and not getting a single win in just 22 mounts, he retires yet another time and drives with Camille from Toronto to New York. Camille stays a week; Noel, who has just separated from his wife, Daphne, stays with Gae and Ron for an entire year. Noel even takes a course in physical therapy so that he can help out more.

For a few days, Ron stabilizes. But five days later, his condition deteriorates again. The headaches worsen. His neck stiffens, and his temperature soars. For days, he is unable to speak. He gets bladder and liver infections, experiences violent back spasms.

With his life in jeopardy, he is given Last Rites by a priest who roams the hallways outside Ron's hospital room.

"We can't keep the meningitis down," Dr. Engler tells Gae. "We need to operate again. We suspect the rods are the problem. We're going to have to remove them."

The second operation takes place on July 31. At the same time, they debride the bone graft. Soon after, the meningitis subsides.

A day later, Rudy drives to New York to see Ron.

"I walked into the hospital and the first thing he does is to try to make me feel good," Rudy tells Noel. "He wanted to cheer me up. God, he's brave. He's in a lot of pain. I remember thinking that he couldn't be as bad off as they said. It hit me when I read in a paper that he couldn't feel anything below his chest. And then I saw him lying there." Throughout August, Ron calls the university hospital home. On September 5, he has recovered sufficiently to be transferred to the New York University Medical Center's Institute of Rehabilitation Medicine — the Rusk Institute, where he begins his long rehabilitation.

His once powerful arms have withered from inactivity. He has lost almost 20 pounds. But the exercise program, especially a lat bar cable-pulley machine, quickly helps rebuild his arms and back latissimus dorsi muscles — the latter the muscles just under the armpits, which spread across and down the back.

"He started on the lat bar using 20-pound weights," says Gene Giamarino, a physical therapist at the Rusk Institute. "In a week, he was up to 40 pounds. Now he's at 50 pounds; he'll go to 60 pounds soon.

"He's a very hard worker. He's an athlete. He knows how to push himself."

Ron is learning to adapt mentally and physically to life in a wheelchair, but pain is still his daily uninvited companion.

He has to learn how to dress and wash all over again. He has to learn how to move from his bed to his wheelchair and back.

Essentially, he has to relearn how to live.

Ron accomplishes in three months what would normally take six.

"This was the most superbly conditioned athlete I ever saw," says Cooperman. "The man was an absolute animal. He is the microscopic version of the Incredible Hulk."

Other people would complain and bemoan their fate. Not Ron Turcotte.

"I'm paralyzed and I have to face that," he says to everyone who calls or visits. "That's all there is to it. There's no sense in brooding about it.

"If you'd asked me before I got hurt, I would have told you 'No, I wouldn't be able to cope.' But God gave me the strength to do it. God gave me the power to cope."

In an interview with racing writer Bill Nack, Ron says: "I've got things to learn. I know that — things to learn as far as getting in and out of the chair. Getting in and out of a car. Being able to wheel that chair around ... It's important to me to get up on my own two feet.

"I just know you've gotta believe to make it anywhere. If you don't believe in yourself, who's gonna believe in you, in your ability.

"I always felt I could ride as good as anybody and better than most. If that's overstating it, I don't know, I apologize, but that was my belief throughout the time I rode. I always believed if it could be done I could do it. Challenge never bothered me.

"What can I be bitter at? Angry at who, at what? It's not the world's fault ...

"So why would I feel anger? I get aggravated and frustrated sometimes trying to do something I can't do ...

"I broke my back. Yeah, I used to run around with six legs, the horse's four and my two and now I've got none ...

"The sad part, the thing I'll miss, is the riding. I love riding. I love being on a horse.

"I'm lucky to be alive, and where there is life there is hope.

"The doctors all say I have no chance of walking again. I don't believe that. Doctors are human; they make mistakes. They can't see what is inside my spinal cord."

The doctors also can't look inside Ron's amazingly strong and indomitable resolve.

"The drive he has, the will to win — that wasn't injured by the accident, and it must play a part in his rehabilitation," says Engler. "I would imagine that he had a tough time growing up: all that energy and ability against all forms of adversity. It helped. I've had patients commit suicide because of problems like this. I've had other people drop out of the world, become recluses. And I've had people like Ron with a will to live and a will to succeed that was there before the accident. A lesser man would have given up."

"I'll walk out of here," vows Ron.

Still going strong, Rudy finishes second — by just three wins — to Chris McCarron in the jockey standings at Bowie, Maryland, in 1978 and ends the year with 128 winners for purses of $792,406.

Among his wins are the $57,050 Gettysburg Handicap with Resound at Pennsylvania's Keystone when he split horses twice to win by a nose; the Maryland Futurity, the richest race for Maryland-breds at Laurel, going wire to wire with Skate; the Meadows Purse; the Mt. Calvert at Bowie; and the W.A. Green Handicap at Rockingham Park, New Hampshire, with Niteangel.

Roger, however, is still in a deepening stupor. Despite winning with his first Alberta mount, his move west is fruitless. In all of 1978, he only wins 24 races from 246 mounts. Typically, Roger leaves a few ounces in the bottle at night so he can have a drink first thing the next morning. Come 10 a.m., Roger is usually standing outside waiting for the liquor stores to open.

Noel isn't doing any better. Mostly galloping horses in the mornings, he rides 22 horses in the afternoons. He has no wins, no seconds and one third for total earnings of $468.

Chapter 29

Two days before Christmas 1978, Ron gets the best present of all. Five months after the accident he is allowed to go home from hospital.

Noel picks him up in Ron's car, another new El Dorado Cadillac, which has been fitted to be completely hand-driven.

The next day Ron, Noel and Al Schwizer, a former jockey, who visited Ron daily in the hospital to play cards, go hunting on Long Island. With Ron shooting through a car window, they bag three deer. A big smile finally creases Ron's face.

It is April 6, 1979. Ron's attorneys file a $100 million suit against Jeff Fell, the jockey of Small Raja, for careless riding. Also named in the suit are David P. Reynolds, the owner of Small Raja, the New York Racing Association, two stewards, the Jockey Club and the Racing Commission for not enforcing rules that strictly prohibit reckless riding or any racing infractions despite numerous warnings. The suit alleges the stewards "failed to maintain compliance with the rules of racing which resulted in Ron's injuries." It also alleges Fell was "a dangerous rider" and was negligent in his riding of Small Raja.

Ron, who has no voluntary reflexes below the waist, didn't want to sue but lawyer Edward Cooperman convinced him otherwise.

What rankles Turcotte the most is there was no inquiry into the race.

"They didn't even look at the race," Ron tells Cooperman. "The winner was the one that dropped me, and they didn't do a thing about it. They took down Secretariat for something he didn't do. But they didn't even look at a spill where somebody was injured for life. If nothing else, I hope my lawsuit helps prevent careless riding. I feel my incident could have been avoided if (Fell) had picked up his head and straightened his horse out. For six months before my accident, the stewards had been too lenient. There were two accidents before mine and there was no inquiry. When that happens, the riders get bold and that's when the trouble starts."

The suit is dismissed.

On June 28 Ron is honored as Canada's Horse Racing Man of the Year.

When you're at the top, the bottom seems an eternity away. It is like looking through binoculars the wrong way.

That is Roger Turcotte's story.

From being North America's leading apprentice jockey and sought by trainers and owners everywhere in 1975, just four years later Roger is a forgotten soul.

The reason is Roger's pernicious Daily Double: weight and drinking problems.

Some days Roger shows up late in the morning in a sport that begins each day around 5 a.m. with grooms and trainers feeding their horses, cleaning stalls and getting the horses ready to gallop or work against a stopwatch.

Some days, hungover from the night before, Roger doesn't show up at all.

"If you don't help yourself, neither I nor anyone else can help you," says his girlfriend, Denise (Ellen) Pierson, whom Roger met last summer in Calgary. "If you aren't around in the mornings you don't get to ride in the afternoons."

"I'll be fine," snaps Roger. "Don't tell me how to live my life."

"You drink too much, and you are getting too heavy. Nobody wants to ride you anymore."

"I don't even care if I don't ride anymore," is Roger's cold retort and far from the truth.

From the time Ron, who is 14 years older than Roger, became Canada's leading rider, a dozen years before Secretariat came along, Roger had only wanted one thing: to be a jockey.

Some alcoholics can fool people. They can get around looking like they are sober. Not Roger. When Roger is drunk, which is most days, he slurs his words and can't walk straight.

He hangs out in the bars at Calgary's Stampede Park or at Edmonton Northlands' Inner Rail and Silver Slipper, where trainers and owners, shaking their heads, can see him drinking.

One of the few trainers who still rides him is Red Robertson, one of Roger's drinking buddies.

"It doesn't matter to Roger if it's a $3,000 claimer or a stake horse," Robertson says. "He rides harder for a man with a small stable than one with a big stable."

But Robertson along with three other trainers with small stables, drinking pals Mark Zimmer, Ed Huckabee and Bill Shapka, are anomalies.

One time at Trout Springs, a half-mile B circuit track west of Calgary, Roger went fishing in the track's infield pond. Hours later they found him, laughing and giggling, with an empty vodka bottle and 30 trout lying beside him.

Even with all of Roger's talent, he doesn't get to show it. Besides being frequently drunk, his weight is up to 120 pounds. When the three and a half pounds of boots, girth and saddle are added to his total weight, Roger can't ride a horse unless it is assigned more than 123 pounds. It is much too heavy.

As the old racing axiom goes, "Weight will stop a train," and Roger is tied to the caboose.

In mid-August, on a two-week vacation from McCain Foods, Yves goes to Calgary to visit Roger and see him ride.

But that doesn't happen very often.

Seeing Roger drink is hard on Yves. Roger seemed destined to be as good as Ron and Rudy. Instead, Yves finds a brother who is seldom sober.

"You've got to quit drinking," he tells Roger. "You've got too much talent. I read all the stories about you in 1975. I read about your win in the Canadian Derby. You were great. Now you are hardly riding at all. You're going to kill yourself if you keep this up."

Yves soon grows impatient and languid. This vacation, which he had looked forward to for months, isn't anything like he had planned. He had looked up to Roger in the same way he had quietly admired Ron and Rudy and Noel.

"I'm bored, Roger," says Yves. "I wish I had never come out here. I want to go home."

"No, don't do that. Don't leave," says Roger, who seems to constantly be combing his thick black hair. "Why don't I get you a job. It'll keep you busy."

"What kind of a job?" answers Yves.

"I don't know but trainers are always looking for good help. Let me ask around."

The next day, Yves finds himself working for trainer Skip Marsh, mucking out stalls, rubbing horses' legs with liniment, brushing their coats and hot-walking horses after they have run or worked.

A week later, Marsh stuffs five $50 bills into Yves' hand.

Yves' face glows. He runs to find his brother.

"Roger. Roger. Skip just paid me $250. For just a week of work. The biggest cheque I ever got from McCain was $260. And that was for 60 hours of hard work. Five 12-hour days. From six in the morning to six at night. Here I come to the track at six o'clock in the morning and I'm done by 10. Then all I have to do is come back to the barn after the races and feed and water the horses. This is crazy. I'm going to tell Mom to call McCain and tell them I'm not coming back. I'm going to fly home, get my car and drive back here. I already asked Skip and he said it would be great if I came back."

He doesn't tell Roger what he has told his mother.

"It's destiny," thinks Yves. "I want to ride horses for a living. I want to win races like my brothers. I want the money that Ron and Rudy are making. And here I am at a racetrack. It's set."

Back in New York, Ron and Gae realize their home in Oyster Bay won't suit a man destined to live the rest of his life in a wheelchair. Ron also wants to go back to New Brunswick, where most of his family still live. Always frugal, Ron and Gae had bought 66 acres of land in Drummond back in 1974, and it is there they start to build a sprawling 18-room house. Their new home will have 5-foot-wide hallways, three fireplaces, three garages and massive rooms — especially one that is a museum containing the hundreds of trophies, memorabilia, artifacts and paintings from Ron's amazing career.

While the house is being built, Ron and Gae move in with her mother, who lives nearby.

The dreams of a new house and returning home buoy Ron. But the pain persists.

"Pains in my back and stomach around the rib cage are pretty constant," he tells his doctors. "It wears me down."

Ron's back is a house of cards in a windstorm. Two vertebrae have collapsed to the size of one. He needs a third operation. On August 27, 1979, at Toronto's Mount Sinai Hospital, two steel rods are reinserted to realign, support and stabilize his spine. Doctors also remove several bone fragments and fuse more damaged discs together. Because his back is so damaged, doctors have to cut through his chest to put the rods back in. To do that they remove some ribs and open his sternum.

The operation is a success, but Ron needs to be in a full body cast to recuperate.

Just as they arrived when he was initially injured and paralyzed, letters arrive by the hundreds from around the world. Some are simply addressed: Ron Turcotte, New Brunswick. Somehow, they reach him. The phone never stops ringing either.

"Look at these letters," he says to Gae. "I can't begin to answer them all. I have more friends than I ever dreamed of."

One of the visitors, unexpectedly, is Yves, who has done what he vowed. He flies back to New Brunswick, picks up his car (a big Buick LeSabre Limited that Camille had bought for $800), quits his job at McCain and heads back to Alberta.

But first he stops in Toronto to visit Ron in hospital.

"Brother," smiles Ron. "What are you doing here?"

"Visiting you. What else?"

"What else?" says Ron. "I hear you've got some big plans."

"Me? Naw. I just drove down to see you."

"Don't lie to me, Yves. Mom already told me. She said you've quit your job and you're working for a trainer in Alberta. She said you want to be a jockey."

"She said that? She told you?"

Ron nods his head.

"You want to end up like me?" Ron asks. "I thought you were going to go to school to be an accountant. When did you change your mind? Why did you change your mind?"

"It's something I've wanted for a long time," answers Yves. "I just never told anybody. I knew nobody would believe me."

"So, you're serious then? You want to be a jockey?"

"Yup," is all Yves says.

"You've been walking horses in Alberta. Do you even know how to ride?"

"Nope. Not really. I guess the last time I rode a horse was when I was 8 years old. One of the horses you sent home."

"You're really serious then," says Ron, stone-faced. "I never thought I'd hear that from you. Noel I could see. I knew Rudy was going to be a jockey. It's all he dreamed about. And Roger, that didn't surprise me either. But you? My little brother? When Mom told me about your plans, I didn't believe her. I said, 'No way. Not Yves. He never said anything about wanting to be a jockey.' But here you are. Standing in front of me, saying straight-faced that you want to ride horses."

"I never really got to know you, Ronnie," Yves says. "I was just born when you left New Brunswick, and I was only 13 when you won the Triple Crown with Secretariat. To me it was still like, 'big deal,' so you won the Triple Crown. So what? I didn't know what that meant. But when Noel followed you and then Rudy and then Roger, that's when I realized being a jockey was what I wanted too. I guess horse racing was in my blood and in my genes all along."

"Well, if you like I could make some phone calls. But I don't want you going back to Alberta," says Ron. "Roger's not a good influence and the season is going to end pretty soon. I'll see what I can do. But tell me again. You're really serious about this?"

"Dead serious," says Yves.

"You know you're going to have to lose a lot of weight. It won't be easy. How much do you weigh anyway?"

Yves says nothing.

"Come on. How much do you weigh?"

"About 130," Yves answers, fudging his weight by at least five pounds.

Hesitantly, the next day Ron places a call to Lucien Laurin and tells him about Yves.

"But I'm worried about him. I don't want him to get into the wrong hands. I've always trusted you and I'm trusting you now. Can you give him a job?"

"Anything for you, Ronnie. Anything for you," replies Laurin. "How are you doing anyway?"

"I'm fine. The third operation was a success. I feel much better."

"We had some good times together, Ronnie," says Laurin.

"Yeah, and some ... how shall I say it, some awkward times too. A couple of times I thought you and Mrs. Tweedy were going to fire me. First with Riva Ridge. Then with Secretariat."

"Nah, I would never have let that happen. You know that."

"Well, I was pretty worried. After the Wood Memorial. After the Whitney. After the Woodward."

"I knew there was something wrong after all three of those races. But it didn't seem like you believed me."

"Ronnie ... No. Anyway, that was a long time ago.

"You tell Yves to come to my farm in Holly Hill in South Carolina. I'll look after him.

"Okay, Lucien. Thanks. Remember what you just said: look after him."

"I will, Ronnie. Don't worry about a thing."

The next day it's all set. Yves will work for Laurin.

Yves couldn't be happier as he points his big boat of a car west and heads back to Calgary for the end of the Alberta racing season to work for Marsh again.

A month later, the first week of October 1979, Ron gets out of the Toronto hospital and goes home to New Brunswick. This time to stay.

It is still potato harvesting season — New Brunswick's main crop, with over 20,000 hectares of land designated across the province for growing spuds. Over 250 varieties of seed, table and processing potatoes are grown. Schools start back in August so that children could help unearth the potatoes beginning each September on land they had cleared of weeds and stones and then seeded. To accommodate potato picking season, even the schools closed. Like the rest of the potato pickers, Yves, pitchfork in hand, started his day at 7 a.m. and was still there 11 hours later.

When he was just 5 years old, Yves used a small tomato basket to put the potatoes in. When he was older, he used a bigger basket. Three of those larger baskets would fill one barrel, which stood almost as tall as Yves. For that he got 35 cents a barrel.

One day Yves picked 80 barrels — his personal best. The family record was 100, set by Albert.

"We kept track," says Yves. "We turned it into a competition."

The picked potatoes would then be trucked to McCain's facility, where many of the Turcottes, and more than half the population of Grand Falls, would work. The person doing the hiring at McCain was a neighbor of the Turcottes, so getting a job there was almost a given. The money made picking potatoes would buy the Turcottes clothes for the school year.

The 1979 Alberta thoroughbred racing season ends in early November. For the entire year, Roger only rides 15 horses; he wins on two of them. Leaving Roger behind, Yves gets behind the wheel and drives to South Carolina — a 35-hour, 2,400-mile trip.

Destiny, he thinks again as the miles swish by.

"I don't know how I'm going to lose 25 pounds. I'm not chubby; I'm fat. But I'll do anything to be a jockey, even if I have to starve myself."

Yves barely makes it to Holly Hill. As he drives into the farm with its smart white-picket fence, the driveshaft on his car conks out. Fortunately, one of the gallop boys is handy around cars and fixes it.

Laurin isn't at Holly Hill when Yves arrives; he is in Florida. Instead, Laurin's brother-in-law, Andre Gauthier, a former trainer in New York, and his wife are in charge.

Yves is given an experienced horse to learn how to gallop: Secretariat's famous docile pony Billy Silver, who is now 12 years old and once even had a song written about him.

First, Yves and Billy Silver spend a lot of time in a corral, Yves just getting his balance. Quickly, he is also learning how to gallop Silver on the farm's five-eighths-of-a-mile track.

Soon he is galloping all of the horses, most of which have been sent to Holly Hill to freshen up while Laurin's main string is racing in Florida.

It all goes smoothly, mostly because all of the horses at Holly Hill are well schooled. Even the two-year-olds. All, that is, except for a two-year-old by the name of Stage Door Johnny, a colt with a bad reputation that throws Yves several times.

One time, on a rainy morning, Laurin makes a rare visit.

"Get back on him," Laurin yells as Yves is covered in mud.

"Get back on him?" Yves thinks. "In the five months that I've been in South Carolina, I've probably only talked to Lucien 10 times. Now all he has to say is get back on this crazy horse. Jesus."

On Saturday, January 5, 1980, Roger and Denise, who were living together in a small apartment near Calgary's Stampede Park, get married.

Before they wed, Denise makes Roger promise to quit drinking. But just three months later, Roger starts drinking again with his buddies Robertson, Shapka and Huckabee.

"You promised, Roger," says Denise. "You promised you would quit. I can't live like this. You're out drinking every night. I hardly see you. I want a divorce."

Roger is finally shaken.

"No, don't leave me. I need you. I want to quit. You're the only one who can help me," he says.

Reluctantly, Denise, as she has so many times before, acquiesces.

"Okay. But no more second, third and fourth chances. First, you have to quit hanging out with those so-called friends of yours. Second, there's no liquor in the house. Third, you're going to start getting up in the morning when the racing season starts again. You're going to work, and you're going to work hard."

"Alright," says Roger. "I'll do it. I'll do whatever it takes."

A few days later, on a bitterly cold evening, Roger goes to an Alcoholics Anonymous meeting.

"My name is Roger. And I'm an alcoholic," he says to six strangers gathered around a table.

On the wall behind him hangs a satin scroll with the letters "AA" in bold.

Chapter 30

The "big horse" is the same dewy wish that keeps all those in horse racing going. It is the dream that lures them like a siren's song.

From dusty half-milers in prairie towns to the moneyed white fences and blue fescue of Kentucky, the big horse drives the grooms down on their knees picking mud and straw from hooves in the pouring rain; the trainers, down on their luck with just two horses in their barn — one with ankles the size of grapefruits and the other pathetically slow and clumsy — believing that tomorrow will be different; and the owners, who keep opening their wallets, certain that this yearling sniffing the air in sales arenas is going to be the next Kentucky Derby winner.

The big horse is a stakes horse that will change people's lives as if they had just won the lottery. It is a horse that reporters will write about and fans will cheer for.

The big horse changes everything.

Ron had Secretariat, Riva Ridge and more than a dozen others. Noel had Belle Geste.

But, for all of his many wins Rudy has never had a genuine star. Then 1980 dawns and out of nowhere up pops a strapping, irascible bay colt named Cure the Blues, owned by Bert and Diana Firestone, the Johnson and Johnson heiress, and trained by Bernie Bond. Rudy, with great success, has been riding first call for Bond in Maryland for years, as far back as when he was just starting out as an apprentice. Bond didn't ride bug boys, but he made an exception with Rudy.

Cure the Blues, however, is far from Maryland. The two-year-old is with the Firestones' powerful main string in Florida with their lead trainer, LeRoy Jolley, for the winter. Bond, a sharp dresser with an even sharper tongue and a keen eye for youngsters, trains their second string in Maryland that do not measure up to the Firestones' more promising runners.

After a series of plodding workouts in New York and Florida, high-strung Cure the Blues, who has shown nothing except for a display of rogue behavior, is one of the culls.

It is almost out of desperation that the Firestones send Cure the Blues to Bond, who has won five training titles at Baltimore's Pimlico racetrack and three more at New Jersey's Monmouth Park.

Bond immediately understands why Cure the Blues is sent to him. So does Bond's top groom, Henry Borden.

"Boss, I can't do anything with this horse," an exasperated Borden, who has been a groom for 25 years, tells Bond. "I've never dealt with a horse like him. He doesn't want to let anyone come close to him. You can't even touch his head or his ears. Today I had to chase him all over his stall. All he wants to do is run away or try to bite me. It took me an hour to put his bridle on. I had to take the bridle apart into three separate pieces. I had to put it on one piece at a time. I got so frustrated this morning that I started crying."

"I know," Bond says, shaking his head sadly. "You can't get close to him. He has no confidence in people. If you raise your hand he runs to the back of his stall and cowers. He does everything wrong."

Two days later, after Borden finally gets the bridle on Cure the Blues, Bond sends him out to gallop one more time. But the nightmare continues: Cure the Blues keeps trying to go to the outside fence, turn around and head back to the barn.

A few days later, Bond calls on Rudy to see what he can do. "Try to gallop him a mile. But hang on tight. This is one very nervous, frightened colt."

Rudy doesn't get far. Cure the Blues rears so high that he loses his balance and flips over backward. Fortunately, neither Rudy nor Cure the Blues is injured.

Weeks roll by. There is little improvement, but Bond decides to try to work Cure the Blues in company with a laggard filly named Rossiter.

"Half a mile. See what happens," instructs Bond.

What happens is a disaster. The cheap filly beats Cure the Blues by 10 lengths.

"He was zigzagging all over the place," Rudy tells Bond.

"One horse can't be that slow," says a disgusted Bond.

"He's cantankerous. It took me two months before I could even put a bridle on him," says Bond. "I kept giving him peppermints as a reward when he did something right. Must have cost me a hundred dollars in peppermints. But for some reason I think there's some talent there. We just have to get it out of him."

For Cure the Blues' next workout, Bond puts plastic blinkers on him. Blinkers can help focus a horse by cutting down on what they can see. Some horses see everything: the jockey, the grandstand, the starting gate or even just a bush inside the inner rail. Cure the Blues seems to be just that kind of a horse.

"He watches everything. When a bird flies by, he'll watch the bird," says Bond. "But I love to fool with 2-year-olds. Hit him on the rump two or three times coming out of the gate," he tells Rudy.

Doing what he's told, Rudy guns Cure the Blues out of the gate.

Remarkably, the blinkers work like a marvel. Cure the Blues is all business. He levels out and digs in down the stretch.

Amazed, Bond glances at his stopwatch. Cure the Blues has just worked in 46 seconds flat.

"I almost dropped my watch," says Bond. "Here was a horse who couldn't go a half mile in 52 (seconds), and he went in 46!" Bond says. "I said to Rudy, 'Uh-oh, we got something here.'"

"What a difference," enthuses Rudy after the work with blinkers. "He's still green as grass. But he traveled so much better. I think you're right. Maybe he really is a runner."

The more Cure the Blues works the better he gets. By early April, Cure the Blues' works are so swift, Rudy tells Bond: "Fastest horse I've ever been on. He does things so easily that you don't realize how fast you're going."

On April 16, Cure the Blues makes his much-anticipated debut in Pimlico. His workouts have been so good that he is sent off at 60 cents on the dollar.

Cure the Blues doesn't disappoint. He wins by 10 lengths under a snug hold by Rudy.

"Rudy, I think we have a runner," says Bond, gasping for breath after running down from the grandstand."

But the race is far from perfect.

"He tried to make a right turn with me three times," Rudy tells Bond. "Each time he opened up a couple of lengths he'd swerve to the right. I had to tap him on the nose with the whip a few times. But when I gave him his head turning for home he was like, swoosh. I could hear the track announcer calling off the margins. Two in front. Four. Six. Eight. Ten."

Persistent foot problems and sore shins send Cure the Blues to the sidelines for five months. But when he returns on September 20, it is more of the same. Cure the Blues wins an allowance at Bowie by 10 lengths at odds of 2-5. Again, Rudy doesn't need to force him.

"All business today, boss," says Rudy. "Those blinkers kept his mind to task."

On October 6 Cure the Blues wins another allowance race at Bowie by seven lengths. But Rudy isn't aboard; instead, Bill Passmore rides because Rudy went to Calgary for a Turcotte Day promotion the previous afternoon where he rode with Roger and Noel. An airline strike then prevented him from getting back to Maryland in time for the race.

Yves, preparing to become the fifth Turcotte to be a jockey, also attends the Turcotte celebration in Calgary.

But when Cure the Blues gets his first stakes test on October 13 in the seven-furlong Maryland Million Nursery Stakes, also at Bowie, Bond, without hesitation, names Rudy.

They win by five lengths. The *Daily Racing Form*'s chart line comments are simply "easily" and "much the best."

"This is my ticket to somewhere," Rudy tells himself.

It is now October 25, the day of the $159,360 Grade I Laurel Futurity. Under damp, spitting gray skies the track comes up sloppy.

Going a mile and a sixteenth, it is the first time Cure the Blues has run farther than seven furlongs.

"He's plenty fast alright but can he carry his speed?" Bond asks Rudy.

"Oh, I think so," quickly answers Rudy. "He's been doing everything on his own. I've never even asked him to show speed in the mornings and he's still been black lettering."

Bert Firestone, a hugely successful industrial real estate agent who won the Kentucky Derby earlier in the year with Genuine Risk — the first filly to win the Derby since Regret 65 way back in 1915 — thinks so too. "His dam, Quick Cure, won at a mile and a quarter. And his sire, Stop the Music, who had the misfortune of having to race against Secretariat, sired 46 stakes winners including Temperance Hill, who we all know won the Belmont this summer going a mile and a half," says Firestone. "Bernie told me he thinks Cure the Blues might be the best horse he ever trained."

Watching the earlier races carefully, Bond knows the inside of the track is especially deep and slow.

"Ordinarily I wouldn't rush him. But today we have no choice; we've got to go for the lead," says Bond. "And after you get the lead take him off the rail."

Cure the Blues' opposition for the Laurel Futurity includes Noble Nashua, who ran second to Lord Avie in the Champagne Stakes, and Well Decorated, who was fourth in the same race.

It is also the race that Secretariat won in 1972, defeating Stop the Music. Secretariat won the Laurel Futurity by eight lengths; Cure the Blues, after a brief challenge by Noble Nashau, wins by six and a half. He is eased up midway down the stretch after Rudy looks over his shoulder and sees no one coming.

He pays just $3 to win.

This time the *Daily Racing Form* says "much the best."

"I've been confident that he'd win this race for the past two weeks," Rudy says after dismounting and doing exactly what Bond instructed — taking the lead and then allowing Cure the Blues to drift to the middle of the track. "He handles kindly and I can do anything I want with him."

Cure the Blues' record is now five for five, by a combined 38 1/2 lengths. He is insured for $5 million.

"I don't think we could have won those races without Rudy; if it hadn't been for Rudy he wouldn't be half the horse he is," says Bond. "We babied him. He got confidence."

The Firestones are voted the Eclipse Award as outstanding owners of 1980; Cure the Blues is runner-up to Lord Avie, who won the Young America, Cowdin and Champagne stakes, as the Eclipse winning two-year-old champion.

"Lord Avie beat Noble Nashua by 2 1/4 lengths; Cure the Blues beat Noble Nashua by 13 lengths," says Firestone, miffed that his colt didn't get the championship.

The Laurel Futurity is Cure the Blues' last start of the year. He will be sent to Florida for some rest ahead of preparations for the Triple Crown.

Not wanting to let Cure the Blues get away, Rudy gives up all the potential winners in Maryland and, instead, goes to Florida with the colt at the request of Bert Firestone in December. Firestone promises Rudy that he will pay off his $40,000 mortgage on his three-bedroom house in Laurel if Rudy wins one of the Triple Crown races.

"I've finally got my big horse," Rudy says to himself, dreaming of winning the Triple Crown just as Ron had seven years ago.

Back in Alberta, Roger holds his promise. Although he stops going to AA meetings, he does stop drinking.

"I just said, 'That's it; I'm going to quit. I'm going to do it by myself,'" he tells Pat McMahon of the *Calgary Herald*. "There's only one thing I want to do and that's ride races. And my marriage wasn't going to work if I didn't quit. So, I did."

In 1980 Roger wins 49 races — 47 more than he won in 1979. He also has 71 seconds and 65 thirds. He shows up in the mornings. He is working hard. The old Roger seems to be back.

"People just didn't want to see a drunk ride a horse," he tells the *Edmonton Journal*. "They didn't want to see a guy coming to work with a hangover. Alcoholism is a disease that eats at you. It gets a hold of your mind and doesn't want to let go. It's especially hard at a racetrack where just about everybody drinks. Racing is fun, but it's a hell of a life."

Noel, who didn't ride at all in 1979 when he went to New Brunswick to help Ron, tries another comeback and wins with his first mount, Countess Questoria, on May 2, 1980.

"I feel young," Noel says after the victory. "I'm 37 but I feel like an apprentice just starting out. I'm determined to stick it out."

The next day, Louis Cauz writes in the *Toronto Star*, "It's a long time between drinks."

Noel rides the entire season but only wins two more races.

Working with Chapman all of 1980 in Toronto, Yves hones his riding skills in the mornings. When the Ontario racing season ends in December, Yves goes with Chapman to Maryland, where Chappy will race during the winter and where Yves will gallop for him.

It isn't the trip Yves had planned. In the middle of a blizzard, Yves rides in the back of a van with six horses. One of the horses isn't Chapman's. It's a standardbred that needs to be dropped off at Roosevelt racetrack in New York.

The horse keeps wanting to lie down.

Yves wants to lie down too. In a warm bed.

Teeth chattering, Yves tries to keep warm, surrounding himself with hay bales, but it doesn't work. He is freezing.

Finally, Yves convinces the van driver to let him ride up front in the sleeping compartment.

When the van finally gets to Maryland, all six horses are sick.

Disgusted, Chapman hastily heads right back home to Toronto. Yves calls Rudy, who is riding at Florida's Hialeah racetrack, to tell him what happened.

"Then you might as well come here," says Rudy. "There are plenty of horses here for you to gallop. There are lots of Canadian trainers down here. Noel is down here too. He's galloping lots and even riding a few horses again. His weight is down. You can leave your car in Maryland and drive my car to Hialeah.

"And I've got Cure the Blues to look forward to riding. He's a machine."

Maybe. But, as 1981 arrives, things begin to unravel.

After a lot of anguish, Bond, who doesn't like to travel, decides he doesn't want to leave Maryland and suggests to the Firestones they send Cure the Blues to LeRoy Jolley, who trains the Firestones' first string in New York for the spring, summer and fall meets and then in Florida in the winter. Bond has the Firestones' second string in Maryland, where he stays year-round.

"It's a relief in a way," Bond tells the *Baltimore Sun's* Ross Peddicord. "Training this colt has made me a nervous wreck. I haven't been sleeping at nights. But now I feel better than I have in three months.

"There is the prestige of training a horse like this, but prestige is one thing and frame of mind is another. I'm 63 years old and to tell you the truth I think this horse needs a younger trainer. LeRoy Jolley has been through all of this before, so I think I am doing what is best for the horse."

In appreciation for what Bond has done, the Firestones promise to still give him 10 percent of the Cure the Blues earnings just as if he were still handling the colt. They also promise to give Bond 10 percent of the commission when Cure the Blues is syndicated and retired to stud duty.

Bond's decision worries Rudy. He knows very well that in New York and in Florida, Jolley's go-to rider is Jacinto Vasquez, who won both the 1980 Kentucky Derby for him with Genuine Risk and the 1975 Derby with Foolish Pleasure — both horses owned by the Firestones. The questions about who will ride Cure the Blues in Florida abound.

"You hear all sorts of rumors," Bert Firestone tells the *Baltimore Sun* on January 8, 1981. "As for Rudy, I like him. I recommended that he come to Florida. Rudy is the only one who gets on the horse. He also breezes, even gallops other horses for us. But I'm not the trainer. I won't tell LeRoy what to do. No decision has been made on who is going to ride and who is not going to ride."

This is the first domino to fall for Rudy.

The second comes on February 27, when the cerebral Jolley replaces Rudy with Ray McKenzie as Cure the Blues' gallop boy. Jolley's answer to why he chose McKenzie is because he wants a heavier rider in the mornings.

Even just a few days before Cure the Blues will make his first start of 1981 in an allowance race on March 26 at Hialeah racetrack, Rudy still doesn't know his fate.

"I don't know who is going to ride him," Rudy tells reporters. "I haven't asked LeRoy if I'm going to ride him. I came down here to be with the horse, but I don't know if I am going to ride him on Thursday."

Jolley, who hates to lose and sulks and throws tantrums when he does, says he isn't sure either.

"I'll give you an honest answer that you won't believe," he says in his slow and soft manner. "I haven't made up my mind. I know it's a late moment but I'm still undecided."

The next day it is Firestone, not Jolley, who breaks the news to Rudy: Vasquez has the mount. Rudy is crushed.

"It's the hardest thing I ever had to do," Firestone tells Rudy. "I asked you to come to Florida. My wife and I both really like you and we appreciate everything you've done for us. We both wanted you to keep riding him. But it's LeRoy's decision. It's a decision the trainer has to make. Not me.

"I'm really sorry. But the deal I made with you still stands. If Cure the Blues wins the Kentucky Derby, Preakness or Belmont I'll still pay off your mortgage. I'll sit down that day and write you a cheque."

Rudy feels like crying — or throwing up.

"I galloped Blues for about a month and then LeRoy took me off," Rudy tells the media, smoking one Marlboro after another, lighting a new one before the first one is even finished. "Maybe I should have realized I was off even then. I didn't say anything to Mr. Jolley because he's a professional trainer and I knew if he wanted to tell me something he would. But he never said anything.

"I began hearing this about two weeks ago, but I still decided to wait until I heard it from someone who knew. Look, it's tough to lose mounts like this. You ride a horse like this and things begin to happen to you. What can I say?

"I really got to love that horse.

"I've got no respect for Jolley."

Rudy returns to Maryland to be with Bond again. Yves goes with him.

Losing the mount hits Rudy even harder when Cure the Blues, with Vasquez aboard, wins his seasonal debut on March 26 at Hialeah by five lengths.

Rudy needs a drink. And then a few more.

Rudy could talk himself onto a good stakes horse and then talk himself right off the horse too. This time his mouth had nothing to do with it.

"That should have been me in the saddle," he tells Yves, who is now living with Rudy and his wife in Maryland. "Damn Jolley."

Cure the Blues, however, doesn't win again. With Vasquez aboard, Cure the Blues gets into a speed duel with Proud Appeal and finishes second, by a nose, in the April 5 Gotham.

The Gotham fractions are ridiculous — half a mile in 45 seconds; three-quarters in 1:08 4/5, with the mile snapping shut in an extraordinary 1:33 1/5.

"The worst-ridden horse I've ever seen," Bond tells Rudy, after the way-too-fast fractions. "I'm sorry I let you down. If I was still training the horse and you were riding, Cure the Blues would have won. You would never have ridden the horse like that."

"And if you were still training him, he wouldn't have run like that," answers Rudy. "Jolley changed his training completely."

The unraveling of Cure the Blues continues. Two weeks later in the Wood Memorial, Cure the Blues is sent off as the 1-5 favorite. In another all-or-nothing, balls-to-the-wall expedition, Cure the Blues takes the lead but then tires badly and gets trounced. In the stretch, Cure the Blues slows almost to a walk.

Now it is Vasquez who gets taken off Cure the Blues.

"The situation just wasn't working with Vasquez," says Jolley, who is well known to quickly pull the trigger with the jockeys if he isn't 100 percent satisfied. "We weren't winning with Vasquez and winning in this business is all that matters."

"I never fit the horse," says Vasquez. "I didn't want to ride him in the first place. I was afraid if I blew the Derby Mr. Firestone would take me off Genuine Risk and some of those good two-year-olds he has. But I guess in this business you're only as good as your last race."

Jolley still doesn't go back to Rudy. Instead, for the May 2 Kentucky Derby, Jolley puts veteran Bill Shoemaker on the colt's back. They finish 15th — defeated by 24 lengths.

On May 25 Cure the Blues, for some reason, is entered against the best and toughest older horses in America in the Met Mile at Belmont. Once again Cure the Blues guns for the lead, this time with Don MacBeth in the saddle. Once again, he collapses in the stretch and finishes a badly beaten fifth.

Sent to Ireland to stand at stud, Cure the Blues never runs again. Despite his disappointment Firestone writes $12,500 cheques — half of the stud fee Cure the Blues will command — to hot walker Sarah Townsend, Borden and Bond's assistant trainer Earl Begley, as well as to Bond and Rudy.

He also gives Rudy a sterling silver ashtray engraved with Cure the Blues' name and the phrase "With the Greatest of Appreciation."

"I have never met more generous people," says Townsend. "I have never heard of giving a hot walker that kind of a gift. It has to be a first."

However, no one will ever know how good Cure the Blues would have been if Rudy, who knew the colt better than anyone, had stayed on his back.

Chapter 31

With the spring of 1981 slipping into summer, Yves is on the precipice of giving up.

Despite gulping Lasix diuretic pills like they were peppermints, sticking his finger down his throat to throw up the last thing he has eaten, stepping daily into the sweat box, driving in his car with the heater turned up hot as he can make it and virtually starving himself, he still weighs 115 pounds. He needs to lose 10 more.

"The weight won't come off, Rudy," a frustrated Yves says to his brother, whom he is living with in Maryland near Bowie racetrack. "The first 10 pounds were easy. But the last 10 pounds ... It's driving me crazy. I'm bulimic and it's messing up my head. I get mad really easy. My stomach hurts. On top of everything else I'm depressed. I can't do it, Rudy. I've tried everything."

"Oh yes you can," Rudy answers quickly. "You've come too far to quit now. I'm getting heavy myself. We'll do this together."

For the next two months, Rudy and Yves jog mile after mile in the hot sun wearing rubber sweat suits or, again with the rubber suits on, ride their bicycles for even more miles. The clothes they wear under the sweat suits are wringing wet.

When they return from galloping and working horses at Pimlico, Rudy drops Yves off five miles from his house; Yves jogs the rest of the way.

One day Yves even takes a bowl of hot soup laced with Tabasco sauce into the sauna with him. Then, after he gets out of the sauna and vomits the soup, he grabs a plastic bag, cuts a hole for his head and two holes for his arms and, exhausted, goes to sleep.

Slowly, the last few pounds slip away. Yves sighs happily as the scale in the jockeys' room shows 105 pounds. He gets off; gets back on. He wants to make sure the scale is correct.

"I couldn't have done it without you, Rudy," says Yves. "I would have quit a long time ago."

With his weight finally under control, Yves makes his first ride on July 23 on Devil's Twin, a three-year-old racing for the first time, who has been flashing so many speedy workouts that he is sent off as the 8-5 favorite at Timonium Race Track, north of Baltimore.

But when the gates clang open, Devil's Twin gets swallowed by the horses on each side of him and finishes seventh.

"And I thought my horse was fast," shrugs Yves, who has to wait 21 mounts and five months before he gets his first win. It comes on December 28 at Laurel with another first-time starter, Greenie's Miss, for trainer R. Carlos Nanez.

It is a masterful ride — the ride of a veteran instead of a first-year apprentice. On the rail in the six-furlong maiden claiming race, Yves duels for the early lead with Undercurrent. With half a mile left, Greenie's Miss appears all done as Undercurrent opens a two-and-a-half-length lead. Not only does Undercurrent pass Greenie's Miss on the outside, so does Hagley Dancer, who slips through a hole on the rail on the inside.

Yves, however, does not give up. Instead, in mid-stretch, he rouses Greenie's Miss one more time and comes back on to win a four-horse photo finish by a nose, rewarding his backers with a $21 payoff.

Five Turcotte brothers have now won a race.

"What keeps me going, I guess, is that the Turcotte name has always stood for something good in horse racing. I've got to keep that part of it up," says Yves.

"I think he might make a rider," says Bond. "He seems to catch on pretty good and he's got a good attitude.

"I guess he's bred to be a rider because he's the fifth brother to make it. He's getting to look pretty good on a horse. He gets some run out of them and he's a good worker. But he's real quiet. Rudy talks all the time."

Two days later, aboard Jet Spray, Yves wins again.

Noel makes yet one more attempt at riding. But it goes no differently than all of his previous comebacks.

Starting off at Florida's Hialeah racetrack, he rides two winners from only 26 starts in 1981 and then heads back to Ontario, where he can't find a winner in seven starts.

Once again, he quits. But this time it is for good. Too heavy and still drinking just as heavily, he resigns himself to galloping horses in the mornings and working as a bartender and waiter in the afternoons at Fort Erie, where he is surrounded by alcohol.

For a while he even tries training. But that doesn't last long either.

Soon, Yves and Rudy find themselves in the same race.

On January 6, 1982, at Bowie, Bond sends out an entry of Dance Pavilion, the program selection and the reason the entry is 6-5, and Gala Event.

Rudy, 32, is on Dance Pavilion; Yves, 21, is on Gala Event, who hasn't shown much.

But at the finish line it is Gala Event by a neck.

"Look at that bug boy on the front-end outride that old jock," laughs one of the riders in the jocks' room watching the replay.

Yves can only smile. It is a years-upon-years grin — more out of relief than anything else.

A sharp January wind blows hard in Calgary as evening settles in.

It is a month after Denise gave birth to her and Roger's first child, Joey, on December 2, 1981.

Raymonde and Gaetan, who came to Calgary for a week to see their nephew, have just left to go back home to New Brunswick.

Roger was on his best behavior, never drinking in front of his brothers. Winning 40 to 50 races a year in Alberta, he seems happy on the surface.

Calgary Herald racing writer Doug Abraham nicknames him "Rocking Chair Roger" for his ability to get horses to the front and then put the rest of the field to sleep. Once in front, he would wiggle his elbows, making it look like he was sending his horses hard. But in reality, it was the opposite, he was actually slowing the pace down.

Few jockeys are as good at breaking away from the starting gate as Roger, and on the five-eighths mile tracks of Calgary's Stampede Park and Edmonton's Northlands Park, speed reigns king.

But inside Roger, the demons continue to churn out of control.

The house is quiet. Denise is upstairs looking after Joey; Roger is downstairs in the kitchen, where he pulls a keen knife out of a drawer.

He slits both radial arteries in his wrists.

For reasons unknown, a feeling comes over Denise that something is wrong, and she comes down the stairs, where she finds Roger, still only 25, lying on the floor with blood soaking his shirt and trousers.

"Roger! No. What have you done?" she screams as she races to phone 911.

An ambulance, sirens crying loudly, arrives in minutes.

"Why, Roger? Why?" Denise asks as the ambulance attendants wrap Roger's wrists in gauze.

Roger says nothing even as they load him onto a stretcher.

Putting Joey in a car seat, Denise follows the ambulance's angry red flashing lights and offensive wails to the hospital where, in her mind, nobody seems to be in much of a hurry. In Canada, there are, on average, 10 suicides a day. Unsuccessful suicides are much more plentiful, with as many as 20 attempts for every suicide death.

Kept overnight in the hospital, Roger is told he seriously needs counseling. He refuses.

Hours later Denise is on her knees, scrubbing the blood out of the linoleum floor.

Chapter 32

On May 30, 1982, an off day at Laurel, Yves decides to go to Toronto to watch Rudy ride in the My Dear Stakes at Woodbine. Rudy wins easily — coming from just off the pace — with Singing Susan, a horse Bernie Bond says is the best filly he has trained. In her only other start, Singing Susan won her maiden race with Rudy aboard at Aqueduct on April 29 by three lengths in a track record performance.

But Yves can't get back to Maryland. Because he doesn't have a passport or any legal documents with him, he is turned away by a border guard.

"I don't know when he will be back," says Yves' agent, Lou Rosenthal.

Left with no way to get back to Maryland, Yves stays in Ontario. He makes his first start at his new home on June 9, finishing sixth with Rexdale Queen.

The next day, he wins his first race in Ontario aboard Sultan's Decree.

With Rosenthal remaining in Maryland, Noel, who has quit riding, becomes Yves' new agent.

"I'm kind of glad all this happened," Yves tells Noel. "This is where I wanted to ride all along. Rudy talked me into going to Maryland first, but Toronto is where I wanted to be."

Until he can find a place of his own, Yves lives with his brother Camille in Georgetown, a small community 45 minutes west of Woodbine. His lodging is a storage room in Camille's two-bedroom apartment. The only things in his room are a single bed and a small dresser.

"We'll do good together," Noel tells Yves. "I've got a lot of good connections here. I'll work hard for you."

With his name and incredible success, Ron had paved the way for Noel, Rudy and Roger. But it wasn't smoothed over for Yves.

"The road was easy for Noel, Roger and Rudy," Ron tells Yves. "Too easy. They were going on my reputation. You had it the hardest. You had to work hard, and you did."

Yves' absence hurts Rudy in a startling way.

Struggling with his weight and without Yves to keep him straight, Rudy, who never turned down an opportunity to party anyway, starts to drink more heavily.

Rudy used to drink to celebrate his wins. Now he just drinks.

As with Roger, it is a deadly combination.

Rudy stops showing up early at Bond's stable, a prerequisite for the strict, former decorated combat captain in the European Theater of World War II.

"You know my rules, Rudy. If you don't show up in the mornings you don't ride my horses in the afternoons. That's always been the case," says Bond. "And you show up late. I can't ride you anymore."

"Bernie, please give me another chance," implores Rudy. "I'll change. I'll come early. Anything, boss. Anything."

"I'm sorry, Rudy. My mind is made up. We've had a lot of success together but that's the past. I can't trust you anymore. I've warned you earlier and you didn't listen then."

With reporters Bond is evasive: "He's a good rider and I don't want to hurt him. My reasons for firing him shouldn't have anything to do with anyone wanting to use Rudy. He has loads of talent. I don't want to go any further on that."

Bond tells Rudy the crushing news on July 15, just three days after Rudy wins the Astoria Stakes at Belmont aboard his Gala Jubilee. Rudy's marriage to Janet, with whom he has two daughters, Stacey and Trudy, is also unraveling.

Used to being a top jockey, one of the best in North America over the years, Rudy, depressed and feeling useless, doesn't care how much he weighs. Never a natural lightweight, his walking-around weight is now 127. One day, earlier in the meet, trying hard to reduce, Rudy got so sick he had to cancel all his mounts.

"It's to the point now that I have to lose five to seven pounds every day," laments Rudy, whose shoe size is just 4 1/2. "In the end, I just couldn't take it anymore."

The smallest of the Turcotte family of jockeys at the beginning, Rudy is now the heaviest.

"Lasix pills. Diet pills. Sweat boxes. I would run in the sauna fully clothed. It could be 90 degrees outside, and I would wear a rubber suit and then put on more clothes and run or drive with the heat cranked up as high as possible."

He is supposed to ride unbeaten Singing Susan again — in the Toddler Stakes at Laurel — but he can't make the weight.

Not getting on another horse in 1982 after winning with Gala Jubilee, it is near the end of a marvelous career.

After the Astoria, Rudy visits his childhood friend, Norbert Laforge, in Grand Falls, sleeping on Laforge's couch. While Laforge is at work, Rudy drinks.

"I had no idea he was drinking so much. Then, one day, Odette phones me. She asks if Rudy is back drinking. I told her 'No.' I told her that we have supper, go for a beer and then go to bed early. That was it. Then Odette asks me to check under the couch where he sleeps."

Shocked, Laforge finds half a dozen empty vodka bottles.

"He was drinking one bottle a day. It was so sad. He had weight problems and the drinking didn't help. He had always been a good buddy. He won so many races and so much money. He often told me that he made millions but that he had lost it all. It was sad to see someone go down like that."

His secret heavy drinking discovered, Rudy returns to Maryland, where he continues to gallop horses. He sleeps in a tack room.

Never good at handling money, Rudy allegedly was bilked by a man who misrepresented himself as a lawyer and convinced Rudy to let him invest the meager amount he had left. The man then disappeared. Unable to put up with his drinking, Janet leaves Rudy, who gives her everything he has left.

Despite winning $1.6 million from his rides, Rudy is suddenly broke.

The Jaguar, his Audi, his station wagon, his Volkswagen Beetle, his house, everything, gone.

"If I had been castrated and there was no booze, I would have been a millionaire," Rudy laments. "I drank so much that I didn't recognize myself anymore. There wasn't enough alcohol in all of Florida for me."

He is depressed and angry.

"Having to lose so much weight it makes me whacky. After losing a lot of weight the first thing you want is a sugar fix. So, I'd take a shot of whiskey to calm me down. Admitting that I was an alcoholic was the hardest thing I've ever had to do," continues Rudy who enters a detox program. "I lost everything. My marriage. My family."

Far from being the Rudy Turcotte who won races everywhere, he gallops a few horses in the mornings and parks cars as a valet in the afternoons at Keystone racetrack in Philadelphia.

It is just the opposite for Yves. In 1982, his first full year of riding, Yves wins 87 races in Ontario even though the jockeys' room is full of other top apprentices, such as Robert Landry, Richard Dos Ramos and Jack Lauzon, who all go on to become very accomplished jockeys.

Yves' success comes without a lot of assistance from Noel, who, like Roger, like Rudy, is also drinking hard.

Two top Ontario trainers, Gil Rowntree and Jacques Dumas, tell Yves he needs to fire Noel and get a new agent.

"I can't do it," Yves replies with a long exhale and a sad shake of his head. "He's my brother."

Immediately Yves loses all his lucrative riding engagements with Rowntree, a Hall of Fame trainer who won most of Ontario's top races including four Queen's Plates, three Prince of Wales and the 1978 Breeders' with Overskate, a two-time Canadian Horse of the Year.

Six months later, with the 1983 Ontario spring meeting beckoning at Greenwood in March, Yves makes the heart-wrenching decision to part ways with Noel and hooks up with Al Duffy, whose brother Lloyd is one of Ontario's best jockeys.

Twenty-five days into the season, Yves loses his five-pound apprentice break. As happened with Roger and with most jockeys, Yves doesn't get the mounts he is accustomed to. Instead of riding in almost every race, he only gets calls on two or three horses a day.

"I knew it would be difficult after I lost my bug," he tells Duffy. "I knew it would take time to get established again. But I didn't know it was going to be this slow."

"Don't worry," Duffy responds. "I'll get you some live mounts." It doesn't happen.

After finishing ninth in the August 7 Prince of Wales, Yves also loses his "big horse," Gone to Royalty, whom he rode to a fourth-place finish in the Queen's Plate and an allowance win.

Nothing is going right.

He only rides one horse on August 20 at Fort Erie. The next day he only gets one mount again. Having gone 26 mounts without a win, Yves tells Duffy that he is going to Alberta.

"I need to find an easier place to ride, Al," says Yves. "I'm hardly riding at all here anymore. I'm going to Calgary. Roger is there and he's doing really good. I just need a change."

When Yves arrives in Calgary in late August it couldn't be more different from when he came to Alberta during his 1979 summer vacation.

Back then Roger was drunk most of the time and hardly riding at all. This time he finds Roger as one of Alberta's top riders. More importantly, he is sober.

Roger also became a father for the second time when Jessica, who would later change her name to Taylor or TJ, is born on June 11.

"I'm a new man," Roger tells Yves. "I couldn't be happier. I'm riding lots. Winning lots. You'll do the same. The Turcottes ride again."

Roger shows Yves just how successful he has been during all of 1983, winning with Cheyenne Autumn the day Yves makes his first ride in Calgary.

Yves only has one mount that day and finishes a close second.

The next day, Roger wins again. While Yves still can't find the winner's circle, he has mounts in six races. One of them, Doxa, is second in the Stampede Park Handicap. He is getting antsy.

A week later, September 2, Yves wins his first race with Alberta Power.

"See, it was only a matter of time," Roger tells Yves.

Between Fort Erie and Stampede Park, Yves had gone 46 mounts without a win.

"The wins will come now," says Roger.

Roger is right. Yves wins again the following day. More wins come regularly.

When 1983 ends, Roger has 119 wins — by far the most since his amazing 290-win apprentice season. His wins include two stakes with the sensational Luke Moser–trained filly Merry-down: the October 8 Great Western Distaff and the October 29 Mount Andromeda Handicap. They are his fourth and fifth stakes wins of the season.

Yves wins 69 races. Still only 23 years old, he becomes a man on the move. When Calgary's thoroughbred racing season ends on November 20, Yves heads back to Ontario for the finish of the Greenwood fall/winter meet. When Greenwood ends, he goes to Boston's Suffolk Downs, braving the freezing winds that howl across the Mystic Lakes.

Meanwhile, refusing to give up, Rudy walks a thin wire. He only gets aboard nine horses in 1983. Clearly showing he hasn't lost any talent, two of them, Autumn Terror and Michael's Playboy, win at Maryland's Timonium racetrack.

At the urging of Noel, a sixth Turcotte makes his debut as a jockey, at Woodbine on June 1, 1984. His name is Daniel David. He is the son of Camilla, making him a nephew to the Turcotte racing family.

He finishes eighth and last.

Three days later, however, he is enticed to ride a quarter horse at Picov Downs in Ajax, Ontario, just east of Toronto. The horse, Rockets Bay Lady, wins easily.

"I didn't even know what a quarter horse was," David tells his uncle Noel. "The trainer just told me to hang on."

David is paid $19 — $10 for the mount and $9 for the victory.

Unable to get any thoroughbred mounts that are less than 30-1, David continues to go to Picov. He keeps winning. He rides three more quarter horses and wins all three. The following week he gets on four and wins all of them too.

"It's fun but I want to ride thoroughbreds. There's no money in quarter horse racing," he says to Noel.

Two weeks later, David finds out differently. He wins the $82,000 Rags to Riches quarter horse stake at Picov on Top Azure Rocket. David's share is $2,500. The next day he buys his first car – a Plymouth Reliant.

Even with that victory, David still can't find a live thoroughbred mount. Riding longshots that run nowhere and living in a tack room at Woodbine, he struggles. From 91 rides, David wins four times. One of them, Marika, lights up the tote board like the fourth of July. The horse pays $282 to win — one of the biggest mutuel payoffs in the history of Woodbine.

Still, his mounts' earnings are just $35,961 for the year.

In 1984 Rudy rides just five times.

The final race of his career comes on June 22, when he finishes last at Bowie, on a maiden named Bright Votre. His spectacular career as one of North America's top jockeys ends in a silent grimace.

David has a breakout year in 1985, winning 94 races in Ontario in his first full year of riding. He is Ontario's leading apprentice and just three wins behind Alberta's Nancy Jumpsen for the most by an apprentice in Canada.

Riva Ridge dies suddenly on April 21, 1985 — just days after his sixteenth birthday — of anaphylactic shock. He is buried in an oak casket at Claiborne.

Still sober after winning 93 races in 1984, Roger wins 91 times in 1985. It seems as though he has finally outridden his past.

After winning 68 times last year, Yves wins 72 races in 1985.

Chapter 33

"Fifteen two, fifteen four and a pair is six," says Yves, playing cribbage in the jockeys' room.

In less than half an hour, he will ride Bill Scott's longshot Postell Man in the June 21, 1986, $20,000 Count Lathum Stakes at Edmonton's Northlands Park. Despite winning the President's Stakes just a month earlier, Postell Man is given no chance by the pundits on this warm afternoon, going off at better than 25-1. Vancouver invader Happy Trap, who has won six of his past seven stakes engagements, is odds-on at 40 cents on the dollar.

"I'm going to win this race," Yves says to anyone who cares to listen as he continues to play cards. "I'm going to beat that Vancouver horse because I've got a game plan. I'm going to take Postell Man way off the pace and let him run late. The only reason he didn't run well last time was because I sent him, and he didn't have the finish."

Yves draws a 29 hand. Moving from seventh at the three-quarter pole, Postell Man has the lead at the top of the stretch.

"I didn't want to move that early," Yves says. "Postell Man just towed me to the top. I actually thought it was too early."

Postell Man obviously thought differently, prevailing by a length and a half, paying $53.70 to win. Happy Trap finishes a well-beaten fourth.

Yves wins four stakes with Postell Man in 1986. Besides the Count Lathum and the President's Stake, they also win the Lotto West Classic and the Victoria Handicap.

In total, Yves wins 10 added-money events in 1986. As well as the quartet with Postell Man, he wins the Lilac Stakes with Time for Words; the Journal with Provocative Prince; the Rundle and Alberta Oaks with Pixindee and the Ken Pearson Memorial and Moraine Lake with Hasty Mort.

It is a grand time.

On September 17, Denise gives birth to her and Roger's third and final child, Danielle Courtney Turcotte, in Calgary.

Danielle has a normal birth but four months later, Denise finds her jerking her arms spasmodically in her crib. Danielle's forehead is burning hot. Grabbing a thermometer, Denise gasps when she sees it read 108° F.

It is just one day after Roger has been released from an alcohol recovery center.

An ambulance arrives, the angry orange and red lights flashing.

"We need to fly," shouts one ambulance attendant.

Denise trembles. Cries.

Roger does the same.

Initially the ambulance heads to Rocky View Hospital, but it is quickly rerouted to the Alberta Children's Hospital. Denise rides with her baby while Roger hurries to find a babysitter for Joey and Jessica.

Every time Denise pokes her head into the emergency room and sees her helpless little girl hooked up to what seem to be dozens of monitors, tubes and IVs connected to her tiny arms and feet, she breaks down in savage sobs.

The initial diagnosis is dire. Danielle has microcephaly, a neurodevelopmental disorder caused by a problem with the brain's central nervous system.

"It seems as if every doctor in the hospital is working on her," Denise says at one point as she walks around the crowded halls while doctors and nurses huddle over her little girl. Danielle's liver and kidneys are shutting down. Her brain is also swelling, and she is having violent seizures.

After a few hours, a doctor gravely approaches Denise and Roger and suggests they call a priest.

"I don't know if your daughter is going to pull through," he says. Again, they cry.

An infectious disease specialist is called in. So is a neurologist. Because Danielle can't swallow, a stomach tube is also inserted.

It takes a full week, but the doctors and nurses manage to get Danielle stabilized. But the prognosis only gets worse as Danielle develops severe cerebral palsy.

The seizures continue, sometimes as many as 100 a day, until changes in medication reduce them to occasional mild attacks.

Denise and Roger are told Danielle will only live until her teens, confined to a wheelchair and in need of constant care. The most they can expect her to do is smile, which she gives when she hears music from toys and Barney the Dinosaur movies.

Roger and Denise are shaken to the core.

Roger starts drinking again. Harder than ever.

Denise is beside herself. Here she has a very sick baby, and all Roger wants to do is drink more vodka. Their marriage is crumbling one more time.

"I've become your babysitter," she angrily tells Roger. "I know you hate me for that but I hate being in this situation. I can't do it anymore. I don't know what to do for you anymore. You can't just have one or two drinks. You have to drink until you're drunk. And then the next morning you are so hungover you can hardly walk. It's crazy, Roger. You need more help."

When this 1986 Alberta season ends, Roger has 69 wins — his lowest total in years; Yves wins 96 races for purse earnings of $619,690. Because of the big year he has in Alberta, Yves decides to try Greenwood again. But after driving all the way from Calgary with fellow Alberta jockey Perry Winters, Yves wins just three races at Greenwood.

Despite his big 1985 season, David struggles in 1986. Weight is already becoming a problem, as is the bottle. His win total is halved.

In 1987, it only gets worse.

In September, he is suicidal. He leaves Toronto to go to Montreal and say goodbye to his parents.

Forever, he thinks.

Then, he follows the sun and heads west to Calgary.

"Hi, uncle," he calls out one day to Yves at Stampede Park.

"Daniel?" replies Yves, who is just three years older than his nephew. "What are you doing here?"

"I've quit riding. I'm going to live in the mountains."

"The mountains?" exclaims Yves. "What are you going to do there?"

"Nothing," replies David. "I've proven everything I have to prove."

"Proven? What have you proven?"

"That I can ride with you guys. My uncles," says David.

"You're not quitting anything," says Yves. "I've got some extra tack and you're going to use it and ride here."

In reality, David does have a plan. Bizarre as it seems, he wants to go to Banff and be eaten by bears.

He keeps that a secret.

But Yves persists. He convinces David to live with him in a house he rents from Alberta-leading jockey Don Seymour, who has moved to Toronto.

David is an instant success in Calgary. Riding against Yves and Roger, in less than two months he wins 20 races, including the Hoofprint On My Heart stakes.

"Horses sure run for you," marvels Yves. "And you wanted to quit?"

Staying until the end of the Calgary meet in mid-November, David returns to Ontario and rides at Greenwood until the season ends. Getting eaten by bears is forgotten. His drinking, however, is not.

In 1988 a breathalyzer is introduced into the jockeys' room. In six months David blows over the limit three times. The Ontario Racing Commission gives David two choices: quit drinking or quit riding.

After a great deal of thought, he enters a rehabilitation program.

In 1987 Yves and Roger have had another resurgence, each winning 110 races in Alberta.

Chapter 34

August 20, 1988, arrives black and bleak at Edmonton's Northlands Park. Yet few of the more than 8,400 people who show up for the $100,000 Canadian Derby, the biggest and most anticipated stakes race in Alberta, seem to care.

The outdoor grandstand is jammed and the cheers cascade like the pelting, callous rain. At least the thunder has passed, muttering its way east.

The Derby is Alberta's pride and joy, but it is also a prodigal son. It has been 10 years since an Alberta horse — Canadian Bill over a similarly muddy track — won the race that local horsemen spend a lifetime dreaming and trying to win.

Since Canadian Bill's win, six Derbies have gone to Toronto horses, two went to horses from the U.S. and one to Victorious Lad from British Columbia.

And that doesn't include Ontario's Laissez Passer, who won with Roger in 1976.

To Albertans the Derby is like Captain Ahab's Great White Whale. It mocks them, swims just close enough that they can get a good look but then stays just out of reach as their harpoons dig into empty spaces.

Today's running certainly seems to offer no relief, with the favorite being Ontario Queen's Plate–winner Regal Intention, who has already won $547,344 — more than the other five entrants combined. Regal Intention is bet down to 40 cents on the dollar.

Everyone else, it appears, is running for second. And another Ontario invader, No Malice, who will be ridden by Julie Krone, the first woman to ride in the Canadian Derby, seems to have that position locked up.

Certainly, Yves' mount, Elmtex, who not long ago ran in a cheap $9,000 claiming race, is one of those who would be happy to finish third. Regal Intention has won 10 times as much money as Elmtex, who is owned by Roy Haeberle, who was born in a log shack during the Great Depression.

"Ride him like you own him," are Elmtex's trainer Bill Matier's only instructions to Yves in the saddle enclosure.

That's more than Matier usually says to him.

"Usually, he says, 'I'm not telling you anything because you don't listen anyway,'" thinks Yves.

But then the darnedest thing unfolds among the rain-soaked umbrellas.

Regal Intention and No Malice duel head-to-head, a tactical mistake it seems, pasted together as a team for the first mile of the grueling mile and three-eighths marathon.

Neither refuses to budge.

Jockey Jack Lauzon tries to get Regal Intention to settle down, but his lines are so wet they keep slipping in his hands. Lauzon wants to be running second behind No Malice. But Regal Intention has a mind of his own and Lauzon can't take him back.

Midway around the final slick turn, Regal Intention finally pokes his nose in front. But the pace has already taken its toll. From far back Elmtex, one of the heaviest horses on the grounds — at one point a staggering 23 lengths off the lead — is suddenly closing the gap with every muddy stride.

It is unexpected. Even Yves is surprised.

"He kept dropping farther and farther back. I wasn't taking him back. He was taking himself back. I said to myself, 'Oh God, I'm in trouble.'"

But that all changes in a flash.

"I chirped, took another cross, and he started running," Yves relates afterward. "Down the backstretch, even though Regal Intention still had me by five or six lengths, I knew I had it all. He was really smoking. What a feeling it was."

The stunned crowd is now riding with Yves as he quickly passes a tired and spent Regal Intention halfway down the stretch and goes on to win easily.

"We finally turned back them guys," says Matier. "They said it couldn't be done, but I always believed in Elmtex. And now we've gone out and done it: beat a Queen's Plate winner. Now isn't that something."

It is one of 124 wins for Yves this year — the most races he has ever won in a season.

Roger wins 78 races — eight of them stakes, including two on the year's champion sprinter, Special Intent.

October 4, 1989. It is a sunny morning, but the air somehow feels bleak and gray. Secretariat, the greatest horse of all time, is dying.

Tears are shed at his home at Claiborne Farm near Paris, Kentucky, where he has stood at stud since 1974.

Since Labor Day, Secretariat has suffered the intense pain of laminitis, which inflames the soft tissue of a horse's foot. It is only a question of when he will have to be put down.

That time comes at 11:45 a.m. when a concentrated barbiturate is injected into his neck. In less than a minute, Secretariat's big copper-red body collapses with a gigantic thud.

He was 19 years old.

The next day, amid national and international coverage mourning his loss — the *New York Times* report reads like a person's obituary — a necropsy is performed by Dr. Thomas Swerczek. The result is stunning. While the rest of his vital organs are normal, his heart is more than twice the size of an average horse's heart, which weighs about eight to nine pounds. Secretariat's heart weighed over 21 pounds, which allowed him to receive more oxygen.

"I think it told us why he was able to do what he did," Swerczek tells Bill Nack, who wrote the definitive book on Secretariat, *The Making of a Champion.*

Secretariat is buried at Claiborne next to his sire, Bold Ruler, his grandsire Nasrullah and his stablemate Riva Ridge.

Tens of thousands of people have since made the pilgrimage to Secretariat's grave, where they leave flowers and his favorite treats — apples and peppermints — around a simple headstone marking his resting spot. He is buried in a 6-by-6-foot oak casket lined with orange silk (the color used by Claiborne's racing stables).

At stud, Secretariat was successful but not overly so.

He sired 53 stakes winners, including 1988 Preakness and Belmont champion Risen Star and 1986 Horse of the Year Lady's Secret, from 663 foals, which won almost $29 million.

He was way more successful as a broodmare sire. In 1992 he was the leading broodmare sire in North America when his daughters produced the winners of almost $6.7 million.

In 1989 Roger wins 73 times. Yves is solid again with 96 victories.

On May 19, 1990, Ron does what he has vowed to accomplish; he graduates from Van Buren High School in Maine.

Chapter 35

Just another race unfolds at Northlands on a clear Sunday afternoon, on May 27, 1990. Roger is in front on the rail with Cusimano when it all changes.

A young horse that, for reasons unknown, is being schooled in an area behind the six-and-a-half-furlong chute suddenly throws its handler and runs away riderless. The horse runs clockwise down the backstretch and around the clubhouse turn.

With the track announcer bellowing as loud as he can to warn the rest of the jockeys about the loose horse, which is on the rail, the unsuspecting field continues to race down the stretch to the finish line. With his head down driving his arms forward, Roger only sees the loose horse at the last second and manages to pull the three-year-old Cusimano slightly to his right.

But it is too late. The pony, in full gallop, slams violently into Cusimano's right shoulder.

As Cusimano falls heavily to the track, Roger is thrown 20 feet in the air; he lands hard on the back of his neck and shoulders. His chin touches his chest. Pinball, one of the horses directly behind Cusimano, stumbles over the fallen horse. Jockey Perry Winters is sent flying too. Cusimano, who had won twice and was showing potential, breaks a shoulder and ribs and has to be humanely put down.

Six horses either fall or have to be pulled up as the race is declared no contest. Somehow Roger, Winters and the other riders in the race are miraculously relatively unscathed.

"We're all very lucky it wasn't worse," says Winters, who, like Roger, was able to get back up on his feet on his own. "If that pony hits another horse head on, he would have killed somebody."

"It was fortunate the pony stayed on the rail," says gate worker Nathan Gross. "If he ducks out and into the pack the whole field might have gone down. You guys are all very fortunate."

"I'm lucky I didn't break my neck," concurs Roger, who chillingly adds: "I could have been paralyzed like my brother Ron. I didn't get much of a chance to see it. All of a sudden, the pony is coming. He looks like he's gonna go to the outside and then he ducks for a hole on the rail. We hit saddles and I went flying."

Just four days after the accident, Roger returns to ride. But it doesn't last. Complaining of excruciating headaches resulting from the spill with Cusimano, Roger rides until June 9.

Then he virtually disappears for two full months.

"Roger, get out of bed," says trainer Mark Zimmer, who shares a two-bedroom unit with Roger and Yves' valet, Billy Ouelette, at the Jockey Club Motel. Just a few furlongs east of Northlands Park, it is a popular spot for horsemen who don't live in Edmonton. The trio's sparse lodging includes a kitchenette in the middle of the two bedrooms. There is also a cot in the kitchenette, which is what Roger has been sleeping on.

The night before, they had been drinking at the Beverly Crest motel.

Withdrawn and reticent outside of a barroom, Roger is a completely different person when he is drinking. While Rudy can easily slide into a room with 50 people he doesn't know and bullshit everybody, Roger is different. But here he walks around the bar singing. As he does, patrons send over trays of beer. He is always a happy drunk.

"You've got to get up," Zimmer tells Roger. "You've got to go to the track and gallop horses. You've got to start riding again. Billy, come over here and help me tip over Roger's cot. He won't listen to me. He won't get out of bed."

Ouelette, who also works for trainer Joan Petrowski in the mornings, complies. Zimmer picks up one end of the cot, Ouelette takes the other and they dump Roger onto the floor.

Still, Roger doesn't budge, feigning sleep.

"Billy, we've got to do something with Roger," Zimmer says as he stands over Roger's prone body. "I think that accident with the pony has him scared. He just wants to hide in a corner someplace. I've tried to talk to him. But he refuses to talk about it.

"You're not hurt, Roger," Zimmer says, now looking back at him. "You got lucky. You can't quit. You're too good of a rider. When you're not drinking you're the best rider out there.

"Get up. Everything is fine."

Roger is not fine.

His marriage to Denise, who stayed in Calgary, is over. He worries about Danielle, who has severe medical issues. He worries about not riding again. He worries about the headaches. He worries about everything.

Two months pass before Roger finally accepts one mount on August 1. In a cheap claiming race, he finishes fourth.

He goes to Calgary when the thoroughbred meet ends in Edmonton, but he doesn't go to the track. In fact, he doesn't ride again for the rest of the year.

Instead, Roger goes to Zimmer's farm east of Calgary and helps break yearlings — getting young horses used to having a bit in their mouths, a saddle on their backs and then someone in the saddle. He also does odd jobs like mucking out stalls for Zimmer's dad, William, whom everyone calls "Red."

He also likes to gallop horses on the farm's half-mile track, which meanders up and down little hills and valleys.

Red tries to pay Roger for his work but Roger refuses.

Instead, all he wants to do is play cribbage with Red or whoever else shows up at the farm. Many times, he will play cards 12 hours a day.

"That crash with the pony took everything out of Roger," Mark tells his dad one night. "He just doesn't have the desire anymore. Maybe you can get him to talk about it to you, Dad. Roger won't listen to me or anyone at the track.

"The crash did him in. It took the fight away. His heart went. It's a tough game. When the horses are running faster than 40 miles an hour, you better have your pumper going. But his ticker is gone."

Mark shakes his big red mustache.

"It's hard to see him like this," says Zimmer. "When he was on and when he wasn't drinking there was nobody better. He went straight for a lot of years in a row. He was rocking and rolling in the mornings, and he was riding as good as anybody in the afternoons and evenings."

"He can sure break babies," says Red. "Better than anyone I've ever seen. He line drives them; teaches them to steer and stop and gets on their backs faster and finer than anyone. He got them all broke like puppies this fall. Even the ornery big stud colt. You can tell all of the babies to whoa and they stop. Now we can put them away for the winter and get started back with them next spring."

"Better than anyone on the planet," agrees Mark about Roger's innate ability to work with young horses. "Absolute."

"I'll try talking to him again, but I don't think I'll get anywhere," says Red. "He doesn't like to even talk about horse racing anymore.

"He's only happy here on the farm."

Surviving at least seven cardiac episodes, Alfred's heart beats for the last time in the middle of August 1990.

But it isn't his heart that lets him down; he passes away from lung cancer at Ron's house in New Brunswick. He has been living for the past 10 years in a separate apartment that Ron had built for him and Rose. He was 79. Yves, Noel, Roger and Rudy and the rest of the family's brothers and sisters also get to see him. Saying their goodbyes, they relive the good days and the bad.

"He was waiting for us to come before he passed away," says Yves. "He talked to us together and he talked to us separately."

Going to Grand Falls probably cost Yves eight winners back home in Alberta but he says, "I don't care if it cost me $10,000. I wanted to see Dad before he died."

Rudy, who, for the past four years has been galloping horses in Ontario and up and down the U.S.'s eastern seaboard, suddenly shows up in Calgary on September 8, where Yves is riding in the Alberta Oaks. Yves' mount is Optimal Power, who was just claimed by Rick Hedge for $12,000.

Despite the big jump in class Optimal Power wins by six and a quarter lengths.

Everyone gives credit to Yves' agent, Ken Deines.

"'Deinsey' was worth every penny of his share today," praises Yves. "He's the one who told Rick that the horse was eligible for the Oaks and that she would run good if he entered her."

Rudy, who is wearing a cast on a broken hand suffered in a galloping spill at the Meadowlands, and Roger, who still complains of whiplash and back injuries, both come into the winner's circle.

"I'm proud of you, Yves," says Rudy. "You gave me chills when you took the lead and opened up so easily."

"I didn't know you were coming out here," says Yves. "Why didn't you tell me?"

"Spur of the moment," answers Rudy. "I like it here. I'm thinking of moving out here next year. "I could gallop horses in the mornings and be an agent at the same time.

"It's not like I've got a lot going on in my life."

"Sure," says Yves, a little unsure. "That would be great."

With nowhere else to go, Roger spends the winter of 1990–91 at the Zimmers' farm.

But when spring 1991 arrives, Roger, as if nothing had happened or changed, shows up at Calgary's Stampede Park ready to ride. Rudy, as he prophesied, also shows up.

As good as he was as a jockey — and he was very good — Rudy is now sought after by many Alberta trainers to exercise their horses, including R.K. "Red" Smith, who is perennially one of the leading trainers. Lianne Knechtel and Barry Brown use Rudy extensively too.

"He has a clock in his head," says Knechtel. "He'd tell you how fast he went, and he was always right on. He knows exactly what he is doing."

But Rudy is fussy.

"Everything has to be perfect; sometimes he drives me nuts," admits Knechtel. "The tack has to be perfect. The bridle has to be perfect. The girth has to be perfect. Same with the reins. After he galloped a horse, he would sometimes say the bit I was using was wrong, and nine out of 10 times he's right."

"Rudy tells the trainers what to do," Yves says to Rudy's girlfriend, Val Cressman, who is a groom for Knechtel and Brown. "He's a lot like Ronnie in that sense. Ron told the trainers what a horse needs and doesn't need. Riva Ridge would never have been the horse he was without Ron. He was the one who got Riva Ridge to relax and to be a great racehorse. And look at how fast he blew out Secretariat before his races. He knew what Secretariat needed. Rudy is the same. He knows a good horse needs to work hard to be better."

Cressman, who also owns a few horses and helps horsemen file their income tax, nods approvingly.

On the second day of the Stampede Park spring meeting Roger wins with Cimerron Rock.

Two racing cards later, he wins again.

But on April 20, a sunny and pleasantly warm afternoon, the perils of being a jockey are once again unleashed.

Roger is traveling comfortably when his mount, Ultimate Victor, suddenly takes a misstep and falls heavily to the track. Roger's injuries are extensive: a broken collarbone, a broken rib, several broken teeth and a chipped ankle. The latter injury may have been self-inflicted. After getting to his feet Roger hobbles to the ambulance, which was quickly on the scene, and frustratingly kicks the bumper. Nobody knows if that might have broken his ankle and not the spill.

Rudy hops over the grandstand fence and sprints to Roger's side.

"Damn it, Rudy. The last thing I needed was another accident," seethes Roger, who picks up a clump of dirt and throws it violently. "There was no warning. You know as well as anyone that if a horse breaks down or something you get a chance to pick up his head. He was running along fine. Then boom."

"Look at that bugger," Roger says, pointing to Ultimate Victor, who got up and was standing there without a care in the world.

"He's fine. He never got hurt at all," he says of the horse trained by Gene White, one of the trainers whom Roger credits for helping his latest comeback.

White, like Rod Cone, Doug Smith, Red Robertson and Dave Nicholson, stuck with Roger through thick (when he fought weight problems) and thin (when he wasn't winning races).

"Why me? Why again? First a pony gets loose and runs into me last year. Now this. I got my weight down. I haven't had a drink in months. I've done everything I was supposed to do. I'm jinxed. I'm frigging jinxed."

"Yeah, and you were just getting rolling," Rudy says, shaking his head, knowing full well that Roger has already won seven spring races.

"I'll be back," Roger vows to *Herald* racing writer Doug Abraham. "It could have been worse. Another horse hit us when I went down. He just missed falling right on top of me."

Abraham asks Roger if he doesn't worry about ending up paralyzed like Ron.

"You can't think about those things," Roger replies in a flash. "Just get back up there and start riding again. Racing is in our blood. I'm a Turcotte. Riding horses is what we do. The doctors say it will take about six weeks to heal but I'm not quitting now."

Instead of six weeks, it takes Roger a full three months to return. He only has two mounts on his July 26 comeback appearance, but he wins with one of them, Whispering Scott.

"I told you I'd come back," he tells Abraham with a wink. "This is only the beginning."

It isn't. Roger only wins one more race all year. And that doesn't happen until August 22. The next day he abruptly quits riding again. Yet when 1992 arrives, Roger returns one more time. It doesn't last long. He rides in 22 races and wins just once. His last mount comes on April 23. It is a cruel ending. Aboard Tenormin, he finishes last in 10th.

Like Rudy, Roger's riding career is over; he is far too heavy to be a jockey, and for the remainder of the year, he and Rudy exercise horses in the mornings.

In the fall, Roger returns to Ontario to gallop horses at Fort Erie.

Before he gets there, he stops at his brother Albert's home in Barrie, Ontario, where Albert owns three Midas automotive service centers.

Albert tries hard to get Roger to quit drinking. But Roger isn't listening, and his visit is very short.

After Roger leaves, Albert calls Yves to talk about Roger's unexpected visit.

"I tried to get him to stop drinking but it didn't work. It didn't matter what I told him. You know him, Yves, life's pressures have got to him. His weight problems. Not riding anymore. His daughter. His divorce. Unable to maintain child-support payments. Everything. I guess he just can't handle it."

"Talking to Roger was like talking to him when he was very young. He still seemed like just a little boy. He never did develop that killer attitude it takes to be a top jockey."

Once in Fort Erie, Roger gets into another accident. Only this time it isn't on a horse. He breaks his pelvis and hip in a car accident. With Rudy staying in Alberta to gallop and continue hustling book, Roger recuperates alone.

Of the five Turcotte brothers that became jockeys, only Yves is left in a race-riding saddle.

Chapter 36

Yves Turcotte is musing.

"This could be my final year of riding," he tells a *Calgary Herald* sportswriter in spring of 1993 at Stampede Park. His face shows little emotion. He is not angry. But he certainly isn't happy. Instead, he is wedged in limbo somewhere in between.

He is 33 and has won well over 900 races.

But business is slow. Most days he is only riding three or four races a day, and the bulk of them are longshots.

"I've had a good run. Pretty good for a fat kid from Grand Falls who everybody said would never be a jockey. I was always heavy. Big in the shoulders and chest. When I was 17, I weighed 135 pounds. I was fat. Not just chubby. Fat. One day Rudy took out a ruler, measured my feet and said forget it. You're going to be too big. Don't even try it."

He talks about how Rudy, who is now his agent, helped him lose weight.

"I was told there was no way I'd get my weight down. But Rudy helped me. We ran miles and miles together in sweat suits to drop weight. We starved ourselves. Did whatever it took to get our weight down.

"When I talk to Ron, he tells me it's him and then me, number one and number two," he says proudly.

Personable, smart and sincere — much like Ron — everybody likes Yves.

"Sometimes people expect a lot of me just because of my name. They expected me to start out like Ron started out. Or Rudy or Roger. Noel got the hang of race riding early too. But it doesn't matter what name you've got. It's what you do in the races."

Yves tells the *Herald* reporter, Gyle Konotopetz, how he worked at the McCain Foods plant loading truck after truck with heavy cartons of frozen french fries and pizza. It was hard work, he says. Exhausting. He talks stolidly of how five children from Grand Falls, New Brunswick, all seemingly destined to be lumberjacks, instead became famous jockeys. They won races across North America but also found a sport where perils lurk around every corner.

Ron, the rider of the greatest thoroughbred in history and so many other champions, is in a wheelchair.

Roger and Noel are together in Fort Erie, both lonely and battling their alcohol addictions, galloping horses and walking them afterward to cool them down. The latter is called "walking hots," a menial job usually reserved for those on horse racing's bottom rung. Certainly not for two jockeys who should have been celebrated for all the races they won.

And then Rudy, every bit as good a rider as Ron — maybe even better — is still galloping horses and working as an agent.

"My other brothers have had so many problems," says Yves, shaking his head. "Drinking problems. Divorces. Ron is proud of me for keeping my life together. I haven't lost my family. I'm happily married with two children," he says of son Dominic, 5, daughter Chantal, 2, and his wife, Lisette, whom he married in 1988 and who has always stuck beside him.

Yves rarely complains. He takes what comes and makes the best of it.

"My valet came in today and said he was at a funeral for a 10-year-old who died of leukemia. So, if I don't win the next race it's no big deal. So what if I don't win?

"Anyway," he shrugs, "I'll never quit until I've got 1,000 wins. After that, if I get an opportunity to start a little business of my own and be my own boss, I'll probably quit."

But he isn't telling the truth. He loves winning and loathes losing. And he isn't really about to quit anytime soon. It's just that this season has him perplexed. The wins simply aren't coming. Until now he has always won at least 68 races every year. This year he will be lucky if he gets half that many.

After getting off to a good start to the year, winning eight races in April, he quickly goes cold. He wins only twice in May and four times in June. Even mellow trainer Freddie Jones, who has ridden Yves dozens of times and who has always run a successful stable, takes him off a couple of horses.

"Jesus. If Fred Jones stops riding you it's time to move on," Yves says to himself. "I've lost my confidence. I used to go to the track thinking I was going to win every race. Now, because I'm not riding many horses — and what I am riding is mostly horses nobody else wants to get on — I don't have the same confidence."

He is 23 wins shy of 1,000.

Disgruntled, Yves takes his tack to Winnipeg on July 3, leaving Rudy behind.

"It's hard having your brother be your agent," Yves tells Rudy. "You drink too much, and you don't show up every morning. People keep asking me, 'Where's Rudy? Where's Rudy?' I worry about you. I'm sorry but I need to get out of here."

The change of scenery doesn't help. Yves only wins twice in each of July and August. It seems to rain every day. Depressing, cold rain.

But he picks up a mount, Gain Respect, in Saskatoon at Marquis Downs in the $30,000 Rainbow of Roses on September 5 and wins by a head over the horse's stablemate.

The next day, he is back in Winnipeg, where he stays until September 26, when he makes another lucrative one-day visit to

Saskatoon and wins the Marquis Debutante Stakes with Gmego. Three days later he is home in Calgary with his wife and kids, ready to give Alberta another chance.

His wins still come in frustrating dribbles.

A good horse can overcome a bad ride, but a good jockey can't overcome a bad horse. Yves is finding a lot of bad horses.

Saskatoon, however, is once again a welcoming ally. So is Gain Respect. On October 11 Yves teams with the horse one more time and wins the Saskatchewan Futurity Stakes.

Two and a half weeks later, with just a few weeks left in the 1993 season, Yves gets his elusive 1,000th win on October 30. Coming from behind, it comes on favorite Right Partner trained by Joan Petrowski. His second win of the day, it comes easily. Stampede Park makes a sign congratulating him on his milestone win. He holds the sign high into the air.

He ends 1993 with just 39 wins.

But he still isn't ready to quit. Instead, he wants to prove that this season was just a bad aberration.

Chapter 37

The starting gate, where thoroughbreds with hearts pounding and chests heaving wait for the bell to send them off, is one of the most dangerous places in horse racing. According to a National Institute for Occupational Safety and Health study in the United States, 35 percent of all jockey injuries occur while entering, within or leaving the starting gate.

Invariably, one or two horses will act up. Some don't want to go into their cages and have to be encouraged. Sometimes two assistant starters, standing at the horse's hip for fear of getting kicked, link their arms behind the balking horse and push it forward. Other times a horse will be blindfolded or led in with the front gates open.

Once in the gate, the assistant starters, wearing flak jackets and helmets, sit on small ledges made of cold steel. They hold the head of one or even two horses looking directly forward. Their job is to ensure the jockeys are safe and secure and the horses are standing still and calm as possible.

Once the head starter is sure the horses are all settled and ready, he presses a handheld button, which cuts an electric circuit and opens the front stall doors simultaneously. A bell rings, and the horses are sent on their way.

But it doesn't always go that easily. The biggest danger, and it happens more often that one would expect, comes if a horse, already in the gate, panics, crosses its legs and flips in the gate, where the stalls are just 34 inches wide. Legs flailing, they thrash wildly until they are either upside down or have completely thrown themselves out the back of the gate.

In summer 1994, aboard a nervous two-year-old filly, it happens to Yves in Edmonton.

The filly rears up and throws Yves off its back. Yves tries to climb onto the starting gate, but his right foot gets wedged in the V formed by the two back stall gates. Two bones on the top of Yves' foot snap like twigs.

Taken to hospital, he is fitted with a cast from his toes to his knee. Fellow jockey Real Simard drives Yves home to Calgary.

A week later, the cast is removed by Dr. David Reid, but the foot is still very much broken. Reid prescribes physical therapy and a steady routine of dipping the foot into ice water and then hot water over and over.

"You shouldn't be riding," says Lisette.

"I have to," replies Yves. "I've got a stakes race to ride in. The Edmonton Distaff on Emily Hares. The horse has a good chance, and she's trained by Rick Hedge. I want to stay in his good books."

"You're in too much pain. You can't even put any pressure on it just walking around the house."

"I'm going to see the track doctor, John Walker, this morning. Maybe he can freeze the nerves."

Walker says he can do that but reminds Yves that horse racing is the most dangerous sport in the world. "The only thing that comes close is racing motorcycles on asphalt," says Walker. "The needle is going to hurt. Your nerves are going to cry a bit."

"Never mind the nerves, I'm going to cry," replies Yves as Walker barely puts any pressure on his foot. "Man, that hurts, Doc. I think I'll just take my chances without any freezing."

Putting some foam into his right boot to act as a shock absorber, Yves rides anyway.

It still hurts like hell.

Finishing sixth, Emily Hares and Yves' foot disappoint.

Yet neither the loss nor his still healing foot does anything to dampen Yves' confidence on June 11 heading into the $30,000 Rundle Heights stakes race — the highest mutuel payoff of the year at Northlands — which pays $73.90 to win.

Despite his 36-1 odds, Yves is sure that his horse, Bankers Blues, is going to win — even when, with a quarter mile left to run, he is trailing 3-5 speedster Tiny Boots and jockey Chris McGregor by five lengths.

McGregor, who nervously looks back three times to see his lead diminish, has nothing left. He is as spent as Tiny Boots' weary legs.

"I knew I had you," Yves yells over to McGregor as they pull up in the backstretch. "Every time you looked over your shoulder I smiled a little more."

On October 16, in another stakes race that he wasn't expecting to win, Yves rides Dana's Pole, who gets up in the final stride, to win the Duchess of York for a $22.60 payout.

The stakes victories, two of his 60 wins on the season — almost twice as many as he won in 1993 — take away some of the pain.

More suffering is coming in 1995.

An afternoon brimming with sunshine is washed away in cold tears on May 28.

One minute, a field of 11 thoroughbreds, their nostrils flaring, thunder around the final turn at Northlands in the featured $25,000 Alberta Breeders' Handicap. Before you know it, Lustrous Bent is dead and two jockeys — Yves, riding the favorite, Mike's Partner, and Perry Winters — are sprawled on the track.

The spill begins when I Hate Music, ridden by Gary Melanson, suddenly ducks to the outside. The three-year-old's right hip collides with Mike's Partner. Off balance, Mike's Partner clips the back heels of I Hate Music, stumbles and falls heavily. Lustrous

Bent, ridden by Winters, tries to hurdle the fallen horse but just misses. Instead, Lustrous Bent is catapulted headfirst into the ground, breaking his neck. Two other riders, Real Simard, aboard Kash B Quick, and Richard Ziegler, aboard the second favorite, Trick Charge, also fall but are, somehow, unscathed.

"I thought Yves' horse had broken his leg," says Winters, lying on a stretcher with his head immobilized and his neck in a plastic brace. "I thought I missed him. Obviously, I didn't. I don't know what happened."

Yves doesn't remember anything.

"Who was I on?" Yves asks gate worker Darryl Jones.

"Mike's Partner," replies Jones. "In the stakes race."

"Mike's Partner?" says Yves blankly. "In a stakes race?" He shakes his head. "I don't know what you are talking about."

Somehow Lustrous Bent gets to his feet and is walked back to Piet Luider's barn, where streams of cold water are poured over the horse's heaving body. A few seconds later, Lustrous Bent falls and lies paralyzed on the ground.

"He was such a good horse. Such a nice horse," says Luider, wiping tears with a handkerchief, the gasps of the crowd still ringing in his ears. "I loved that horse. And now he's dead. I finally get a good horse and then this happens."

"I'm so sorry, Piet," says veterinarian Trish Arnold as she wraps her arms around Luider's shaking body. "So very, very sorry."

The stewards disqualify I Hate Music, who finished third, and place him last. But they do not fine Melanson or give him a suspension. That rankles several jockeys.

"I don't understand it," vents Winters. "Four jockeys go down, they take the horse's number down, but they don't give the jockey a suspension. I'm very upset. My horse is dead because of it. Yves and I got lucky. It could have been much worse. One or both of us could be dead."

Winters doesn't miss a day; Yves is sidelined two weeks with a concussion.

It is one of two times Yves is injured this year. The second is a complete fluke. On post parade at Stampede Park in the third race on October 18, he is aboard Formula One Regent, a dark bay maiden claiming two-year-old. Abruptly, the filly sees something out of the corner of her eye and ducks out. Yves squeezes his knees to try to regain control. Then he hears a ripping noise — like Velcro coming unfastened. Unknown to Yves, he has torn cartilage in his knee. Feeling a little sore, he rides the filly to a fifth-place finish. He has eight mounts that day. He rides them all and then goes home and makes a cup of coffee. He turns to reach for the cup and suddenly is on the floor — his knee buckling.

"Lisette," calls Yves. "I can't get up. It's my knee."

Two weeks later, Dr. Reid operates. Yves doesn't ride for the rest of 1995. He finishes with 55 wins.

The therapy — exercising on a stationary bike and swimming hundreds of laps in a pool — is so strenuous that Yves loses almost 10 pounds. At 107 pounds, he is the lightest he has ever been.

In 1996 Rudy goes to Japan for the fourth straight winter. There Alberta horseman Yvan Loranger brings some of the best jockeys to help teach young want-to-be jockeys how to ride.

"Rudy was such a good horseman," says Loranger. "I remember the first time I saw him work a horse at Northlands and I said, 'Wow, who is this guy?' He was just breezing the horse, but it was unreal. He was one with that horse. He switched sticks so fast. It was beautiful to watch."

What wasn't pleasant to see was Rudy's drinking.

"In the end, I needed to have a drink in the morning to start the day," Rudy says. "At night, I needed a drink to go to sleep. It wasn't anything for me to drink six beers and then half a pint of vodka straight up. Losing weight and reducing all the time made the effects of alcohol even worse. It hit me even harder."

Chapter 38

It is an unseasonably cold May 11, 1996, afternoon in Fort Erie. Gray clouds hang against a marbled sky. Overnight the temperature dropped to freezing, and the rain, which has overtaken the area, turned to sleet.

Not having spoken to or seen Roger for a couple of days, Noel goes to his brother's apartment and raps on the door. Silence.

Maybe Roger is sick. Maybe he is hungover and sleeping. Roger's car is parked outside his apartment, so Noel knows he is around somewhere.

"Roger," Noel calls out. "Answer the door, damn it. Come on, open up. I'm freezing."

Noel tries the door and it opens easily.

The next sound is a horrified gasp.

"Oh shit. No. No. No."

Noel sees Roger's body hanging limp from the ceiling in the threshold of the doorway between the living room and the kitchen. A green nylon rope one centimeter in width is tied around his neck. A knot just above his Adam's apple has left a deep ligature mark parchment brown in color the same width as the rope. A cordless drill, which he used to bore through the ceiling, lies on the carpet below him.

"Roger! Roger!" Noel shouts to no avail. Dressed in a white, long-sleeved turtleneck shirt, blue jeans and black socks, Roger is dead — his tongue black where he has bitten through it.

A Timex watch showing the correct time is around his left wrist.

Nearby is a handwritten suicide note and a microcassette tape indicating his intentions.

In the note, he says he is sorry and apologizes for what he has done.

There are two pennies in his pocket — about all the money he has left. In his wallet is a card that reads: "When our lives seem to take a rough or wrong turn it's good to remember that we just might be earning a higher reward for the lesson we are learning. So, instead of complaining, or quitting and crying, blaming ourselves or moaning and sighing we should trust in the Lord and just keep on trying. For the hard times are only a way to start growing and if God is testing us it is our one chance of showing that when the going gets tough, the tough get going."

A postmortem examination, done the next day, shows a moderate quantity of alcohol in his blood as well as traces of diazepam, which Roger used to treat his anxiety. There is also a small amount of bloody fluid in his pharynx.

For two decades, Roger walked a thin tightrope, aching because of the contrariety of his life. On one hand, he still possessed more talent than the vast majority of jockeys. Just 18 years old in 1975, he led all apprentice jockeys in North America, broke Chris McCarron's record in Delaware and was sought after by trainers from California to New York. But here he was, 40 years old and broke, galloping horses in the morning with Noel at Fort Erie. A nobody, he believed.

He last rode in a race in 1992.

"That's the thing with riders," says Yves after hearing about Roger's suicide. "They are young when they start. They get to the top of the mountain. Everybody loves them. Everybody praises them and then it's a long way down. It's hard when people start to look the other way. I always had it in the back of my mind that he couldn't get out of the hole. God knows we tried to help him. I know I did. We all did. But you can try so much and then you give up. You realize he has to help himself.

"He tried to straighten out many times," Yves says before pausing. "But this time he couldn't do it."

Roger leaves behind three children: Joey, 14, Jessica, 12, and Danielle, 10.

Five months after Roger's death, Yves wins the $100,000 Alberta Derby in Calgary on Letkingo after being last in eighth during the early going.

"I wasn't worried because I had a lot of horse," Yves tells reporters after the race. "And the pace was fast."

At the quarter pole, Yves had turned Letkingo loose and went on to win by three-quarters of a length for a $33.40 payout.

"Still ready to quit?" someone asks, a smirk hanging on the question.

"Not now," he says quickly. "This is too much fun."

On March 8, 1996, Rose, the matriarch, passes away at one o'clock in the morning.

She has been in a nursing home in Grand Falls for four years, suffering first from Alzheimer's and then three long years with Parkinson's.

The Alzheimer's comes in a blink.

"One night I had dinner with her and she seemed fine," says Gaetan, who kept her company throughout her illnesses. "The next morning I got a phone call saying my mom doesn't know where she is. I drove her to the hospital and within days she was in the nursing home and never got out.

"Two weeks before she passed she stopped eating and refused even a sip of water. She lapsed into a coma and that was it. There was nothing anyone could do."

Rose was 81.

Chapter 39

And then there were none.

After winning 73 races in 1996, then 54 in both 1997 and 1998, it all comes to a cold, abrupt end for Yves Turcotte.

In the first race in Calgary on September 18, 1999, the field is sent away at exactly 1 p.m.

At the sixteenths pole, Yves finds a hole between two horses in front of him. Riding trainer Red Smith's Covumel, Yves aims for it. But as quickly as Yves reacts to the opportunity, the hole slams shut when Chris McGregor's horse, Remarkable Writer, drifts to his left. The hole is now a wall and Covumel clips heels with Remarkable Writer.

Covumel stumbles and falls to his knees. Yves falls with him. "Like a bag of potatoes," he says.

As Yves tumbles off his saddle, Covumel strikes Yves' head with its hip. Yves is knocked out before he hits the ground — again striking his head.

The next thing he remembers is waking up in hospital with doctors and nurses hovering over him. Noting that the time is now 3:05 p.m., he has been unconscious for more than two hours.

He has a skull fracture and three bleeds in his brain.

"They wanted to make sure the bleeding in my brain didn't get any bigger," he tells Al Dahl of the *Calgary Sun* four days after the spill. "That kind of scared me. I've had concussions before but nothing like this."

After Yves is released from hospital, one of the first phone calls he gets is from McGregor.

"Yves, I'm so sorry. The horse just swerved," McGregor says. "I tried to straighten him out, but I couldn't. Please forgive me."

"Don't worry, Chris. It happens," Yves replies. "I know you didn't do it on purpose. I know you wouldn't do anything stupid.

"Don't lose no sleep over it. I'm alright. I just won't ride the rest of the year," says Yves, who has won 50 races so far this year including four stakes on Alberta's Older Mare of the Year, Betty J.

For the next three months Yves doesn't remember anything about the accident. Not the spill. Not the ambulance ride. Nothing.

What he does remember is being flat on his back inside a tunnel-like CAT scan machine, which detects the three bleeds.

"I'm claustrophobic," he told the doctors. "I'm scared. It's like getting into a casket."

He wakes up every morning with a virulent splitting headache and it's there all day. When he gets tired, he gets dizzy. His balance is also gone. He has post-concussion syndrome and there is no timetable for how long it will last.

"I'm trying to remember who I was talking to half an hour ago and I can't," he frustratingly tells Lisette.

At the close of 1999, ESPN counts down the Top 50 Athletes of the 20th century. Secretariat is the only nonhuman on the list at No. 35. He is placed just ahead of Oscar Robertson, Mickey Mantle and Ben Hogan, and just behind Lou Gehrig and Mark Spitz.

The following spring brings no relief to Yves. The doctors tell him that he can't ride for at least six months.

"That takes me into September," he tells the *Edmonton Journal* on April 6. "So, I'm done for at least this year. After that who knows?"

The doctors know. So does everyone else. Everyone except Yves. One day he is watching a horse race on TV and suddenly exclaims, "I'm coming back."

Lisette shouts, "No! There's no way you're riding again."

"I'll quit when I'm ready to quit," he answers curtly.

Then he phones Ron. "I want to come back," he says.

Not even a nanosecond goes by.

"Are you stupid?" shouts Ron. "Do you want to be like me? Confined to a wheelchair? Get those thoughts out of your mind and quit now while you can."

Yet Yves still isn't willing to let it go. He seeks a second opinion that will be in his favor.

It isn't.

The doctor Yves sees shakes his head emphatically. "There's no way you should ride again. Take one more fall, one more bump on your head, and it's going to be way worse. I'm talking seriously worse."

With that Yves finally — reluctantly — gives up. At 39 years of age, he is done after 18 years as a jockey.

"I'm glad the doctors made the decision for me," he continues to the *Journal* sportswriter. "That's when I accepted it. But if it was up to me, I'd probably still go back. Just because I want to ride that much. It's hard to let go. Especially when it's about the only thing you've done in life. I went to Calgary a couple of weeks ago. It broke my heart watching those horses go around. Everybody is getting pumped up and here I am, doing Mr. Mom. I want to go back. But deep down I don't trust myself. I've also got a wife. Two kids. And then there are the guys I'd be riding against. I'd be putting every one of their lives in jeopardy. Right now, there is no way I could be out there and be safe. It's the right thing to do but ... There's always those 'buts' in there."

Finally, even those buts are gone.

"Until you go down once, you think you're Superman," he says. "Then you go down a couple of times and you get smart."

For the first time in almost 40 years, as the 2000 racing season opens in Calgary, there is no Turcotte in the saddle anywhere.

Retiring to Key Largo, Florida, trainer Lucien Laurin dies after complications from hip surgery on June 26, 2000. He was 88.

Chapter 40

The Turcottes' world shudders one more time.

Noel, who hasn't ridden since 1981 and not to any consistent degree since 1975, isn't even galloping horses anymore at Fort Erie, Ontario. Because of a bad back he is down to just walking hots.

It is August 7, 2001, clear and sunny.

Owning no vehicle, Noel walks the mile and a half back and forth from the track to his spartan apartment on Goderich Street, not far from the Peace Bridge, which separates Ontario from New York. It is the same complex where his on-again, off-again girlfriend, Dianne, who works as a groom, lives. They had been living together but now occupy separate lodgings.

But this afternoon, trainer Rod Cone, who came to Fort Erie from Alberta the previous fall, sees Noel walking with two beers in a paper bag in one hand and stops to give him a ride.

Cone has regularly used Noel as a hot walker.

"Hop in," says Cone. "I've got to make a quick stop at the hardware store; I need some screw eyes for the barn."

"Hey, I know a guy at a hardware store that's not far from here," says Noel. "We're friends. He'll give you a good price. It's just down this street and then left at the lights. I need to pick something up too. My girlfriend wants a clothesline, so I need to get some wire."

"Perfect," says Cone.

While Cone is paying for the screw eyes, Noel appears beside him with a long length of quarter-inch steel cable normally used for fences.

"That's going to be one heavy-duty clothesline," Cone laughs. Noel chuckles back.

"Hey, boss," Noel tells the store's owner. "I don't have any money on me. Can I pay you later?"

The owner nods. "Wait until payday and then you can settle with me later."

"That's okay, Noel," interjects Cone. "I'll buy it for you."

Sheepishly, Noel thanks Cone.

"I'll pay you back," Noel says.

"Oh, don't worry about that," says Cone. "It's no problem at all."

Transactions done, Cone takes Noel home.

It is the last time that Cone sees Noel. Most likely the last time anyone sees him.

The next morning Noel doesn't show up at the track.

"I didn't think much of it," says Cone. "I just thought he was hungover."

When Dianne doesn't see Noel either, she goes to his apartment late in the day. She raps on the door but gets no answer. She tries to open the door, but it is blocked by a heavy couch.

Panicking, Dianne forces her way in. She sees Noel hanging limp — a rope tied around his neck — outside of the bedroom door.

"My God, no!" she cries.

Hoping against hope, Dianne checks to see if Noel is still alive. Tears streaming, she calls the police on another heartbreaking evening.

The coroner's report is succinct: "Known alcoholic, chronic disability due to remote back problems as a jockey ... No postmortem was ordered after discussion with police personnel at the scene."

That said, a lot of things don't add up with Noel's suicide.

"He just got new teeth," says Rudy. "They aren't cheap and it's not something someone who is going to kill himself would do. Noel was so mad that Roger had killed himself. I wasn't surprised that Roger had given up. But Noel? I had no idea. I never saw that coming."

"He also bought a new cell phone," says Yves, obfuscating matters further. "That's not something someone who is going to commit suicide would do either."

Cone is jolted. "I'm shocked. I was with him yesterday. Drove him home," he tells a group of silent men hanging their forearms over the outer railing, drinking coffee and watching their horses gallop or work against the clock. The sun has barely poked its head above a gray-laced horizon. "He seemed fine. He was cheerful. Content. Like always. He was always friendly."

Cone pushes his tan straw hat back as he nods his head.

"He sure didn't look or sound like a guy who was giving up. It's weird. It just doesn't make sense. I never would have guessed he was going to kill himself."

Another trainer, an older man who has been around the track for a long time, shakes his head sadly. "He was a great rider. Not just good. Great," he says, looking at the ground.

"King of the turf course here," someone else says. "I don't think there was another jock that won as many races on the grass as he did."

"Yup," agrees an older horseman wearing pressed Levi's.

"Belle Geste," he says, and they all bow their heads in obeisance, remembering the grass-loving champion filly who set several track records on the turf at Woodbine with Noel on her back. "I'll never forget the 1972 Canadian Maturity. Hooked up with Kennedy Road coming out of the gate and ran head and head for 10 furlongs. Won by a neck. That track record lasted for 16 years. It was Noel that won that race. Noel carried her. Just like he did the year before in the Breeders'. Against the boys then too. Set the track record then too and that one stood for 20 years."

"It's a shame he couldn't handle the booze," says Cone. "His career would have gone a lot longer. He was a real gentleman. He always had a good attitude when he was riding regularly. He went out with that confidence on every horse he rode. I don't think he was ever the same since he found Roger hanging in 1996. When Roger died Noel's drinking really got bad. Sad."

Dried dirt on their boots, they all nod again.

Chapter 41

Noel is gone. Roger is gone. Ron is in his wheelchair in New Brunswick.

Rudy, who has stopped showing up to exercise horses in the mornings in Alberta, moves back to Ontario and then quickly follows the sun south to the warmth of Tampa Bay, where, needing money, he continues to gallop horses.

It is now the summer of 2002.

Fred Hilts, who is an agent for jockeys Peter Wong and Stephan Heiler, becomes Northlands' racing secretary, replacing Alan Bott.

Almost three full years after his 1999 career-ending head injury, which continues to torment him with excruciating headaches, nausea and dizziness, Yves decides he is well enough to take over the jockey's book for both Wong and Heiler. Hilts recommends Yves to both of them. Having ridden against Yves and also having received riding tips from him, they readily accept.

Early every morning, trying to find the best mounts for both, Yves pounds the barn area, cozying up to the top trainers who have the best horses. He is a salesman selling the services for his two jockeys — a good salesman.

Wong has his best year, winning 45 races; Heiler wins 74.

On a frigid February 27, 2003, afternoon the heat goes out in the recreational vehicle Camille Turcotte is living alone in while he rents out his cottage on Lake Erie near Simcoe, Ontario.

While trying to fix the propane tank it explodes. Badly burned from head to toe, he lapses into a coma he never comes out of. A short, stout man, Camille was 61.

Wong's win total of 59 in 2003 is another career best. Heiler is even better. He wins 91 times and his mounts earn a career-best $1.13 million.

But as well as he is doing, Yves knows an agent's life is not for him.

"I can't do it anymore," Yves tells Heiler and Wong in the autumn. "I hate the job. It's the worst job you can get. You have to kiss everyone's ass for somebody else. Just to keep the mount. You have to defend your jockey's rides. You take a lot of crap."

Unless you have a very good jockey, the pay for an agent isn't much either. While many of the top jockeys arrange their own deals with agents, the standard contract gives an agent 20 percent of what their jockeys make. With Heiler, one of the top riders in Alberta, taking home 10 percent of what his horses make, he nets $100,000 in 2003. So, Yves' cut is $20,000.

When jockeys dry up or run cold, the agent falls with them. A jockey gets $50 for a losing jock mount. Twenty percent of that leaves just $10 for the agent.

"I don't know what I'm going to do but it's not being an agent," he says to Heiler. "You guys are going to have to find another agent."

In spring of 2004, Yves takes the job as clerk of scales for Calgary and Edmonton, making sure the rider's weight is correct. Bored, this job isn't for Yves either. He's been standing on scales most of his life.

The following year he is hired by Horse Racing Alberta as a security supervisor.

"You'd do that?" asks chief steward and racing supervisor Conrad "Dude" Dick.

"Of course," says Yves. He knows it is another rung up the ladder in his post-racing career, one step closer to his goal of being a steward: the referees of a racetrack, making sure all rules of horse racing and wagering are followed.

Being a steward is a prestigious position in horse racing. Level-headed, smart, confident and as knowledgeable of the rules as anyone, Yves seems the perfect candidate.

Joey Turcotte, Roger's son, tries to be a jockey beginning in the summer of 2005. He rides for three years with limited success, winning 15 times in 196 starts, all on Alberta's B circuit in Grande Prairie and Lethbridge.

Chapter 42

Horse racing is an addictive but unforgiving sport, especially for jockeys, whose careers are generally short. Once it's in your blood, it stays there.

Some fortunate jockeys become trainers, some successfully.

Others, like Rudy, settle for galloping horses. Still others, like Daniel David, hold on to the role they know: hot-walking horses.

Many, like Ron and Yves, are forced to the sidelines because of injury.

And then there are jockeys like Roger and Noel who can't accept their fates.

Most jockeys only know horse racing. They arrive young, most with little education. And when the door closes tight, whether because of weight, injuries, declining abilities or addiction, they don't know where to turn. The spotlight that once glared bright is snatched away. The music stops. All too often they are broke.

One minute trainers are falling over themselves to ride you. The next you are old and forgotten.

"You can't ride forever," says Yves. "The sport tells you when it's time, and most of the time it's before you want it to end. The outside world can be a scary place to dwell. The racetrack is their comfort zone. So, they keep hanging on.

"Noel kept making comebacks. He refused to let it go. Rudy and Roger kept trying to make comebacks too. When I got hurt and they told me I couldn't ride anymore, I was scared too. I wasn't ready to retire.

"But the fact is that no matter what the sport is, it's the game that all too often retires you. It's other people who make the decision for you. Not a single one of us left on our own terms.

"And when it does end, most riders aren't prepared. Most never did anything outside of riding horses. Ron worked hard when he was growing up in the woods and the logging camps. Real hard. He knew what it was like to work. He knew what a dollar meant. I worked hard too. I worked 60 hours a week for $3.65 an hour. In cold storage where it was minus-10. And when I graduated, I weighed 140 pounds.

"But Noel, Rudy and Roger never had jobs before they became jockeys. They didn't know what it was like to do anything except ride horses. They didn't know what it meant to have to work a 9-to-5 job. None of them had outside-world skills.

"After Ron quickly became Canada's leading rider, Noel came along. He was going to be an electrician, but when he saw what Ron did, he became a jockey and won lots of races.

"And after Noel, here comes Rudy. He knew he was going to be a jockey when he was just a kid. He was an instant success. Except he was never happy unless he was the leading rider, and it went sideways for him.

"And then Roger. He quit school in Grade 10. Like Rudy, all Roger thought about was being a jockey and making money like Ron. In just his second year of being a rider he was North America's leading apprentice rider.

"It was one Turcotte after another after another. But in the end, they didn't know what to do when they had to quit.

"Ron paved the way for Noel, Rudy and Roger. By the time I came along that road was broken. Things had all gone bad for

Noel, Rudy and Roger. All three of them didn't grasp how lucky they were to be in the position they were in."

.

Epilogue

In the spring of 2008, Rudy leaves Florida and stays a short time with his brother Aurele in Quebec — just seven miles from the New Brunswick border.

Then, Rudy moves into an apartment in Grand Falls to be closer to Ron, who gives him some odd jobs. It doesn't go well, especially after Rudy drives Ron's tractor into a pond.

In 2010, after taking a course, Yves realizes his long-sought ambition. He is hired as a steward by Horse Racing Alberta, replacing Al Lennox, who retires. Former jockey Bobby Noda and former trainer Wayne Armstrong are the other stewards.

Yves goes home with an enormous grin.

Daniel David retires at the end of 2013 with 1,220 wins as a thoroughbred jockey and 42 more on quarter horses.

Diagnosed with diabetes, he struggles with weight and a plethora of injuries — mostly torn groin muscles and the after-effects of a 2009 spill when he broke his collarbone in 20 pieces, five ribs and a knee. He was in a hospital for nine weeks.

"My body is done," David announced. "I'm sore everywhere. I'm riding through a lot of pain. I can't do it anymore. I just woke up one morning, and my life hurt too much."

Despite his 9,119 mounts earning just under $20 million, he is now broke and living in a dormitory on the backstretch of Woodbine.

"I don't know where the money went. I spent it as fast as I made it. It's all gone."

In 2015 a statue of Secretariat and Ron crossing the finish line in the 1973 Belmont is erected in downtown Grand Falls.

That same year, Ron breaks both legs in a single-vehicle accident in New Brunswick when his truck flips over after hitting a snowbank.

Penny Chenery, one of the first women admitted as members of the Jockey Club, dies on September 17, 2017, at her home in Boulder, Colorado. The first female president of the Thoroughbred Owners and Breeders Association (1976 to 1984), she is honored with an Eclipse Award of Merit for a lifetime of outstanding achievement in thoroughbred racing and bestowed a Pillar of the Turf award — the highest honor given to owners and breeders of thoroughbreds.

She was 95.

Raymonde Turcotte dies of cancer on September 16, 2018. She was 65.

Because of his drinking, Rudy's health deteriorates quickly. He forgets or simply doesn't want to take his medication. Unable to live on his own, he is moved into a group home in Grand Falls.

Shortly after 5 a.m. on February 13, 2019, Rudy dies at 69 of pneumonia and kidney and liver failure. He is survived by two daughters, Stacey and Trudy, son Rudy Jr. and four grandchildren.

There is a sign on Rudy's bedroom wall: "Yesterday is history. Tomorrow is a mystery. Today is a gift."

Daniel David's son, Michael, becomes a jockey. Despite also battling weight problems, he wins 12 of 99 races in 2021 and is Ontario's leading apprentice rider.

Selfless and proud, Ron remains in the village of Drummond, population 700, where he is loved and respected.

He motors around in a red Ford van specially fitted with hand controls, sporting license plates that fittingly read "Big Red."

At his sprawling ranch, one room is a shrine with trophies, awards, newspaper clippings and citations. Among them are a dozen Hall of Fame honors, as well as the Order of Canada, the country's highest civilian commendation for "outstanding achievement and merit of the highest degree, especially in service to Canada or humanity at large."

Ron is in the National Museum of Racing and Hall of Fame, the Canadian Horse Racing Hall of Fame, the Canadian Sports Hall of Fame, the New York Sports Hall of Fame, the Long Island Sports Hall of Fame, the Hawthorne Racing Hall of Fame and the New Brunswick Sports Hall of Fame. His hall of fame inductions cap a career that included winning the Paul Harris Fellowship Award, the George Woolf Memorial Award, a Sovereign Award as horse racing's Man of the Year and the inaugural Avelino Gomez Memorial Award.

"I am just an ordinary man who was lucky enough to accomplish something," he says. "I'm just a simple farmer or lumberjack. That's all."

Despite his paralysis, he never laments his fate.

Asked if he is in constant pain, Ron quickly rebuffs the question.

"That would be complaining. And I never complain. What good is complaining? It's not going to help you. All my life, I took it one day at a time.

"Every day I thank God that I can open my eyes."

"I'm proud of what Noel, Rudy and Roger — and especially Ron — accomplished on the track," says Yves, looking back on his brothers' careers. "I'm not so proud of what happened to Noel, Rudy and Roger off the track.

"Alcoholism is a sickness. A disease. Roger is a perfect example. He was an alcoholic, but I think he suffered from deep depression too. I think it was the same thing with Noel.

"But in those days, nobody talked much about mental health. Back then, when you needed help, people would tell you to pull up your pants and get going. You wouldn't see a doctor. You'd just have another beer to try and forget about it.

"There were a lot of triumphs for my brothers and me. Some very big moments. But there was a lot of tragedy there too."

One day ends. The next one begins.

Career Statistics

Ron Turcotte		
YEAR	**WINS**	**EARNINGS**
1961	0	$0
1962	180	$396,135
1963	263	$684,019
1964	250	$1,292,264
1965	153	$1,139,116
1966	157	$1,049,821
1967	158	$1,383,392
1968	149	$1,380,643
1969	163	$1,368,347
1970	166	$1,904,175
1971	156	$2,042,917
1972	178	$2,789,332
1973	259	$3,393,368
1974	177	$2,432,874
1975	171	$2,115,991
1976	237	$2,903,539
1977	155	$2,388,296
1978	60	$941,976
TOTAL	3,032	$29,606,205

Noel Turcotte		
YEAR	**WINS**	**EARNINGS**
1964	51	$104,160
1965	142	$347,251
1966	134	$435,905
1967	68	$258,808
1968	63	$227,873
1969	63	$179,627
1970	104	$410,571
1971	109	$432,404
1972	65	$336,741
1973	98	$427,401
1974	21	$109,132
1975	17	$99,911
1976	0	$6,662
1977	5	$9,476
1978	0	$468
1979	0	$0
1980	3	$23,493
1981	2	$17,144
TOTAL	945	$3,427,027

Rudy Turcotte		
YEAR	WINS	EARNINGS
1968	3	$11,570
1969	110	$733,392
1970	116	$872,172
1971	205	$1,134,919
1972	178	$864,732
1973	166	$1,042,032
1974	98	$651,766
1975	232	$1,268,727
1976	115	$1,063,395
1977	145	$881,806
1978	128	$792,406
1979	53	$417,671
1980	70	$512,253
1981	77	$831,201
1982	42	$515,003
1983	2	$6,608
1984	0	$726
TOTAL	1,740	$11,600,379

Roger Turcotte		
YEAR	WINS	EARNINGS
1974	2	$13,446
1975	290	$1,536,362
1976	54	$365,597
1977	12	$43,154
1978	24	$89,738
1979	2	$7,672
1980	49	$180,963
1981	42	$226,863
1982	53	$321,713
1983	119	$664,398
1984	93	$494,329
1985	91	$410,190
1986	69	$338,047
1987	110	$695.726
1988	78	$502,037
1989	73	$442,063
1990	16	$93,011
1991	9	$49,223
1992	1	$6,538
TOTAL	1,187	$6,481,070

Yves Turcotte		
YEAR	WINS	EARNINGS
1981	2	$13,314
1982	87	$819,161
1983	69	$567,882
1984	68	$394,143
1985	72	$406,689
1986	96	$619,690
1987	110	$605,210
1988	124	$786,122
1989	96	$457,304
1990	89	$478,000
1991	70	$400,381
1992	79	$454,800
1993	39	$227,663
1994	60	$340,807
1995	55	$326,198
1996	73	$588,945
1997	54	$525,232
1998	54	$4441,034
1999	50	$412,640
TOTAL	1,347	$8,866,446

Turcotte Brothers Total
8,251 Wins
$59,981,127 Purses

Index

Acknowledgments

Ron Turcotte, who I spent three days with at his home in New Brunswick, thank you for your hospitality and the time it took to give me all the details I asked for. I cannot express my thanks enough.

Yves Turcotte for the hundreds of invaluable hours of getting together and the phone calls, the emails and the texts. Thank you for your patience.

Gaetan Turcotte for sharing your photos and filling in so much previously missing information.

Odette Turcotte for her wonderful and informative book on her family's history.

Rudy Turcotte for letting me visit with him in New Brunswick as well, and the many, many phone calls.

Roger Turcotte for the time and dinners we spent together.

Gae Turcotte for her unwavering hospitality.

Kelly Coffman, research Services Librarian for Keeneland, for the many back and forth emails and the statistics for the Turcotte family of jockeys, all the past performance lines for numerous horses.

Brian Tucker, former colleague at the *Edmonton Journal*, for eight straight days of six hours a day editing the book.

Darcy Shea, editor at Firefly Books, for his painstaking work editing the manuscript.

Lionel Koffler and Firefly Books for the opportunity to publish this work.

Bruce Walker, former publicity director of the Ontario Jockey Club, for picking up numerous mistakes and giving me my job as his assistant in Toronto 40 years ago.

Hal Walker, Bruce's father, for giving me my start in journalism as a summer student at the *Calgary Herald*.

Pat McMahon, my mentor at the *Herald*.

The Edmonton Public Library for helping me with their archives.

Linda Rainey of the Ontario Jockey Club for digging up information in their archives.

Moe Morrison, who introduced me to the world of horse racing.

My wife of 30 years, Barb Wilkinson, for helping me with computer issues, and my wonderful children, Dallas and Maia.